Paulina's promise to her grandfather, Jesus

by Dylan Stephens

Infinite SOULutions
508 Rainbow Dr
Sedro Woolley, WA. 98284
USA

CONTENTS

Advice on navigating this book

Given that Paulina's book presents an alternate story of Jesus that clearly challenges the accepted version, the supporting material had to be more than some obscure footnote that would take time for the reader to look up or find from the library, if that were even possible. Thus this book is presented in a two column format with story on the right and the contents of the supporting material on the left.

It is hoped that the reader will find this book to be both scholarly and enjoyable. And for those who feel that the distortions of modern day "Christianity" have become archaic and unsatisfying for today's world, this story will present the real Jesus and his hoped-for mission of peace and love from the loving words of his granddaughter (who really existed), the daughter of St. Paul and Jesus' first child, Phoebe.

(Front cover: Paulina & her father St. Paul from the Basilica of St Pudenziana in Rome named after Paulina and her sister using their student names: Pudenziana and Praxedis)

ACKNOWLEDGEMENTS

I am grateful to my grandmother Yeva and my father Peter John for instilling in me Faith, Love, and Hope in the Scriptures. They taught me not to take the Biblical verses on face value, but to look for spiritual meaning within them.

I will always remember fondly my friend and teacher, Dr. Barbara Thiering, and our hard work to bring her web site: *The Pesher Technique* to the world. She showed me not to be afraid 'to think out of the box' and, though we had our differences on her Rules of Pesher, I could not have created this book without her groundbreaking work. It is from her work that, by inductive reasoning, I was able to uncover *The Pesher of Christ* that revealed such secrets as Mary Magdalene's mother and her grandchild, Paulina, born of her daughter, Phoebe, and St. Paul.

I am thankful for the support that I had from my Wendy-Bird and our three children Kes, Nirvana, and Tarot and my grandchildren. 'Where's Dylan?' they would ask and then answering in unison, 'He is lost again in his Pesher studies.'

BIOGRAPHY

With a Jesuit education from Fordham Prep School and Georgetown University earning a Bachelor of Science degree (having graduated in the same class of 68 with President Clinton), I pursued a career in computer systems and GIS programming. However, this did not stop me from becoming a songwriter of 500 songs with a recording contract from Columbia Records and becoming part of the inner circle of the metaphysics teacher G.I.Gurdjieff. My uncle, Richard Waring, was a Hollywood actor and my grandfather, Thomas E. Stephens, was friend and portrait painter of Eisenhower. My half-brother Anton Holden and my father Peter John Stephens are published authors. As a website builder and founder of the non-profit organization Infinite SOULutions Foundation, I built the web site for Dr. Barbara Thiering that expands the concepts of the 'pesher technique' from her published books. While continuing to write, I have illustrated, designed, and photographed picture stories for my songs on YouTube. My web site: pesherofchrist.com is the authoritative source for the Pesher of Christ™.

PREFACE

"The seventh angel blew his trumpet; and there followed loud voices in Heaven which said, 'The sovereignty of the world now belongs to our Lord and His Christ; and He will be King until the Ages of the Ages." Revelations 11:15. (The Restoration of Israel thought to be 3920 at 44/45AD)

Svensk Filmindustri (SF), 1957

As the granddaughter of Jesus, I now sound this 'last trumpet' of Matthew Annas and my father Paul that will prevail against all the theories, translations, and distortions of the vested clergy and degreed scholars. My heredity is the key that will unlock the truth by means of the seven facts that follow. Thus the Restoration of the true Christian Church that was founded by Jesus, Paul, Peter and John Mark can begin anew. As with the promise to my grandfather, these facts will be verified in this book.

Signed, Paulina

1. *My great-grandfather, Joseph, conceived Jesus with my great-grandmother, Virgin Mary.*
2. *My grandfather, Jesus, was married to my grandmother, Mary Magdalene.*
3. *My mother, St. Phoebe, was the child of Jesus and Mary Magdalene, conceived before the Crucifixion.*
4. *My father, St. Paul, did actually marry and to 'his yoke-fellow', my mother, St. Phoebe.*
5. *My great-grandmother, Helena, is St. Salome, St. Martha, the wife of Zebedee, the Syro-Phoenician woman, the woman of Samaria, the Menstruous Women, Luna, Justa, but most importantly, the mother of Mary Magdalene, and thus the mother-in-law of Jesus.*
6. *My step-great-grandfather is Simon Magus, Lazarus, the young man at the sepulchre, Zebedee, the step-father of James and John, Simon the Canaanite/Zealot (one of the twelve disciples), Simon of Cyrene, Simon the leper, Simon the tanner, Demetrius the silversmith, Ananias, 'the great power of God', 'Beast 666', and the Pope of the early Church before the Christian Church of Antioch and Rome, which began at Qumran where the Dead Sea Scrolls were hidden.*
7. *And last but not least: My mother, St. Phoebe, had a child with my father, St. Paul: Me!!*

My dear grandfather, Jesus, I made a promise to you and now I must stand up to my Church and accept their anger, their beatings, their imprisonment, and possible death for your name and for the Kingdom. But first, let me begin with a prayer:

In the name of Jesus, St. Peter and St. Paul, and God within us all, let the Church live again! Amen.

Jesus

Chapter 1 - Herald of the Coming Good.
(My Grandfather's Request & Fulfillment of My Promise.)

I am the Alpha and the Omega, the First and the Last, the Beginning and the End.
I, Jesus did send my messenger to testify to you these things concerning the churches;
I am the root and the offspring of David, the bright and morning star! (Revelation 22:13,16)

Christmas day, AD 71

As I enter the hall, Jesus rises and walks towards me. Taking both my hands, he kisses me on the mouth, for he would always welcome brothers and sisters of the Church with a kiss on the mouth, as he had taught his disciples to do. Some of the members look up disapprovingly for I was a young girl and Jesus was now quite old, but he was also my grandfather.

Jesus would tell us, "the purpose of the kiss on the lips is to honor the Logos which is the Word of God which comes from the mouth." My father Paul would say, "From this 'holy kiss' we are perfected by the grace that is in one another."

Years ago when my grandmother Mary Magdalene was alive, public shows of affection were frowned upon, but Jesus was not one to follow tradition. His disciples, being always worried about what the Essene leaders would think, saw only that Mary Magdalene was his wife, and mistook these kisses to her. They complained, "Why do you love her more than us?"

Certainly, the Nazarite-Essene sect of Jesus had certain prescribed times that a David king and queen would be allowed to be in the married state, but Jesus saw no difference between male and female in the Faith. His rebuke to them had been swift, "Do I not also kiss you on the mouth?"

It had been especially hurtful when Judas Iscariot had kissed Jesus on the mouth to betray him. It had showed him that Judas had never grasped the purpose of the 'holy kiss' of grace within all those who seek the Kingdom of Heaven.

As I look into my grandfather's eyes, I sense that he is clearly anxious to talk with me. Jesus takes my hand and gently leads me back to his red velvet chair, decorated with gold leaf, and gestures for me to sit down next to him.

His hold is gentle and, although his body is frail, his touch evokes a deep peacefulness and love in me. His hands and arms are quivering somewhat from old age, but mostly from the irreparable damage to the nerves of his hands from the nails of the cross.

Jesus speaks to me softly while staring lovingly into my eyes, "Dear granddaughter of mine, I have something very important to ask of you."

"As Grandmother Magdalene called you, you are Rabbuni, my Teacher", I answer Jesus immediately.

***********Reference Column***********

The Church includes all

(All members are important to the Church: *1Corinthinans 12:8-12*) For to one is given through the Spirit the word of wisdom, and to another the word of knowledge, according to the same Spirit; to another faith, by the same Spirit; and to another gifts of healings, by the same Spirit; and to another workings of miracles; and to another prophecy; and to another discerning of spirits; to another different kinds of languages; and to another the interpretation of languages.

But the one and the same Spirit works all of these, distributing to each one separately as he desires. For as the body is one, and hath many members, and all the members of that one body, being many, are one body: so also is Christ.

***********Reference Column***********

Paul's work

(Paul's toils: *2Corinthinans 26,27*) In journeying many times, perils of rivers, perils of robbers, perils from kindred, perils from nations, perils in city, perils in wilderness, perils in sea, perils among false brethren; with labor and toil, with many a sleepless night, in hunger and thirst, in frequent fastings, in cold, and with insufficient clothing.

(Paul's work: *Epistle of St. Clement to the Corinthians, 5*) Paul by his example pointed out the prize of patient endurance. After that he had been seven times in bonds, had been driven into exile, had been stoned, had preached in the East and in the West, he won the noble renown which was the reward of his faith, having taught righteousness unto the whole world and having reached the farthest bounds of the West.

***********Reference Column***********

Thy will be done

(The Lord's Prayer: *Matthew 6:9,10*) After this manner therefore pray ye: Our Father who art in heaven, Hallowed be thy name. Thy kingdom come. Thy will be done on earth as it is in heaven.

***********Reference Column***********

He has risen from the dead!

(After Jesus is rescued and the tomb is empty Simon Magus speaks: *Matthew 28:2,5-7*) Behold, there was a great earthquake, for an angel ... rolled away the stone from the door, and sat upon it and answered the women, 'Do not be afraid, for I know that you seek Jesus, who has been crucified. He is not here, for he is risen, as he said ... Go quickly and tell his disciples, "He has risen from the dead", ... Remember, I have told you.'

☧ Jesus smiles and continues, "I remember the strong-willed Peter and the patient-loving Paul that my Father in Heaven had sent me. Now that they are gone in my old age, He has blessed me with my granddaughter Paulina, who is the sum total of both!"

"You only say that because I am your granddaughter!", I laugh. "My feet are too small for their footsteps!"

☧ Jesus looking at her kindly, "I see so much of your father Paul in you. It seems only yesterday that I placed on his shoulders my mission to the Gentiles. He was only twenty-two, and he never failed me. Now you are seventeen and, though I know that women grow up faster than men, I should not be placing my burden on your shoulders."

"It is all right, Grandfather", I said soothingly to him.

☧ Jesus smiles, "You are very sweet, my granddaughter. Clearly you also possess your mother Phoebe's strength and courage!"

☧ Jesus pauses, reminiscing, "Paul endured so much for me. His devotion to me was always unfailing. Even if he disagreed with me, he would faithfully present my views on the direction that the Church needed to follow.

"I remember how we fought with the Church on policies like circumcision and membership fees and how they hated us for standing up for the rights of Gentiles and women."

☧ Jesus pauses again as a wave of sadness comes over his face, "I loved your father Paul, that dear, sweet man. I truly have been lost without him."

"I know; I miss him too", replying to Jesus as tears come to my eyes.

☧ Jesus looks over to me as tears are now in his eyes as he says, "Oh, dear Paulina, I am so sad that you lost your father because of me."

"The will of God is above all else", I say as a tear falls down my cheek.

☧ Jesus reaches over and hugs me, "Sorry I brought us to tears. That was not my purpose."

☧ Jesus pauses again then begins again in earnest, "Please forgive me Paulina, but I must continue: You know the story of my Crucifixion and Resurrection of how I had been taken from the cross, as if dead, and how I was revived and rescued from the cave. And how, later, when the women came to the cave and found it empty, there was Simon Magus, speaking as the Pope (an angel of God), sitting on the blocking stone that had fallen flat after having been pushed by Theudas ('Earthquake'). Simon, having been crucified with me and placed alive in the adjacent tomb, said, 'He is risen from the dead' and, then, thinking how perfect this would be, he had instructed the women to tell the others these exact words."

(The true story that Jesus did not die on the cross: Eusebius, Fragments Of Papias, Church History XXXIX 8-10) It is worth while however to add to the words of Papias given above other passages from him, in which he records some other wonderful events likewise, as having come down to him by tradition. That Philip the Apostle resided in Hierapolis with his daughters has been already stated; but how Papias, their contemporary, relates that he had heard a marvellous tale from the daughters of Philip, must be noted here. For he relates that in his time a man rose from the dead, and again he gives another wonderful story about Justus who was surnamed Barsabas, how that he drank a deadly poison, and yet, by the grace of the Lord, suffered no inconvenience. Of this Justus the Book of the Acts records that after the ascension of the Saviour the holy Apostles put him forward with Matthias, and prayed for the (right) choice, in place of the traitor Judas, that should make their number complete. The passage is somewhat as follows; And they put forward two, Joseph, called Barsabas, who was surnamed Justus, and Matthias.

(Lazarus (Simon) in the tomb: Clement Letter: Secret Gospel of Mark 2.26b,3.01a) And immediately a great sound was heard from the tomb,

Revived, but not resurrected

(Jesus is rescued from the tomb: Gospel of Peter 35-37,39,41)
And in the night in which the Lord's day was drawing on,
as the soldiers kept guard two by two in a watch,
there was a great voice in the heaven;
And they saw the heavens opened,
and two men (Peter and beloved disciple) descend from thence with great light and approach the tomb.
And that stone which was put at the door rolled of itself and made way in part;
and the tomb was opened,
and both the young men entered in.
And, as they (the soldiers) declared what things they had seen,
again they see three men
coming forth from the tomb,
and two of them supporting one (Jesus),
and a cross following them.
And they heard a voice from the heavens, saying,
'Hast thou preached to them that sleep?'
And a response was heard from the cross, 'Yea.'

"Certainly it was a wonderful story!", I exclaim.
"Grandmother Magdalene told everyone at the convent at Hierapolis in Phrygia under St. Philip about the miraculous survival of Justus Barsabas. She told how, after he had been given poison on the cross and placed in the cave as if dead, he had vomited up the poison. Of course, I knew it was you because your brother James was stoned to death.

℞ Jesus exclaims, "Yes, you see! That was all part of the cover-up! Even Magdalene was sworn to secrecy, that I had not died! Alas, it seems that people are always too eager to take things literally, especially when it is what they want to hear. Since she had promised Simon to hide the truth, she used the family name Barsabas and my brother James' title Justus as crown prince. You, of course, know the secret that it is common to substitute the name of your Great Uncle James instead of me in order to disguise that I am alive."

℞ Jesus continues, "When I wrote the Gospel of John with Simon Magus, I was encouraged by him, who was always the magician and illusionist, to write in the style of many writers of the day, telling of my reforms of the Church as if they were miraculous healings."

"Of my amazing recovery after appearing to die on the cross, I told of it as if it were a Resurrection from the dead. After all it had seemed that way to me."

"Naively, I just assumed that these stories would be taken as symbolic rather than real."

"When I brought Lazarus out from the tomb, I thought it would be obvious to the readers that this was Simon Magus' symbolic reentry into the Church after his excommunication. I assumed everyone knew the Essene saying:
'Outside the Church is death; In the Church is life'".

"Even if outsiders might not understand, at least, each event would be a miraculous story that would interest them in joining the Church. I never expected that those inside the Church would not to be able to see the truth. Somehow it all got out of hand and there was no turning back."

"My survival from the Crucifixion was a miracle, but, after that, I walked around in my physical body and Thomas touched the wounds in my hands. Yet, as the legend grew that I was resurrected, then it somehow became a requirement that I would have to ascend to heaven within a short period of time in my physical body because I was also a spirit.

"Yes, I had risen from a deep coma, but I was still alive. I did not 'Ascend', but I did rise in status, merely because I had been reduced in status during my three years in my prior married state."

"And besides all this, when Peter wrote his Gospel of Mark, he had explicitly shown many events not as miracles, such as Lazarus speaking from the tomb and the two men (Peter and John, the beloved disciple) who went into the tomb and helped me out, but all this was removed by the Church leaders."

***********Reference Column***********

The Secret Gospel of Mark and The Gospel of Peter (continued)

***********Reference Column***********

For Paul, Resurrection is the key

(Paul declares that mankind is saved by faith in Christ's Resurrection: 1Corinthians 15: 13,14) But if there is no resurrection of the dead, neither has Christ been raised. And if Christ is not raised, then is our preaching vain, and your faith is also vain.

***********Reference Column***********

Paul defines the 'Pesher of Christ'

(Paul defines a need to a deeper meaning: Hebrews 6:1-3) Therefore leaving the principles of the doctrine of Christ, let us go on unto perfection; not laying again the foundation of repentance from dead works, and of faith toward God, of the doctrine of baptisms, and of laying on of hands, and of resurrection of the dead, and of eternal judgment. And this will we do, if God permit.

***********Reference Column***********

Paul defines himself as an apostle

(Jesus' appearances: 1Corinthians 15:5-8) And was seen by Peter, and then by the Twelve. Afterwards he (Jesus) was seen by more than five hundred brethren at once, most of whom are still alive, although some of them have now fallen asleep. Then he was seen by James; then by all the Apostles. And last of all he was seen of me (Paul) also, as of one born out of due time.

***********Reference Column***********

Metaphoric description of Jesus

(The description of Jesus: Revelation 1:12-18) And I turned to see the voice that spoke with me. And having turned, I saw seven golden candlesticks; And in the midst of the seven golden candlesticks, one like to the Son of Man, clothed with a garment down to the feet, and girt about the paps with a golden girdle. His head and his hair were white as white wool, like snow. His eyes were like a flame of fire. And his feet like fine brass, as if they burned in a furnace; and his voice as the sound of many waters. And having in his right hand seven stars, and out of his mouth a sharp two-edged sword is proceeding, and his countenance is as the sun shining in its might. And when I saw him, I did fall at his feet as dead, and he placed his right hand upon me, saying to me, 'Be not afraid; I am the First and the Last, and he who is living. and I did become dead, and, lo, I am living to the ages of the ages. Amen! ...

"It is fortunate", I add, "that these sections still survive under the names of 'The Secret Gospel of Mark' and 'The Gospel of Peter.'"

ℙ Jesus continues, "Yes, but still it is not enough. When I expressed my concerns with your father Paul, he begged me to allow him to continue to teach my Resurrection as truth. He would tell me that the Resurrection worked well to inspire the people and that his 'babes in Christ' need a mythic story. He said that the Egyptians, Greeks, and Romans had resurrection stories of their many gods, and therefore it was important that I should match these miracles for the people to believe in Jesus Christ."

"Paul claimed that those who were in the inner circle, would apply the principle expressed in the 'Pesher of Christ' and uncover the truths."

"At that time, I agreed with Paul for it was more important that the teaching of agape-love be spread to the four corners of the earth. Unfortunately, we misjudged those elders who found that they could lord it over others by keeping them in the dark."

"These elders, even found a way to exclude Paul!" I exclaim. "They made up the absurd rule that there could be no discipleship without being instructed by you in person!"

"My mother Phoebe would tell me how much this infuriated my father Paul, who, of course, was actually the most instructed of any of the apostles. By claiming your 'Ascension' happened, they could disqualify your personal teaching sessions with him as just séances with your 'Spirit.'"

ℙ Jesus pauses for a moment, reaching down into the center of his being.

As I look up at him I notice that he is just as described in Revelation.

His hair is tinged with white and somewhat curly, but soft like a lamb.

His eyes glow like the flame of a candle.

I imagine how he could walk across the fires of hell and lift himself up to the stars of the Pleiades.

His countenance is like the sun and his voice is as the sound of a river.

***********Reference Column***********
Jesus faints on the cross

(On the cross Jesus forgives his accusers and then faints from the poison: Luke 23:34,44-46) And Jesus said: Father, forgive them, for they know not what they do ...
It was now about the sixth hour,
and darkness came over the whole land until the ninth hour.
and the sun was darkened,
and the veil of the sanctuary was rent in the midst,
and Jesus cried out in a great voice,
and said, 'Father, to Thy hands I entrust my spirit.'
And after uttering these words He yielded up His spirit.

***********Reference Column***********
Life is imperfection, but salvation awaits

(Parable of the tares in the wheat: Matthew 13:36-40) Then Jesus sent the multitudes away, and went into the house. His disciples came to him, saying, 'Explain to us the parable of the tares of the field.'
He answered and said to them, He that soweth the good seed is the Son of Man;
The field is the world; the ideal seed are the children of the kingdom; but the tares are the children of the that were led astray;
The enemy that sowed them is the opposing evil force; the harvest is the Last Judgement; and the reapers are the angels. As therefore the tares are gathered and burned in the fire; so shall it be at the Last Judgement.

***********Reference Column***********
Jesus is physically alive

(Jesus as 'the suffering servant' lives after death with his children: Isaiah 53 6,7,10) All we like sheep have gone astray; we have turned every one to his own way; and the Lord has laid on him the iniquity of us all. He was oppressed, and he was afflicted, yet he opened not his mouth; like a Lamb that is led to the slaughter, ... when he makes himself an offering for sin, he shall see his offspring, he shall prolong his days; the will of the Lord shall prosper in his hand;

St. Stephen is Jonathan Annas

Greek for crown is stephanos, Jonathan (Jacob of Alphaeus) is priest and king.

***********Reference Column***********
Meaning of 'Justus'

(Joseph is James, brother of Jesus) They put forward two, Joseph called Barsabbas, who was surnamed Justus, and Matthias.
('Justus' is the term for crown prince. His younger brother James had this title, but it would pass to Jesus' son.)

Speaking in his 'great' voice, Jesus says, "Did I have to die on the cross to save the world? Is it not a greater miracle that I survived?"

"As my sight blurred on the cross from the poison and the pain subsided, I looked down at the blurred image of my dearest Magdalene standing there and, as my world went black, I imagined that I was talking to the child inside her womb, the child who would be your mother Tamar-Phoebe. I tell her, 'I will not leave you; I will survive this; I will see your birth.'"

"Now is it possible that you, her daughter, my dearest, dearest grandchild, Paulina, can understand the regret I feel to have lived this lie of my death and Resurrection? Can I ask you, Paulina, to make me a promise?"

As the strong wave of his emotional pain touches my heart, I say to him, "Of course, my dearest, dearest Grandfather, you have suffered enough; I will promise you anything."

Jesus asks his question softly, "Dearest grandchild, will you promise me to reveal the truth about the Resurrection after I am gone?"

I think in silence, imagining that I could be an author like Jesus. I lean over and kiss his cheek, "Dear Grandfather, you may go to the Father in peace. I promise you that I will reveal the truth to the world. Although the Resurrection has been believed for too many years now, the Truth always has the power to separate the tares from the wheat. I would love to be your angel so that there can yet be a great harvest."

Jesus smiles with tears falling down his cheeks, "You have been reading my parables I see." He reaches over and puts his arms around me and hugs me and kisses me on both cheeks and then on my lips. "Thank you, my brave Paulina. My heart is at rest now. May the Last Judgement bring peace to us all."

I still remember this day vividly. It is hard to believe that my grandfather Jesus was still alive in AD 71, when the rest of the world, in spite of the many clues to the contrary, is convinced that, in AD 33, he had died on the cross, had resurrected, and then ascended. The prophesies of Isaiah were correct in total: that the 'suffering servant' would 'see his offspring'. The Church conveniently ignores this point.

We, my mother Phoebe and my younger sister, had journeyed down from Lugdunum Convenarum to celebrate the Feast of St. Stephen on this Christmas Day, AD 71. At the celebration with Jesus were also Uncle Jesus Justus with his betrothed and Uncle Joseph, Clement, and many other trusted Church leaders. None of us expected that this would be the last day that we would see my grandfather Jesus alive, as we thought he would live forever.

Of my two uncles, Jesus Justus, being the eldest was just getting used to his honorary role as the 'David king' and Uncle Joseph had just returned from a mission in Britannia at Glastonbury. Jesus Justus was a helper to Paul in Rome and Paul acknowledges him as a Jew, but he really meant that he was of the line of David like his father Jesus.

The births of my uncles being male heirs to the throne of David are indicated as the 'Word of God' in Acts. As Jesus was the 'Word', so would be his heirs. Having named his eldest son after him, he is 'Jesus Justus' as crown prince.

At the Pentecost after the Resurrection, two names had been put forward as a replacement for Judas Iscariot, both were brothers of Jesus: James (Joseph) and Joses (Matthias). The title 'Justus' meaning crown prince was often used as a surname as implied Acts. The term 'James the Just' was a very popular name for James to distinguish him from St. James who was the twin brother of St. John and thus it was also used for Uncle Jesus Justus for the obvious reason.

The fact that James retained the title 'Justus' after the birth of Jesus' son is primarily due to the pretence of Jesus' Ascension and not having an heir, but also because the detractors of Jesus were grooming James for the throne. Due to James' attitude of acting as if he were above Jesus, he would be humorously called 'James the Little' to emphasize his position as younger than Jesus and below him.

My Uncle Joseph was born while the 'Schism of the Churches' had begun, just prior to Mary Magdalene's divorce from Jesus, and thus my grandmother Magdalene, heavy with child ('from joy'), is shown as not recognizing Peter at the gate of the convent (house) of Mother Mary under John Mark, 'the beloved disciple'. She is called Rhoda being the head of the Church at Rhodes, indicating her separation from Jesus.

As the Schism of Churches had begun, Mother Mary, Mary Magdalene, and John Mark, having declared that they would be remaining in the Church of Simon Magus, would therefore not be accepting of Peter who would be leading the opposing Church. This is the reason that Acts says Mary Magdalene would not let him in and ran to get the others.

Since Uncle Joseph had the same name as Jesus' father, he was immediately confused by the Celtic Saints in Cymry with the 'Joseph of Arimathea' who asked for the body of Jesus. However, 'Joseph of Arimathea' was the same person as James, the next younger brother of Jesus. Uncle Joseph had been introduced to the Celtic Saints by my teacher Claudia who was the daughter of the famous Celtic leader Caractacus.

The marriage of Uncle Jesus Justus was held on June AD 73, as told in Revelation, which says "Let us rejoice and be exceedingly glad, and let us give the glory to him. For the marriage of the Lamb has come, and his wife has made herself ready".

The presence of Uncle Jesus Justus in Revelation was 'Name' as he had the name Jesus, but was acting on the side of the Zealots, which my grandfather Jesus did not approve of.

The son of Uncle Jesus Justus, my cousin, was born in AD 77 and his wedding would be scheduled when he was 36 years of age in AD 133. The son of Jesus Justus was called 'Words' because he was following more in the path of Jesus, who was known as the 'Word'. The duplicate is in the plural form as it was for Qumran being in the plural form of Jerusalem.

My great-grandmother is Helena, Mary Magdalene's mother, and my step-great-grandfather is Simon Magus.

In Simon's eyes, his consort, Helena, was a goddess, the incarnation of Helen of Troy and of Sophia (wisdom- the first principle). Helena was also known as 'Luna' and 'Justa' in the 'Clementines'. (The 'Clementines' are the writings of Pope Clement and will be discussed in a later chapter.)

More importantly, she was the Syro-Phoenician woman who asked Jesus to heal her daughter. The amazing implications of this request will be revealed later on.

The use of the title 'Justa', the feminine of 'Justus', in the Clementines indicates that Helena (Mary Salome) was in a position to have a major role in the Gospels and clearly she did as consort of Simon Magus and mother-in-law of Jesus! There were many discussions that she had with Jesus in the Gospels, but disguised as generic people like 'the Syro-Phoenician Woman', 'the Samaritan Woman at the well', 'the Menstruous Women', or the 'Martha' (which is a title above the 'Mary').

As the daughter of Phoebe, who is the daughter of Jesus, I am a descendant of the royal line of King David. Jesus is my grandfather and thus Joseph is my great-grandfather and Mother Mary is my great-grandmother. My great-great grandfather is Heli.

The grandfather of Jesus, Heli, had been allowed under King Herod to be the 'David king' in the mission to the Diaspora, who were the Jews outside of Judaea. His title was 'Jacob', the patriarch, whose sons became the twelve tribes. Herod did this to appease the Jews as he was not a Jew himself. Obviously, the Zealots would find good use for a king to lead them into battle and it was for this reason that Heli, Joseph, and Jesus had to take a neutral position. It was Joseph who often stepped over the line and this led to his death in AD 23.

The younger brother of Jesus, who was James, had the real name of Joseph, but took the title of 'Jacob' for he was my great-grandfather Joseph's protégé. The name Jacob is also the name James.

In the generations of Jesus in the beginning of the Gospel of Matthew, Heli's name is shown as Jacob.

Matthew has enhanced Jesus' generations by splicing it to those of David's son Solomon instead of his son Nathan as in the Gospel of Luke, however, Nathan is the correct one.

Our home in Lugdunum Convenarum is a large Roman town to the west of Lyons near the border of Espana. Founded by Pompey in 72 BC, it is a thriving town, tolerant of Jews and Christians. You may know it as the place where Herod Antipas and his wife Herodias were exiled by Caligula in AD 37.

Herod Antipas was the tetrarch of Perea and Galilee during Jesus' ministry, being involved in the imprisoning of John the Baptist and of the taking of 'his head' metaphorically, by deposing him, but not his murder.

***********Reference Column***********
Joseph is murdered

(Herod Agrippa murders Joseph from Galilee: **Luke 13:1**) And there were present certain at that time, telling him about the Galileans, whose blood Pilate did mingle with their sacrifices;

Herod Antipas in Lugdunum Convenarum

(Herod's banishment to Lugdunum: **Josephus Antiquities of the Jews, 18, 7, 2**) .... Herod (Antipas) admitted that he had the arms in his armory; he could not do otherwise as the facts were there to confute him. Gaius (Caligula), accordingly, accepting this as proof of the accusation of conspiracy, deprived him of his tetrarchy, which he added to Agrippa's kingdom; he also presented the latter with Herod's wealth. He further punished Herod by banishing him for life, appointing Lugdunum (Convenarum), a city of Gaul, as his place of abode.

***********Reference Column***********
Paul does get to go to Spain

(Paul wishes to go to Spain: **Romans 15:24**) I hope, as soon as ever I extend my travels into Spain, to see you on my way and be helped forward by you on my journey, when I have first enjoyed being with you for a time.

***********Reference Column***********
The manner of death for Peter and Paul

(The deaths of Peter and Paul: **The Teaching of Simon Cephas in the City Of Rome**) And, when Caesar had commanded that Simon (Peter) should be crucified with his head downwards, as he himself had requested of Caesar, and that Paul's head should be taken off, there was great commotion among the people, and bitter distress in all the church, seeing that they were deprived of the sight of the apostles. And Isus the guide arose and took up their bodies by night, and buried them with great honor, and there came to be a gathering-place there for many.

***********Reference Column***********
Mary Magdalene landing in France

(**St. Lazarus of Bethany, Catholic Encyclopedia**) St. Lazarus of Bethany, reputed first Bishop of Marseilles, died in the second half of the first century. According to tradition, or rather a series of traditions combined at different epochs, the members of the family at Bethany, the friends of Christ, together with some holy women and others of His disciples, were put out to sea by the Jews hostile to Christianity in a vessel without sails, oars, or helm, and after a miraculous voyage landed in Provence at a place called to-day the Saintes-Maries.

Agrippa, who later became King Herod Agrippa, was the one who had John the Baptist killed and the Herod who mocked my grandfather Jesus at the Crucifixion trial. He was also the one who killed my great-grandfather Joseph, when he would not release the Church money to him. Later, by accusing Antipas to Caligula, he took Antipas' lands and riches and Antipas was exiled to the town we live in now.

Herod Antipas had helped his brother-in-law Agrippa with a job as magistrate of Tiberius, the city he had built in Galilee for the emperor Tiberius. It was due to the confusion of this position that Pilate turned Jesus over to Herod Agrippa for trial.

My father Paul had stopped at our future home town on his way back from Spain and been welcomed by Herod Antipas' son.

Paul told us that if things became too dangerous in Rome that we should go there as the Herod family promised to look after us.

Nero's reign of terror against Christians, which began with the great fire of Rome in AD 64, was the end of our happiness and it almost destroyed our Church. I cannot look back on these times without feeling again the anxiety that we felt. It was as if the floor had been pulled out from under us.

It is said that the fire burned for six days and that Nero played the lyre in stage costume as the city burned.

My dearest father St. Paul was beheaded on the Ostian way outside the walls of the city and a monument marks his grave on Lucina's land.

Our courageous St. Peter was crucified upside down at Nero's Circus and nearby is his grave marked with a red stone.

I remember the tears and courage of my mother Phoebe as she took us by boat from Rome, landing at Oppidum-Râ near the mouth of the Rhone, in the south of Gaul, then north to Lugdunum Convenarum. The metaphor of 'a vessel without sails, oars, or helm' refers to the leaders Peter and Paul being killed.

The followers of the Church of Simon Magus offered to help us in deference to my grandmother Mary Magdalene who had gone over to Simon's Church in AD 44 in the Schism of the Churches. The bishop Lazarus had taken one of Simon Magus' names.

***********Reference Column***********
Simon battles Peter

(Simon flies and Peter prays: The Acts of Peter, Vercelli III.32) ... a great multitude assembled at the Sacred Way to see him (Simon Magus) flying ... raised up above all Rome ... the faithful looked toward Peter ... And he fell from the height and brake his leg in three places ...

***********Reference Column***********
Jesus guides Paul

(Paul's conversion after meeting with Jesus: Acts 9:3-6) But on the journey, as he was getting near Damascus, suddenly there flashed round him a light from Heaven; and falling to the ground he heard a voice which said to him, "Saul, Saul, why are you persecuting Me?" "Who art thou, Lord?" he asked. "I am Jesus, whom you are persecuting,' was the reply. But rise and go to the city, and you will be told what you are to do."

***********Reference Column***********
Clement made Pope

(Peter makes Clement Pope: Epistle of Clement to James, Chap II) But about that time, when he (Peter) was about to die, the brethren being assembled together, he suddenly seized my hand, and rose up, and said in presence of the church: "Hear me, brethren and fellow-servants. Since, as I have been taught by the Lord and Teacher Jesus Christ, whose apostle I am, the day of my death approaching, I lay hands upon this Clement as your bishop; and to him I entrust my chair of discourse,"

***********Reference Column***********
The Bernice is criticized

(The affair of Bernice and Titus: Revelation 17:5) 17:5 And upon her forehead was a name written, 'Mystery, Babylon the Great (Rome), The Mother (Superior) of Harlots and Abominations of the Earth'.

The Church of Simon Magus is gone

(The affair of Bernice and Titus is over. Jesus' blood would be joined with the prophets at his death: Revelation 18:23,24) The light of the candle shall no more shine (removed from church leadership); and the voice of the bridegroom (Titus, the son of the Espousing, the emperor of Rome) and of the bride (Bernice, the exiled of queen of Judaea, "the harlot of Babylon-Rome") will be heard no more at all in you (for Titus is unwilling to marry her); for your merchants (East Manhesseh) were the princes of the earth (controlled the mission in Rome); for with your poison all the nations were deceived. In her (the deception) was found the blood of prophets and of saints, and of all who have been slain on the earth.

Simon Magus, who was the same person as Lazarus and the step-father of Mary Magdalene and thus my step-great-grandfather, died shortly before Paul in the famous battle in the sky with Peter.

In this staged event Simon had used wires and pulleys to appear to be flying in front of the sun. Unfortunately, the wires broke and he fell and broke his leg in three parts. This was, of course, attributed to Peter's prayer.

Thank God that we have continued to be blessed with Jesus' presence, in person, to console us with the immense void that Peter and Paul left behind at the height of their missions.

Although this has been known only by those in the inner circle and his relatives, it has been through us that the Church, which Jesus had envisioned, has been nurtured.

While Jesus was alive, there were different methods that would show his active guidance, for instance the 'visions of Jesus' at Paul's conversion, or just simply the 'ascended Jesus'.

After the deaths of Peter and Paul, Clement, the younger brother of St. James and St. John, became Pope. Although he died last year in AD 99, with his able leadership our Church has survived all attempts to suppress it.

In fact, after the Emperor Domitian's death in AD 96, times have been peaceful under the Senate appointed Emperor Nerva.

And now, for the last two years, with his successor, his adopted son, the Emperor Trajan.

Because Simon Magus' Church had supported the failed Zealots and also the failed affair of Bernice with the Emperor Titus, it was clear that our Church would become the predominant one.

Most of all, our elders were pleased that my grandfather had stepped down. You see, it was always an embarrassment to the Church for Jesus to be present in his human body when he was supposed to have been resurrected!

The triumph of the Church is told in the eighteenth chapter of Revelation and proceeds to blame all deceptions and mistakes on Simon Magus and his followers.

They did not suspect that I would later be a threat to them when I would expose the Resurrection as a lie. After all, I was just a female.

***********Reference Column***********

Final public appearance of Jesus

(Jesus' final public appearance: Revelation 7:14)
They will make war upon the Lamb (Jesus), and the Lamb will triumph over them; for He is Lord of lords and King of kings.
And those who accompany Him --called, as they are, and chosen, and faithful--shall share in the victory.'

Earlier in December AD 71, Jesus, who was also called 'the Lamb' in Revelation to indicate the 'suffering servant of Isaiah', had still been active at the Church Council, advocating again for peace and not to support the Zealots who had managed to cause the destruction of Jerusalem last year.

Shortly after this Council, Jesus realized that he was no longer up to the stress of advisor to the Church and had officially retired. My grandfather's position had been turned over to Uncle Jesus Justus, the crown prince.

Sadly, Jesus would pass away in the next year having lived for 78 years to be reunited with God in AD 72. His body would be placed next to the bones of St. Peter.

New Year's day, AD 100. The fulfillment of my promise to my grandfather.

***********Reference Column***********

The predicted Eschaton

(The Eschaton: Revelation 20:7,11) But when the thousand years are at an end ... Then I saw a great white throne and One who was seated on it, from whose presence earth and sky fled away, and no place was found for them.

***********Reference Column***********

Jesus is the Lamb of God

(John the Baptist calls Jesus 'the Lamb of God': John 35,36)
Again, on the next day, John was standing with two of his disciples, and he looked at Jesus as he walked, and said, 'Behold, the Lamb of God!'

***********Reference Column***********

The Kingdom of Heaven

(John the Baptist proclaims the Kingdom of Heaven: Matthew 3:1,2)
About this time John the Baptist made his appearance, preaching in the Desert of Judaea. And saying, Repent ye: for the kingdom of heaven is at hand.

(Jesus proclaims the Kingdom: Matthew 4:17)
From that time, Jesus began to preach, and to say, 'Repent! For the Kingdom of Heaven is at hand.'

(The Kingdom is within you: Luke 17:20)
Being asked by the Pharisees when the kingdom of God would come, he answered them, 'The kingdom of God doesn't come with observation; Nor will they say, 'See here!' or 'See there!' --for the Kingdom of God is within you.'

(The Kingdom is to be born anew: John 3:3)
Jesus answered him, 'Most assuredly, I tell you, unless one is born anew, he can't see the kingdom of God.'

It is now the year AD 100 and I am 46 years old. The emperor of Rome is Trajan. It was supposed to be the Eschaton, the rapture, when the kingdom of God would be established on earth. Of course, the Church, having made up some excuse, has settled for AD 114. By then I would be 60 years old and, when I see the wrinkle lines in my face, I know that I cannot wait any longer.

My grandfather would have loved to hear their excuses. Jesus warned me not to rely on prophecies as the adjustment to a prophecy inevitably results in the death of a 'scapegoat' like John the Baptist and himself.

He would smile then, and say that 'fortunately, he was only a Lamb'.

We once imagined, as John the Baptist and Jesus did, that the 'Kingdom of God was at hand'. We believed that if enough people embraced 'agape-love' as brothers and sisters, evil would be erased from the world. Sadly, time has shown that this has not been possible to achieve. The Church has been a vehicle for good, but has also been a vehicle for evil.

There are those in the Church today who have chosen to manipulate the faithful by means of dogma to achieve their own egotistical goals for wealth and power and abuse. They resent the descendants of Jesus who hold their lies up to the mirror.

Jesus taught us that the kingdom of heaven is within us and that unless we cast off the false beliefs that enslave us and be born anew, we will not be able to enter into the Kingdom of Heaven.

We must embrace a new paradigm that moves from exclusion to inclusion and that reflects the purity and truth within our cooperative Being. This is what Jesus and all religious leaders hoped for us.

The Knowledge of Good and Evil

(The Tree of the Knowledge of Good and Evil: Genesis 3:4-7) But the serpent said to the woman, "You will not die. For God knows that when you eat of it your eyes will be opened, and you will be like God, knowing good and evil." ...

The stars rule the night

(The fourth day of Creation: Genesis 1:16) And God made the two great lights, the greater light to rule the day, and the lesser light to rule the night: the stars.
(*Assuming the lesser light is the moon, although the moon only reflects light, they added 'he made the stars also'.*)

The Resurrection is to come

(DSS Resurrection fragment: 4Q521)
...For the Lord will consider the pious and all the righteous by name. Over the poor His spirit will hover and will renew the faithful with His power And he will glorify the pious on the throne of the eternal Kingdom... He will heal the wounded, and revive the dead and bring good news to the poor...

Matthew the writer of the Gospel

(Matthew: Matthew 9:9) As Jesus passed by from there, he saw a man called Matthew, sitting at the tax collection office. He said to him, 'Follow me.' He got up and followed him.

Mark the writer of the Gospel

(Mark: Papias of Hierapolis (c.60-135) quoted Church History Eusebius, III.39.15)
"Mark, having become the interpreter of Peter, wrote down accurately, though not indeed in order, whatsoever he remembered of the things said or done by Christ."

Luke the writer of the Gospel

(Luke in Paul's Epistle to the Colossians 4:14) Luke, the beloved physician, and Demas greet you.

John and James

(John#1, brother of James: Matthew 4:21) Going on from there, he saw two other brothers, James, the son of Zebedee, and John, his brother, in the boat with Zebedee, their father, mending their nets. He called them.

John the writer of the Gospel

(John#2, 'the disciple that Jesus loved': John 13:23) One of his disciples, whom Jesus loved, was at the table, leaning against Jesus' breast.

It is not the triumph of good over evil that matters because evil and good will always exist side by side. The tree of the knowledge of good and evil that was placed in the Garden of Eden is to remind us that it is from the choice to do good and not evil that a substance is created within us that survives our death.

My quote from Genesis reminds me of the need to wary of Bible translators who, even on the fourth day of Creation, have led us to accept the silly idea that the moon has its own light and rules the night. Their biased thinking made them add 'he made the stars also' when it really just says 'stars' and thus they removed the stars from ruling the night!

I have dreamt of the day when the angels of heaven would blow their trumpets to herald the freeing of all religions from the chains of dogma that separate us from each other and the Kingdom of Heaven. For it is then that we can be joined with all the other souls who have struggled also to rise above hate and greed with love and generosity.

In every hour of my day for the last twenty-eight years between my prayers to God, to Jesus Christ, to Moses, to the Prophets, to Buddha, to the Angel Gabriel, and to the Angel Michael, and to all our grandmothers and grandfathers who endured Hell on Earth to show us the way to Heaven, I have been secretly compiling the truths that are not only of the Resurrection, but for all of the New Testament.

Please forgive me if my presentation is perhaps too detailed, but I hope that you, my dear reader, will not fault me for meticulously including all written references to everything I have written.

When one deals with history, and especially religious history, there are some facts that are believed to be true without a doubt, but many of these 'facts' may be the result of bias, 'hearsay', or merely wishful thinking. It is therefore safer, whenever possible, to apply the rule of law relating to 'indirect or circumstantial evidence' that states 'the existence of any fact must not be assumed to be true until it can be deduced by a process of probable reasoning'.

The New Testament is supposed to be the truth because it was canonized by the Church or approved by the ordained disciples, and to have mystically become 'the word of God' like the Ten Commandments transmitted directly from God to Moses on Mount Sinai. However, in every situation, there is at least one intervening person between Jesus and his words.

Who is it that you trust? According to church doctrine, your Matthew, Mark, Luke, John, and Paul have 'testified'. They being a reformed tax collector: Matthew; and two persons probably Gentiles: Mark and Luke, who could not have met Jesus before the Crucifixion; and John, one from two possible Johns (the one listed with James or 'the one that Jesus loved'), with scholars thinking that John's style of writing was written long after the others when these Johns would have been dead. As for my father Paul's letters, he was not even allowed to be one of the twelve because he was not with Jesus before the 'Ascension' and made up his own doctrines.

Would it not be important to know the authors of the Gospels in order to understand their personal biases and their connections to Jesus? The truth about these persons is one of the reasons for this book:

1. Matthew was a Sadducee priest and one of the twelve who led the Church and attempted to keep all the Christian groups together.

2. Mark was the scribe of Peter, carefully conserving of the 'Secret Gospel of Mark' and the 'Gospel of Peter'.

3. Luke was the physician of Jesus, who also worked closely with Paul.

4. John, 'the beloved disciple', whose name is revealed in Acts as John Mark, is also known as 'Barthomew', one of the twelve. He had left Jesus' Church with Simon Magus, but was later reconciled.

5. Paul was Jesus' right-hand man and was instructed for the duration of his life by Jesus, who survived the Crucifixion.

And I knew them all!

Addition by the Editor

In AD 114, the people, believing that the Eschaton was occurring, rioted as they had done in Nero's time. In the chaos that ensued, the godless leaders betrayed Jesus' brother Simon-Silas to be martyred by the governor Atticus.

Having been born in AD 22, Simon was 92 years old. (His age of 120, given by Hegesippus, was misinterpreted as Jesus' age if he was still alive!) He had been made Bishop of Jerusalem after the death of James, the brother of Jesus. Simon was also known as Cleopas like James being 'son of a renowned father' (Joseph), and the youngest brother of Jesus, as his age proves.

With his death, 'the generation of those that had been deemed worthy to hear the inspired wisdom with their own ears had passed away' and the corrupt leaders could preach whatever they wanted.

It was during this time that, having heard of the books that Paulina had written, these corrupt leaders arrested Paulina and her sister. In an effort to find out where the master copies of these books were hidden, they subjected the sisters to all sorts of torture. Both sisters being true Sisters of the Church became martyrs for Christ, but did not reveal the location of the books.

***********Reference Column***********

The Basilica of Santa Pudenziana

(Rome of Pilgrims and Martyrs, Ethel Ross Barker, 1913) Even before the Peace of the Church many a private house, whose natural construction of inner court and portico lent itself so admirably to purposes of Christian worship, had been consecrated permanently. Thus the house of the patrician lady Cecilia, that of Pope Clement, that of Pudens (the host of Peter), all became churches which are still standing today.

***********Reference Column***********

The Basilica of Santa Pudenziana

(Tourist guides) The seventh-century itineraries to the graves of the Roman martyrs mention in the catacomb of Priscilla two female martyrs called Potentiana (Pudenziana) and Praxedis (Praxidis). The Basilica of Santa Pudenziana is located near Santa Maria Maggiore. A mosaic in it is the oldest Christian mosaic in Rome showing the two sisters, one on each side. In the back there is a fresco of the sisters Pudenziana and Prassede flanking the Virgin and Son and a fresco of Pudenziana resting her head on St Paul.

A church in Rome called the Basilica of St Pudenziana is named after Paulina and her sister using their student names: Pudenziana and Praxedis.

Their town of Lugdunum Convenarum was later called Saint Bertrand de Comminges with a cathedral on a hill above the Roman ruins. Nearby is Lourdes, the greatest Christian pilgrimage destination in the world.

Paulina's spirit was tied to the earth near this town waiting to fulfill her promise to Jesus.

Her spirit waited until 1858 to be revealed to Bernadette as 'a small young lady'. It was in the village of Lourdes, near to the town of Saint-Bertrand-de-Comminges that this fourteen year old girl thought she saw the spirit of the Virgin Mary, but the spirit was that of Paulina, her great-grandchild.

She showed Bernadette the hiding place of her books in the cave and warned her not to tell anyone and to keep them safe for future generations. She did.

Phoebe and Paul

Chapter 2 - "Like oxen yoked in the Faith."
(My parents: St. Phoebe and St. Paul.)

Jesus said, 'Take up my yoke upon you, and learn from me, because I am meek and humble in heart, and ye shall find rest to your souls' (Matthew 11:29). *** Paul said, 'I commend to you Phoebe our sister, who is a servant of the church which is at Cenchrea' (Romans 16:1). *** 'Yes, I beg you also, true yoke-fellow, help these women, for they labored with me in the gospel, with Clement also, and the rest of my fellow workers, whose names are in the book of life.' (Philippians 4:3)

**********Reference Column**********
Origin of Tamar-Phoebe

(David's daughter: 2Samuel 13:1) And it came to pass after this, that Absalom the son of David had a fair sister, whose name was Tamar.

(Artemis is mentioned in Acts 19:24) ... all with one voice for a time of about two hours cried out, 'Great is Artemis of the Ephesians!'

(First Horsemen of the Apocalypse: Revelation 6:2) And I looked and a white horse appeared, and its rider carried a bow ...

**********Reference Column**********
Mary Magdalene's marriage

(Song of Solomon image at three month pregnant: John 12:3) Then Mary took a pound of ointment of spikenard, very costly, and anointed the feet of Jesus, and wiped his feet with her hair: and the house was filled with the odor of the ointment.

**********Reference Column**********
Three Marys: mother, sister-in-law, wife

(Three Marys: Gospel of Philip, 36) There were three Marys who walked with the Lord at all times: his mother and her sister (in-law), and Magdalene, this one who is called his consort. Thus his Mother and Sister and Wife are each a Mary.

**********Reference Column**********
Mother of sons of Zebedee = Salome (Helena)

(Three at the cross 1-Mary Magdalene, 2-Mother Mary (mother of Jesus' brothers: James and Joses), and 3-the mother of the sons of Zebedee (Helena-Salome foster mother of James and John, consort of Simon Magus): Matthew 27:55,56) And there were there many women beholding from afar, who did follow Jesus from Galilee, ministering to him, among whom was Mary the Magdalene, and Mary the mother of James and of Joses, and the mother of the sons of Zebedee.

Phoebe, my mother, the daughter of Jesus and Mary Magdalene was named after Tamar (in Greek Damaris), who was the daughter of King David. She took the name Phoebe, when she was married to Paul to honor her own grandmother Helena who was a Vestal Virgin in the temple of Artemis. (Helena will be discussed in another chapter.)

In the Greek mythology, the Titan goddess Phoebe was the grandmother of the goddess Artemis, one of the most widely venerated of the Ancient Greek deities, depicted as a huntress carrying a bow and arrows, known to the Romans as Diana.

The conception of Tamar-Phoebe's is implied when Mary Magdalene, being three months pregnant, anointed Jesus with spikenard as she celebrated their permanent marriage. As Jesus was a descendent of King David, she was following the tradition in the Song of Solomon. This was just days before the Crucifixion in March AD 33. It is true that she also did this at the early part of his ministry in Luke but this was merely their betrothal.

It is amazing to think how my mother Phoebe was inside Mary Magdalene's womb during the Crucifixion. The energy of despair all around could have made any baby want to abort, but Grandmother Magdalene told me that it was as if Tamar-Phoebe jumped for joy inside her when Jesus spoke to her from the cross. It was a glow within that warmed the coldness and chaos of the day. I must describe this scene in greater detail now as it reflects on the misunderstandings of the translators.

At the Crucifixion, Jesus had below him three mothers: his mother Mary, his mother-in-law Mary Salome, who was the mother of Mary Magdalene, and the mother-to-be, Mary Magdalene. The Gospel of John says that Mary Cleopas (the betrothed of his younger brother James) was also there.

The three Marys, who are common to all three Gospels, were the Marys that the Gospel of Philip says walked with Jesus at all times.

Mother Mary was 'the mother of James and Joses', her second child and third child. This is a fact that would be obvious to all except for those who hold on to the 'uncle' or the 'perpetual Virgin Mary' theory.

Mary Salome is my grandmother Helena, the sister-in-law of Mother Mary, but not her natural sister, though they would have been Sister nuns. Since Mary Salome had adopted James and John, and was the consort of Simon Magus, also known as Zebedee, she would also be 'the mother of the step-sons of Zebedee'.

Common belief is that Jesus was addressing his mother from the cross, asking John to look after her as a son would. The translation is "he said to his mother, 'Woman, behold your son!'; to the disciple 'Behold thy mother'". The stylish phrasing for someone in agony on the cross seems strange when "John, take care of my mother" would suffice. Actually, his mother would be cared for by her mentioned sons, James and Joses, in addition to the convent.

The knowledge that Jesus is married to Mary Magdalene and that she is three months pregnant with his child, changes the translation: Jesus sees 'the mother and the disciple (John) standing by, whom Jesus loved, he says to 'the mother', not to Mother Mary, nor to his mother-in-law Mary Salome, but to the most important mother in his life: Mary Magdalene who is three months pregnant with Tamar-Phoebe, "Behold the son of you!" Expecting to die soon, Jesus was finding comfort from the excruciating pain in knowing that he would leave behind a son. Needless-to-say it was a daughter, my mother Phoebe, but then my grandfather also survived the cross! John Mark is already Mary Magdalene's chaperone and he will watch over Mary and the baby, my mother inside her.

The name Cleopas, meaning 'renowned', is clearly a title for Joseph, the father of Jesus, as can be seen by this name being used for his youngest son, Simon.

After Great-Grandfather Joseph's death, his second son James took this title, as he is shown with this title after the Resurrection on the Emmaus road to Jerusalem, not recognizing Jesus, and his betrothed is shown as the wife of Cleopas in the Gospel of John as the fourth Mary at the cross named Suzanna.

At the Ascension, my grandfather Jesus had returned to the celibate monastic existence at Qumran and then moved to Damascus with Simon Magus the next year. In September, my grandmother Mary Magdalene had given birth to my mother Phoebe. Since this birth was a girl, Jesus would leave his monastic existence in three years to try again for a male heir. Knowing this fact, Peter decides to announce that Jesus will return again at the 'Times of Restitution'. Ironically, Jesus' calendar time for this had failed on Good Friday, but given the different calendar prophecies of the different sects, why not make up a new timeframe that was predictable. He could later announce this date as 36 AD.

After all, the Magi had tricked Herod the Great on the date that Jesus would be born in Bethlehem by using their calendar. Thus Herod would wait two more years. When he figured out that he had been tricked, he had to have all the children two years or younger slaughtered in Bethlehem. Even if he had the right dates, he still did not have the true location for the birth which was at the Queen's House near Qumran.

**********Reference Column**********

Paul meets Seneca

(Paul's debate in Athens: Acts 17:23) For as I passed along, and observed the objects of your worship, I found also an altar with this inscription: 'To An Unknown God.' What therefore you worship in ignorance, this I announce to you.

Phoebe meets Paul

(Tamar-Damaris-Phoebe meets Paul: Acts 17:34) But certain men joined with him, and believed, among whom also was Dionysius the Areopagite, and a woman named Damaris, and others with them.

**********Reference Column**********

The Letters of Paul and Seneca

(2nd letter, Paul to Seneca) I received your letter yesterday with pleasure ... I reckon myself very happy in having the judgment of so valuable a person, that you are delighted with my Epistles: For you would not be esteemed a censor, a philosopher, or be the tutor of so great a prince (Nero), and a master of everything, if you were not sincere. I wish you a lasting prosperity.

(3rd letter, Seneca to Paul) I have completed some volumes and divided them into their proper parts. I am determined to read them to Caesar, and if any favorable opportunity happens, you also shall be present, when they are read;

**********Reference Column**********

Paul and Phoebe betrothed

(Aquila and Priscilla are the chaperones: Acts 18:2) And found a certain Jew named Aquila, born in Pontus, lately come from Italy, with his wife Priscilla.

**********Reference Column**********

Essene view on marriage

(Essene view on marriage: Josephus, Jewish War 2,8,2) They (Essenes) shun pleasures as a vice and regard temperance and the control of the passions as a special virtue.
Marriage they disdain, but they adopt other men's children, while yet pliable and docile, and regard them as their kin and mould them in accordance with their own principles.
They do not wholly condemn wedlock and the continuance thereby of the human race, but guard against women's wantonness, being persuaded that none of the female sex keeps her plighted troth to one man.

It was in AD 51 in Athens that Paul met my mother Phoebe-Damaris when she was 18 years old. Paul had just experienced his first successful debate that would begin his friendship with Seneca, the Younger, a famous Stoic philosopher, who was also tutor and later the advisor to Nero.

Seeing an altar inscribed: 'To An Unknown God', he declared to the crowds of Epicureans and Stoics that this was God the Creator who did not dwell in their temples and could not become a graven image.

Paul's friendship with Seneca would prove to be very valuable for he could be advised of the disposition of the leading characters in Rome and the emperor because of his connections in Rome.

What is not well known is that Seneca, as the tutor and advisor of Nero, had actually shown Paul's Epistles to the Emperor. Seneca had meant well, but this would turn out to be a fateful move. For, when Seneca fell out of favor and Nero turned on the Church, Paul would be considered as dangerous to him as Peter.

Seneca also suffered a similar fate to Paul when he was unjustly accused of plotting against Nero and ordered to commit suicide. He had previously been exiled by Claudius at the behest of his third wife Valeria Messalina, but had been recalled by his fourth wife, Agrippina the Younger, as a tutor to Nero.

Paul and Phoebe were betrothed in Corinth in March AD 52 and chaperoned by the married couple Aquila and Priscilla soon to be his step-uncle and step-aunt. Paul's relationship to Aquila and Priscilla would then be by marriage since the twin brothers, Aquila and Niceta, baptized as John and James, the disciples, had been adopted by my great-grandmother, Helena. (The story of these twins and of their younger brother Clement, who would later to be Pope, is in the chapter on the 'Clementines'.)

Phoebe and Paul's marriage was truly a match made in heaven: the daughter of Jesus to be married to Paul, whom Jesus counted on for his mission after surviving the Crucifixion! Paul would be 36 in AD 53, the age for a dynastic marriage and thus was born in AD 17.

Their betrothal would last three years, which was similar to the three years of betrothal for Jesus and Mary Magdalene, which began when he had left the monastery. Jesus also used this three years to gather and teach his disciples, for which the Church will be eternally grateful.

When Phoebe was three months pregnant with me, thus having confirmed her ability to carry to term and thus eligible to be permanently married by Essene rules, my mother Phoebe and my father Paul were married in Ephesus.

***********Reference Column***********

Essene Rules of Marriage

(Three month probation before marriage: Josephus Wars 2,8.13) There is yet another order of Essenes, who, while at one with the rest in their mode of life, customs and regulations, differ from them in their views on marriage. They think that those who decline to marry cut off the chief function of life - that of transmitting it - and furthermore that, were all to adopt the same view, the whole race would very quickly die out.

They give their wives, however, a three month's probation, and only marry them after they have thrice undergone purification (no menstruation), in proof of fecundity (of pregnancy to term).

They have no intercourse with them during pregnancy, thus showing that their motive in marrying is not self-indulgence but the procreation of children. In the bath the women wear a dress, the men a loincloth.

***********Reference Column***********

(Nazarite vow: Numbers 6:1-5) And the Lord said to Moses, "Say to the people of Israel, When either a man or a woman makes a special vow, the vow of a Nazarite, to separate himself to the Lord, he shall separate himself from wine and strong drink; he shall drink no vinegar made from wine or strong drink, and shall not drink any juice of grapes or eat grapes, fresh or dried. All the days of his separation he shall eat nothing that is produced by the grapevine, not even the seeds or the skins. All the days of his vow of separation no razor shall come upon his head; until the time is completed for which he separates himself to the Lord, he shall be holy; he shall let the locks of hair of his head grow long."

***********Reference Column***********

Paul prepares for marriage

(After Paul's Nazarite vow, his head is shaved (unholy) before his wedding to Tamar: Acts 18:18,23) And Paul, having yet stayed there many days, took leave of the brethren and sailed thence to Syria, and with him Priscilla and Aquila, having shorn his head in Cenchrea, for he had a vow... and went over all the country of Galatia and Phrygia in order, strengthening all the disciples.

***********Reference Column***********

Paul waits for the birth

(Paul visits the convent in Phrygia for the birth of Paulina: Acts 18:23) After spending some time in Antic, Paul set out on a tour, and went over all the country of Galatia and Phrygia in order, strengthening all the disciples.

As strict Essene rules shun any association with females for fear of sexual arousal, marriage was only allowed for members of the royal line of David and for the priestly lines for their continuation and then strictly controlled to limit its defiling influence. A set of laws were developed which were a combination of Jewish and Essene principles.

These marriage rules allowed a three year betrothal period with sexual relations, being allowed only after the holy month of October and a period of Nazarite purification. The three month rule before marriage was to ensure the espoused wife's ability to successfully carry to term before they were tied by marriage rules.

Also, there would be a period of six years abstinence, counting from conception, after the birth of a son or three years after a daughter, since a son is preferred.

Abstinence would most certainly begin no later than the third month of pregnancy to protect the fetus, but preferably at the first missed period.

My great-grandmother Mary had gone to the hill country with Elizabeth for this purpose to avoid my overly amorous great-grandfather Joseph, although he did respect the three month rule. (More on that later.)

Prior to coming together with Phoebe, Paul had gone into the wilderness, as Jesus had done before his engagement to Mary Magdalene, with a Nazarite vow like Samson. He would then shave his hair and beard before they could have sexual relations.

This use of the Nazarite vow prior to marriage explains the confusion of Jesus being called Jesus of Nazareth, as he was really Jesus the Nazarite when in that state. Jesus was born and lived near Qumran on the Dead Sea, not in Nazareth.

This Nazarite vow was used quite often by Bernice, the twin sister of Agrippa II, as penance for her diverse sins. She was the one who was called the 'Whore of Babylon' in Revelations. She had an affair with Titus, the son of Emperor Vespasian, while Titus was destroying Jerusalem and almost married him. She was also accused of incest with her brother.

Bernice was head of a rival Church in Rome that had similar views as Simon Magus' Church, having the audacity to be its female Cardinal, thus 'arrayed in purple and scarlet'. Uncle Jesus Justus was quite infatuated with her as were all men.

When close to deliver, Phoebe traveled to the convent at Hierapolis in Phrygia in Asia Minor to be with her mother, Mary Magdalene, for the birth. Paul took this opportunity to visit Galatia first and then Phrygia to the Churches of Colossae, Laodicea, and Hierapolis in Phrygia in order to be in Hierapolis at my birth.

***********Reference Column***********

Phoebe is deaconess at the Church

(Phoebe takes Paul's Epistle, Romans, to Rome: Romans 16:1-4) I commend to you Phoebe, our sister, who is a lay deacon of the assembly that is at Cenchreae, that you receive her in the Lord, in a way worthy of the saints, and that you assist her in whatever matter she may need from you, for she herself also has been a helper of many, and of my own self. Greet Priscilla and Aquila, my fellow workers in Christ Jesus who have for my life laid down their own necks: unto whom not only I give thanks, but also all the churches of the Gentiles.

***********Reference Column***********

Phoebe & Paul 2nd child

(Phoebe is not at the designated meeting place to try for their second child: 2Corinthians 2:12-14) Now when I came to Troas for the gospel of Christ, and when a door was opened to me in the Lord, I had no relief for my spirit, because I didn't find Titus, my brother, but taking my leave of them, I went forth into Macedonia. But thanks be to God, who at all times is leading us in triumph in the Christ, and the fragrance of His knowledge He is manifesting through us in every place,

***********Reference Column***********

Mary Magdalene is ill

(Phoebe and Paul go to Hierapolis to try for their second child and to visit Mary Magdalene who is ill: Acts 19:22) So he (Paul) sent into Macedonia two of them that ministered to him, Timothy and Erastus; but he himself stayed in Asia for a season.

***********Reference Column***********

Mary Magdalene' funeral

(Simon Magus (Demetrius) makes golden statues of Mary Magdalene: Acts 19:24-28) For a certain man named Demetrius, a silversmith, who made silver shrines of Artemis, brought great business to the craftsmen, whom he gathered together, with the workmen of like occupation, and said, 'Sirs, you know that by this business we have our wealth. You see and hear, that not at Ephesus alone, but almost throughout all Asia, this Paul has persuaded and turned away many people, saying that they are no gods, that are made with hands. Not only is there danger that this our trade come into disrepute, but also that the temple of the great goddess Artemis will be counted as nothing, and her majesty destroyed, whom all Asia and the world worships.' When they heard this they were filled with wrath, shouting, 'Great is Artemis of the Ephesians!'

I was born in the month of September AD 54 at Hierapolis. It was just a month before the hated Nero, at the age of 17, became emperor of Rome.

Being prohibited from sexual relations for three years after the birth of a daughter and also busy with Church affairs, Phoebe and Paul left me at the monastery at Hierapolis under the care of my grandmother Mary Magdalene.

In March AD 57 Paul sent my mother Phoebe to Rome carrying the Epistle to the Romans. Aquila, her step-uncle, and Priscilla his wife would watch over her while she is there. Aquila was the real name of St. John, the twin of St. James. Paul was expecting her to return to renew their marriage, being three years after my birth. He would be 40 years old.

The schedule was tight considering the time it took to go to Rome and back to Asia Minor. In September AD 57, when Phoebe did not return to Troas as scheduled with her chaperone Titus, Paul in 2Corinthians describes his concern that the allotted time would be missed to conceive a second child and how he had crossed over to Macedonia and found her there. Note the subtle use of 'triumph, manifesting' (a hoped for son); 'fragrance' (spikenard: marriage); 'Christ's knowledge' ('Phoebe, Jesus' conception: Biblical 'to know').

Word came to Phoebe shortly after this that her mother Mary Magdalene was ill, so Paul departed with Phoebe to travel to Hierapolis, putting Timothy and Erastus to be in charge at Macedonia. I was so pleased that I was able to see my mother and father again!

I was too young to really remember Grandmother Magdalene, but I think of her fondly. I was told that, when she was feeling poorly, I insisted on sleeping by her side. She always gave me big hugs and kisses.

The nurse nun watched over us, while Paul and Phoebe were together in the next room. It was in Hierapolis that my parents conceived my younger sister.

Mary Magdalene's illness did not improve and she died shortly after this. John Mark-Bartholomew, 'the disciple that Jesus loved', who was always by her side and who had also watched over Mother Mary in Ephesus, decided to take her body there to be buried next to Mother Mary. The two Marys had remained good friends even after her divorce with Jesus.

In Ephesus my step-great-grandfather Simon Magus (Demetrius) had his people make up silver statues of Mary Magdalene. They became so popular and in demand by the people that it started an uproar with the townspeople who worshiped Artemis (Diana). They felt that it was an affront to the goddess Artemis whose major temple was in the city for Mary Magdalene to be venerated more than her.

Paul had tried to persuade Simon Magus to stop making these idols as he felt that this would reflect badly on the Church to be breaking the Second Commandment. Simon's influence in Ephesus was too strong and most of the Church members ignored Paul's advice anyway as Mary Magdalene was much loved. The town clerk merely dismissed the complaining mob.

***********Reference Column***********
(Mary Magdalene (daughter of Philip who lived in the Holy Spirit (married to Jesus) buried in Ephesus: Polycrates, Eusebius, Church History II 31.1)) The time of John's death has also been given in a general way, but his burial place is indicated by an epistle of Polycrates (who was bishop of the parish of Ephesus). In this epistle he mentions him together with the apostle Philip and his daughters in the following words: "For in Asia also great lights have fallen asleep, which shall rise again on the last day, at the coming of the Lord, when he shall come with glory from heaven and shall seek out all the saints. Among these are Philip, one of the twelve apostles, who sleeps in Hierapolis,' and his two aged virgin daughters, and another daughter who lived in the Holy Spirit and now rests at Ephesus; moreover John, who was both a witness " and a teacher, who reclined upon the bosom of the Lord, and being a priest wore the sacerdotal plate; he also sleeps at Ephesus."

***********Reference Column***********

Mary Magdalene divorce

(John Mark leaves Paul to accompany Mary Magdalene who has divorced Jesus: Acts 13:13) From Paphos, Paul and his party put out to sea and sailed to Perga in Pamphylia. John, however, left them and returned to Jerusalem.

***********Reference Column***********

John Mark = beloved disciple

(John Mark, the beloved disciple at the Last Supper: John 13:23-25) One of his disciples, whom Jesus loved, was at the table, leaning against Jesus' breast. Simon Peter therefore beckoned to him, and said to him, 'Tell us who it is of whom he speaks.' He leaning back, as he was, on Jesus' breast saith unto him, Lord, who is it?

(John Mark, the beloved disciple at the Resurrection: John 20:1-5,8) Now on the first day of the week, Mary Magdalene came early, while it was yet dark, to the tomb, and saw the stone taken away from the tomb. She ran therefore, and came to Simon Peter, and to the other disciple whom Jesus loved, and said to them, 'They have taken away the Lord out of the tomb, and we don't know where they have laid him!'
Peter and the other disciple started at once to go to the tomb, both of them running. And the two ran together, and the other disciple ran forward faster than Peter, and came first to the tomb. And stooping down he sees the linen cloths lying; he did not however go in. ... Then the other disciple also entered in therefore, who came first to the tomb, and he saw, and believed.

At the funeral were Simon Magus and his consort my great-grandmother Helena, now quite frail; my father Paul and mother Phoebe; my grandfather Jesus and his new wife Lydia; John-Aquila and Priscilla; Peter and Andrew, and many other important elders of both Churches.

The beloved disciple, John Mark-Bartholomew, was there, of course, with his subordinate, Philip, who was the head of the Churches in Asia including Hierapolis, which at that time were under Simon Magus.

It was a time when the two opposing Churches could for that brief moment join in a common prayer for their dearest Mary Magdalene and reflect on the days when they were one Church, optimistically expecting the Kingdom of Heaven on earth.

It must be understood that Christianity was merely a concept before the Crucifixion and did not become a working entity until AD 44 in Antioch after the Schism of the Churches. Even then, the fine details of the Faith still needed to be worked out by Jesus with the help and advice of Peter and Paul.

No one could really blame Mary Magdalene for staying with her step-father Simon Magus and her mother Helena during the Schism of the Churches. She had, after all, served her purpose of giving birth to my mother Phoebe and my uncles Jesus Justus and Joseph. It was a hard choice to leave Jesus, but it had to be. (John's leaving, being Magdalene's guardian, 'the beloved disciple', shows when Mary Magdalene left Jesus' Church; just as his return showed her death.)

With Mary Magdalene gone, John Mark, the beloved disciple, who had been torn with his duty to Mary Magdalene and his dedication to Jesus, would no longer need to stay in Simon Magus' Church. He would now come back to the Church of Peter and Paul in March AD 58. Philip, his subordinate would also come with him.

The term 'beloved disciple' only appears in the Gospel of John where he is clearly as important as Peter, however, in the other Gospels he is shown only in the list of disciples as Barthomew. He was next to Jesus at the Last Supper, where Peter asks him to question Jesus about Judas, and he was the one who rushed up to the tomb after the Crucifixion. As the 'beloved disciple' he was the one who would stand in for Mary Magdalene at occasions that females were not allowed and to be her chaperone.

It is clear that John-Bartholomew is more important than the John who appears with James and therefore must be the one who is assigned as the author of the Gospel of John. The removal of his name in the Gospel of John and the disguising of his name as Bartholomew in the other Gospels is because he was gone with Mary Magdalene when the Gospels were canonized.

**********Reference Column**********
John Mark as Eutychus

(John Mark, the beloved disciple returns as Eutychus: Acts 20:8-12) And there were many lamps in the upper chamber where they were gathered together, and a youth of the name of Eutychus was sitting at the window. This lad, gradually sinking into deep sleep while Paul preached at unusual length, overcome at last by sleep, fell from the second floor and was taken up dead. Paul, however, went down, threw himself upon him, and folding him in his arms said, 'Do not be alarmed; his life is still in him.' Then he went upstairs again, broke bread, and took some food; and after a long conversation which was continued till daybreak, at last he parted from them. They had taken the lad home alive, and were greatly comforted (not a little comforted).

**********Reference Column**********
Paul waits three months

(Paul waits in Macedonia to be there for the three month viability celebration of his second child: Acts 20:1-3) After the uproar had ceased, Paul sent for the disciples, took leave of them, and departed to go into Macedonia. When he had gone through those parts, and had encouraged them with many words, he came into Greece. And there abode three months. And when the Jews laid wait for him, as he was about to sail into Syria, he purposed to return through Macedonia.

**********Reference Column**********
Phoebe's 2nd child

(Paul stops at Tyre for the birth of his second child: Acts 21:3-9) After sighting Cyprus and leaving that island on our left, we continued our voyage to Syria and put in at Tyre; for there the ship was to unload her cargo. Having found disciples, we stayed there seven days. These said to Paul through the Spirit, that he should not go up to Jerusalem (Qumran).
When it happened that we had accomplished the days, we departed and went on our journey. They all, with wives and children, brought us on our way until we were out of the city. Kneeling down on the beach, we prayed... After saying goodbye to each other, we went on board the ship, and they returned home again.
When we had finished the voyage from Tyre, we arrived at Ptolemais. We greeted the brothers, and stayed with them one day. On the next day, we, who were the companions of Paul, departed, and came to Caesarea. We entered into the house of Philip the evangelist, who was one of the seven, and stayed with him. Now this man had four virgin daughters, who prophesied.

The return of John Mark is told as a humorous story about Eutychus. It was well-known that my father Paul liked to speak at length and Luke, when writing Acts, decided to make fun of this by saying that John Mark, the beloved disciple, whose real name is Eutychus, fell asleep during his speech and fell from the second floor.

Actually, it was not this at all, but a metaphor for John Mark's reinstatement in the Church. The second story of the church was where the clergy of higher rank stood. He fell from this position when he left with Mary Magdalene to go over to Simon Magus' Church, thus the metaphor that he died and was a youth.

When Paul said "his life is still in him", it meant that he was not totally corrupted by Simon Magus' church. There was still not much difference between the two Churches. Clearly, the immense joy at his return is shown, but the expression as a double negative: 'they were not a little comforted' indicates that his return also brings the sadness of the death of Mary Magdalene and the way things used to be.

After the Mary Magdalene's funeral, Paul went to Macedonia and Phoebe took me along to her Church of Cenchreae near Corinth. Paul was biding his time in Greece to wait for Phoebe's three month viability celebration for his second child that he hoped would be his male heir.

My mother and father were pleased when the three month viability was reached. However, there was too much unrest in Corinth and it was decided that Phoebe should go by ship to Tyre. Paul would backtrack through Macedonia until it was time for Phoebe to deliver.

With Phoebe approaching her due date, my father Paul, who had been given a mission to bring money to Jesus' brother James at Jerusalem (Qumran), gave a farewell sermon in Miletus and finally arrived by ship at Tyre, just as Phoebe went into labor.

And then to my joy, I had a baby sister! In seven days, my mother was ready to travel. Phoebe and Paul, carrying my baby sister, and I boarded a ship to travel to Caesarea to stay with Philip. The brothers and sisters of the Church who had helped Phoebe with the birth came down with us and watched us board the ship.

When John Mark and Philip returned to Jesus, they also brought their Church in Caesarea with them. My mother Phoebe, being Jesus' daughter, was asked to take over Mary Magdalene's role of Mother Superior at their Church as 'a virgin daughter of Philip', the abbot.

***********Reference Column**********
Do not go to Jerusalem

(Matthew (Agabus) warns Paul: Acts 21:10-14) As we stayed there some days, a certain prophet, named Agabus, came down from Judaea. Taking Paul's belt, he bound his own feet and hands, and said, 'Thus says the Holy Spirit: 'So will the Jews at Jerusalem bind the man who owns this belt, and will deliver him into the hands of the Gentiles.' When we heard these things, both we and they of that place begged him not to go up to Jerusalem.Then Paul answered, 'What are you doing, weeping and breaking my heart? For I am ready not only to be bound, but also to die at Jerusalem for the name of the Lord Jesus.' and he not being persuaded, we were silent, saying, 'The will of the Lord be done.'

***********Reference Column**********
Jesus on shipboard

(Paul picks up our family at Sidon and drops us off at Myra: Act 27:1-6) Now when it was decided that we should sail for Italy, they handed over Paul and a few other prisoners into the custody of Julius, a Captain of the Augustan battalion; and going on board a ship of Adramyttium which was about to sail to the ports of the province of Asia, we put to sea; Aristarchus, the Macedonian, from Thessalonica, forming one of our party. The next day, we touched at Sidon. Julius treated Paul kindly, and gave him permission to go to his friends and refresh himself. Putting to sea again, we sailed under the lee of Cyprus, because the winds were against us; and, sailing the whole length of the sea that lies off Cilicia and Pamphylia, we reached Myra in Lycia. There the centurion found a ship of Alexandria sailing for Italy, and he put us on board.

***********Reference Column**********
Cornelius is Luke

(Cornelius meets Jesus: Acts 10:30,31,33) Cornelius said, 'Four days ago, I was fasting until this hour, and at the ninth hour, I prayed in my house, and behold, a man stood before me in bright clothing, and said, 'Cornelius, your prayer is heard, and your alms are remembered in the sight of God. ... Therefore I sent to you at once, and it was good of you to come. Now therefore we are all here present in the sight of God to hear all things that have been commanded you by God.'

***********Reference Column**********
Apollos accuses Paul

(The viper in the fire is Apollos: Acts 28:3) ...there came a viper out of the heat and fastened on his (Paul) hand.
(Alexander the coppersmith: 2Timothy 4:14) "Alexander the coppersmith did me much evil: the Lord reward him according to his works."

Matthew (Agabus), coming from Jerusalem, warns Paul not to go there for Paul was being implicated in the assassination of Jonathan Annas. Clearly, Paul was not part of it in December 57 AD as he was sharing my mother's bed.

Phoebe also tries to dissuade Paul from going, which brings him to tears. However, he insists that it is his duty to go and declare his innocence. It turned out to be a grave mistake that led eventually to his death.

When Paul arrived at the Temple of Jerusalem, he was immediately arrested and put in prison. He was even in danger of being executed.

Our despair turned to joy when in the Fall of AD 60, after not seeing Paul for two years, we were picked up by him at Sidon. So here we were, my mother Phoebe and my father Paul and my baby sister of two years, all sailing on a ship towards Rome!

At six years old, I had no idea of the gravity of the situation. All I knew was that my father Paul was with me. Also on board was my grandfather Jesus who was also going with Paul to Rome.

This was also my first meeting with my grandfather. A fond remembrance I have is when Jesus picked me up to show me the dolphins that were swimming by and taught me a parable about the big fish that had swallowed up Jonah.

The story of Jonah had to do with God's mercy and compassion, but I imagined how much fun it would be to live inside a whale. Jesus often kidded Peter by calling him 'the son of Jonah' because he was so contrary.

We mostly were relegated to the stern of the boat being females, but this was also fun because Luke, the beloved physician, whose other name was Cornelius, was sitting there writing down the diary of the travels of Paul and Jesus. This book would be known as the Acts of the Apostles. Luke would often stop writing and read to us from this book that told amazing stories of places that my father Paul had traveled to while preaching the gospel.

Sadly, the time went by too quickly and we had to disembark at Lycia, but Paul stayed with us for a while until the centurion found a ship of Alexandria sailing for Italy. I cried as Paul hugged me goodbye. He called out to Phoebe, "I will send for you in Rome as soon as I can."

When Paul is shipwrecked on Malta, Apollos, a friend of the accused procurator Felix, implicates Paul in the killing of Jonathan Annas. (Being from Alexandria, he is a Therapeut like Theudas and, being third in gold, silver copper, he reports to Simon Magus, silversmith.) It is not a literal shipwreck, but the wreck of the hopes of those who had counted on the Eschaton by the end of the year.

***********Reference Column***********
Paul is freed

(Paul is freed for two years to take up his mission again: Acts 28:30) And Paul dwelt two whole years in his own hired house, and received all that came in unto him, preaching the kingdom of God, and teaching those things which concern the Lord Jesus Christ, with all confidence, no man forbidding him.

***********Reference Column***********
Pudens and Claudia

(Epistle of St. Paul urging Timothy to come for his second trial in AD 63 showing my teachers Pudens and Claudia: 2Timothy 4:21) Make haste to come before winter. Eubulus and Pudens, and Linus and Claudia, and all the brethren, salute thee.

(Pomponia Graecina accused of foreign superstition: Annals of Tacitus, Book VIII.32) and a lady of distinction called Pomponia Graecina, wife of the Aulus Plautius, whose ovation over the Britons I have recorded, having been accused of some foreign superstition, was handed over for trial to her husband. So in accordance with ancient practice, Plautius sat in judgment on his wife's status and reputation in presence of her relatives, and pronounced her innocent.

***********Reference Column***********
Claudia daughter of Caractacus

('On Claudia Rufina'. Book XI, poem LIII by Martial) "Although born among the blue-eyed Britons, how fully has Claudia Rufina the intelligence of the Roman people ! What beauty is hers ! The matrons of Italy might take her for a Roman; those of Attica for an Athenian. The gods have kindly ordered that she proves fruitful to her revered husband, and that, while yet young, she may hope for sons-in-law and daughters-in-law ! May heaven grant her ever to rejoice in one single husband, and to exult in being the mother of three children."

***********Reference Column***********
Paul goes to Spain

(Paul's Departure from Rome to Spain: The Acts of Peter, Vercelli III.1 ... And when he had fasted for three days and asked the Lord what was right for him, Paul then saw in a vision, the Lord saying to him, 'Paul arise and be a physician to those who are in Spain.'

***********Reference Column***********
Description of Paul

(Description of Paul: Acts of Paul and Thecla) And he saw Paul coming, a man small in size, bald-headed, bandy-legged, well-built, with eyebrows meeting, rather long-nosed, full of grace. For sometimes he seemed like a man, and sometimes he had the countenance of an angel.

When Paul arrived in Rome he was put in prison awaiting trial and then freed for two years, having shaken off 'the viper', Apollos, and suffered no harm. When my father was freed, he sent word to Phoebe to join him. So my mother took my sister and me to Rome and we stayed at the house of Pudens.

I was hoping that Paul and Phoebe would conceive a brother, but, sadly, it did not happen.

I enjoyed my studies under Pudens and Claudia and my sister and I were welcomed by many brothers and sisters in Christ. By now there was a large following of Christians in Rome who were converted by Peter when he came to Rome in AD 44 after his escape from King Herod Agrippa.

My teacher Claudia had married a Roman centurion Aulus Pudens, a friend of Pomponia Graecina and Aulus Plautius, who had received an ovation for conquering the Britons. Pomponia Graecina had been accused of 'some foreign superstition', which we all knew to be Christianity. She was exonerated by her husband at the trial.

The beautiful, blue-eyed Claudia was the daughter of Caractacus, that famous Celtic leader, the son of Cymbeline, who bravely fought with the Silures in South Cymry in Britain against the Roman armies of the Emperor Claudius.

Caractacus was betrayed by the Brigantes and brought in chains to Rome with his wife and child. He was pardoned due to his heroic speech and his child had taken the name Claudia to honor the Emperor.

Our family seemed almost normal with Paul visiting for a few days at a time, but he and Phoebe were always busy doing something and I was often left to look after my sister.

One day my father Paul announced that he was setting off to Espana as it was what he had always wanted. He left Linus in charge at Rome. When he returned, we had barely enough time to hear his travel stories before he was arrested again.

My father Paul looks just the same as the pictures and statues of him because he was well-known throughout the Mediterranean world. He was small in size, bald-headed, bandy-legged, well-built, with eyebrows meeting, rather long-nosed. His face was narrow, ending in a pointy beard, except that his forehead was quite predominant with deep wrinkles. His dark eyes and composure were full of grace.

(Description of Jesus: Ascribed to Publius Lentulus, a governor of a province of Rome) There has appeared in our times, and there still lives, a man of great power (virtue), called Jesus Christ. The people call him prophet of truth; his disciples, son of God. He raises the dead, and heals infirmities. He is a man of medium size; he has a venerable aspect, and his beholders can both fear and love him. His hair is of the color of the ripe hazel-nut, straight down to the ears, but below the ears wavy and curled, with a bluish and bright reflection, flowing over his shoulders. It is parted in two on the top of the head, after the pattern of the Nazarenes. His brow is smooth and vary cheerful with a face without wrinkle or spot, embellished by a slightly reddish complexion. His nose and mouth are faultless. His beard is abundant, of the color of his hair, not long, but divided at the chin. His aspect is simple and mature, his eyes are changeable and bright. He is terrible in his reprimands, sweet and amiable in his admonitions, cheerful without loss of gravity. He was never known to laugh, but often to weep. His stature is straight, his hands and arms beautiful to behold. His conversation is grave, infrequent, and modest. He is the most beautiful among the children of men.

(Concerning Virginity: First Epistle of the Blessed Clement Chap. 6) The womb of a holy virgin carried our Lord Jesus Christ, the Son of God; and the body which our Lord wore, and in which He carried on the conflict in this world, He put on from a holy virgin. From this, therefore, understand the greatness and dignity of virginity. Dost thou wish to be a Christian? Imitate Christ in everything. John (the Baptist), the ambassador, he who came before our Lord, he "than whom there was not a greater among those born of women," ' the holy messenger of our Lord, was a virgin. Imitate, therefore, the ambassador of our Lord, and be his follower in every thing. That John (Mark-Bartholomew), again, who " reclined on the bosom of our Lord, and whom He greatly loved," — he, too, was a holy person (a virgin). For it was not without reason that our Lord loved him. Paul, also, and Barnabas, and Timothy, with all the others, " whose names are written in the book of life," — these, I say, all cherished and loved sanctity," and ran in the contest, and finished their course without blemish, as imitators of Christ, and as sons of the living God.

Sadly, there is no official image of Jesus, as he mostly kept in seclusion, not wanting to be recognized at the risk of exposing the story of his Resurrection. However, I can tell you my description of him in his later years, which does correlate with others.

Jesus' appearance is not the stern look that is portrayed in the popular stylized icon of him, as his appearance is gentle and kind. His face is roundish and he is tall and average stature. His hair is of the color of the ripe hazel-nut, straight down to the ears, but below the ears wavy and curled, showing no signs of gray. It is parted in two on the top of the head, after the pattern of the Nazarenes. His brow is quite prominent and his eyebrows, quite full, were tinged with gray. His beard is abundant and the color of his hair, not long, but divided at the chin, showing tinges of grayest white. His bluish hazel eyes glow with an incredible inner depth.

People often say that I look more like Jesus on my mother's side of the family than of Paul, but my nose is more like Paul's. My hair is light brown and my eyes are hazel. But that is enough about me.

With virginity and marriage being direct opposites according to the strict Essene principles, Paul was concerned that the congregation would not understand that his marriage was a special situation that, of necessity, would ensure the continuance of the royal family of David as it would be also for the priestly lines. The path of virginity would still be practiced with the exception of the times that they would get together to conceive a child.

These rules, based on Nazarite principles, specified the times and circumstances that marriage would be allowed. Thus my mother Phoebe would still be called a Virgin like her mother Mary Magdalene (in spite of the Church's prostitute slurs), and, of course, her grandmother was the Virgin Mary.

This also meant that Paul could call himself a virgin being married to the David line, as could my great-uncle Barnabas (Joses). Also, John the Baptist, being of the Zadokite priestly line would also follow the same rules and call himself a virgin. Others like John Mark and Timothy and Clement would observe virginity at all times.

***********Reference Column***********
Phoebe is yoke-fellow

(Paul calls Phoebe his yoke-fellow while under house arrest In Rome: Philippians 4:3) Yes, I beg you also, true yoke-fellow, help these women, for they labored with me in the gospel, with Clement also, and the rest of my fellow workers, whose names are in the book of life.

***********Reference Column***********
Paul denies marriage

(Paul denies that he is married: 1Corinthians 7:8,9) But I say to the unmarried and to widows, it is good for them if they remain even as I am. But if they don't have self-control, let them marry.

***********Reference Column***********
Jesus = 'Word'

(Derived code word for Jesus: John 1:1) In the beginning was the Word, and the Word was with God, and the Word was God.

(Epistle of St. Paul showing that he is imprisoned, but saying in code that Jesus (the Word) is still alive in AD 63: 2Timothy 2:9) For preaching the Gospel I suffer, and am even put in chains, as if I were a criminal: yet the Word of God is not imprisoned.

***********Reference Column***********
Jesus as the Holy Spirit

(At Pentecost Jesus (the Holy Spirit) directs the disciples to include all races: Acts 2:4) They were all filled with the Holy Spirit, and began to speak in foreign languages according as the Spirit gave them words to utter.

David as the Holy Spirit

(Jesus explains to the scribes that Holy Spirit as the third position, at the right hand of the priest (God): Mark 12:36) For David himself said in the Holy Spirit, 'The Lord said to my Lord (the priest as Lord), Sit at my right hand, Until I make your enemies the footstool of your feet.'

(Peter identifies the title of Holy Spirit as derived from King David: Acts 1:16) 'Brothers, it was necessary that this Scripture should be fulfilled, which the Holy Spirit spoke before by the mouth of David concerning Judas, who was guide to those who took Jesus.

***********Reference Column***********
The Trinity

(Melchizedek: DSS 1QMelch) The Day of Atonement is at the end of the tenth Jubilee, when all the Sons of Light and the men of the lot of Melchizedek will be atoned for.

Clearly many followers had seen Paul and Phoebe together, but Paul denied being married. He used the term "yoke-fellow for my mother Phoebe to disguise the fact that he was married to her.

Paul encouraged the brothers and sisters of the Church to follow the celibate path that Pope Clement and John Mark-Barthomew had recommended, but did not explain to them, in order to prevent confusion, that being married to Phoebe of the David line meant he was exempted from celibacy at certain times.

Since Jesus was alive during the lifetimes of Peter and Paul. They would both have the opportunity to be personally directed by Jesus. It would be through them that Jesus would communicate his directions for the Church. Jesus could not appear in public because he was supposed to have been Resurrected and Ascended. Thus certain devices needed to be used to indicate the presence of Jesus in the flesh.

I have previously shown how 'the Word' was used to indicate the birth of Jesus' sons: Jesus Justus and Joseph. It is also used for Jesus who was referred to as 'Word of God' as expressed in the first chapter of the Gospel of John: "In the beginning was the Word, and the Word was with God, and the Word was God." Thus when Paul wrote from Rome, "the Word of God is not imprisoned", he was saying that Jesus was safe.

The 'Holy Spirit' had always been Jesus' designated position in the Church as the 'Son of Man' who reported to 'the Son of God'. It was a position that had been handed down from King David as Jesus explained to the scribes who questioned him and Peter describes in Acts. It was logical to continue its use after the Crucifixion as Jesus still held this position.

At the Pentecost meeting, even though Jesus had survived the Crucifixion, his position as 'Holy Spirit' was substituted for him to disguise his presence in the flesh. It was not a new entity, but merely Jesus!

Much later, with the strengthening of the Resurrection story, a whole new entity called the 'Paraclete' was created, which is translated as 'Comforter' and implied to be the same as the Holy Spirit. It is in Chapters 14 -17 of the Gospel of John that this new entity was added.

This addition of the 'Paraclete' forms a huge break in the action in the Gospel of John between the Last Supper and the Garden of Gethsemane. Its style and its use of the question and answer technique of the disciples, which is so prominent in gnostic literature, shows that it was added later to support the concept of Trinity being one and the same.

The three important positions in the Church are Priest, Levite, and Holy Spirit known as God, Son of God, Son of Man. As angels they are Michael, Gabriel, Sariel or Raphael and the combination of all three, which was Jesus' ultimate goal: Melchizedek, the Trinity.

Clearly it should be evident that, if Jesus himself uses the expression 'Son of Man', he is not the 'Son of God' and is thus only third in importance in the Church structure. This negates the common belief that he is the Son of God or even God.

It is others in the New Testament that call Jesus the 'Son of God', which has to do with the confusion with Jonathan Annas (Nathanael, one of the twelve) who, as a Sadducee priest, had the title of 'God', similar to the Jesuit title of 'Father'. Yet Jonathan's position in the Church was 'Man' (Gabriel) which is second in importance as 'Son of God'.

Caiaphas tries to get Jesus to say he is the 'Son of God' at the trial, but this was to trap him into admitting that he took orders from Simon Magus who had already been convicted of sedition against Rome.

You may be horrified to find that the position of 'God' was held by Simon Magus before being excommunicated as Lazarus. Then he was the esteemed and respected leader, but at the Schism of the Churches he was derided as '666'.

Apparently, even Peter was confused and called Jesus, "the Christ, Son of God". After Jesus expressed displeasure, he quickly added 'Living' in front of God. This Jesus could accept because 'Living God' meant the position of 'Man', being the 'human' form' (i.e. 'living') of God, his messenger Gabriel, the levite.

Then Jesus, calling Peter, 'the son of Jonah' meaning contrary one, congratulates Peter for finally understanding the difference between what is 'God' and what is 'Man'. He reluctantly puts Peter being in charge of his Church, but is relieved when my intellectual father, Paul, joins him.

In major situations concerning changes of direction, another device to show the presence of Jesus in the flesh is indicated by the 'visions' to Peter and Paul. In the situations that follow, Peter and Paul and Simon actually debate with these visions of Jesus concerning his directives and this should alert us that they are discussing the issues with Jesus in person. A true vision would be one-sided and unchangeable and welcomed; to argue might result in its disappearance.

When Saul is blinded, a 'vision' directs Ananias to name him Paul and accept him into the Church so that he can be his 'chosen vessel' to 'the nations and kings, and the children of Israel.'

Ananias (Simon Magus) objects, saying to Jesus, that he must be mad to take in this man who has been persecuting the Church, but agrees to Jesus' request.

Peter sees a vision of a sheet with four corners with wild beasts on it and a voice saying unto him 'slay and eat' and he replies 'Not so Lord' and the voice replies 'What God has cleansed, call not common.'

Again, in this argument, Peter vehemently opposes 'the vision of Jesus' since, up to this point, he had only been proselytizing the Jews. Jesus was now insisting that Gentiles be included as equals regardless of the issue of circumcision. Baptism would cleanse these 'wild beasts'.

***********Reference Column***********
Jesus & Paul & Luke = 'We'

(The "we-passages" - Paul, Luke, & Jesus - of Acts 16:10-17; 20:5-15; 21:1-18; 27:1-28:16. Shown: Acts 16:9-40) Here, one night, Paul saw a vision: There was a Macedonian who was standing, entreating him and saying, 'Come over into Macedonia and help us.' So when he had seen the vision, *WE* immediately looked out for an opportunity of passing on into Macedonia, confidently inferring that God had called us to proclaim the Gospel to the people there ... A certain woman named Lydia, a seller of purple, of the city of Thyatira, one who worshipped God, heard us; whose heart the Lord opened to listen to the things which were spoken by Paul ... It happened, as *WE* were going to prayer, that a certain girl having a spirit of divination met us, ... crying aloud, 'These men are the bondservants of the Most High God, and are proclaiming to you the way of salvation.' ... The multitude rose up together against them, and the magistrates tore their clothes off of them, and commanded them to be beaten with rods ... Suddenly there was a great earthquake, so that the foundations of the prison were shaken; and immediately all the doors were opened, and everyone's bonds were loosened.

***********Reference Column***********
Jesus' Rules of Marriage

(Jesus' view on the divorce as set down by Paul: 1Corinthians 7:10,11) But to those already married my instructions are - yet not mine, but the Lord's - that a wife is not to leave her husband; (but if she departs, let her remain unmarried, or else be reconciled to her husband), and that the husband not leave his wife.

***********Reference Column***********
Paul's Rules of Marriage

(Paul's view on the divorce: 1Corinthians 7:12-15) But to the rest I - not the Lord - say, if any brother has a wife that believeth not, and she is content to live with him, let him not leave her. The woman who has a husband that believeth not, and he is content to live with her, let her not leave her husband. For, in such cases, the unbelieving husband has become, and is, holy through union with a Christian woman, and the unbelieving wife is holy through union with a Christian brother. Otherwise your children would be unholy, but in reality they have a place among God's people. If, however, the unbeliever is determined to leave, let him or her do so. Under such circumstances the Christian man or woman is no slave; God has called us to live lives of peace.

Interestingly, right after one of Paul's visions, Luke, the author of Acts, starts to use the pronoun 'we', which implies that Paul and Jesus are acting together, with Luke writing it down. (Luke, 'the beloved physician', a Gentile, had replaced John Mark, 'the beloved disciple' after he had left with Mary Magdalene in AD 44 when she divorced Jesus.)

In the 'vision', Jesus begs Paul to come over to Philippi, the chief city of Macedonia to consecrate his betrothal to Lydia in March of AD 50. Lydia was a member of Simon Magus' Church under Bernice who allowed women to be bishops. Thus she is called 'a seller of purple'.

The healing of the soothsayer women by Paul is a metaphor for Paul exercising his right as a bishop to baptize Lydia into the Church of Peter and Paul and to illustrate his discourse to justify Jesus' remarriage.

The justification of this marriage was, of course, difficult to do because Jewish rules forbid divorce and remarriage if the spouse were still alive and Mary Magdalene was. (Paul's defense of Jesus in 1Corinthians is discussed shortly.)

The flogging and arrest of Paul and Silas (Simon, Jesus' youngest brother) are also a metaphor for the anger and discord that arose between the two Churches.

Jesus' decision to marry Lydia did prove to be a mistake as she only produced a daughter, but it came out of the disappointment of losing his dear Mary Magdalene.

The crisis of Mary Magdalene's divorce of Jesus was considerable, but Jesus' remarriage was even worse. To justify the marriage, Jesus even declared a new marriage rule, through Paul's 1Corinthians, with the formula that: the man could not leave, but if the women left the man, as she would be allowed to do as long as she did not marry, then the man was free to remarry. This covered Jesus' situation since it was Mary Magdalene who left. The somewhat obscure nature of this new rule clearly indicates that it was made for a specific purpose, namely for Jesus to marry Lydia.

Paul, however, disagreed with Jesus' marriage rule and wrote after this in 1Corinthians that: if one of the married persons was of a different Church, the couple should stay together because one would sanctify the other. However, he adds, for Jesus' sake that 'marriage is not bond like slavery' and that 'God has called us to live lives of peace.'

One can almost see my father, Paul, writing this Epistle with my grandfather, Jesus, standing next to him, while dictating the words and then Paul insisting that he put in his own opinion after it.

***********Reference Column***********

Epistles are Jesus & Paul writing

(Letters of Paul and Seneca: 1st letter, Seneca to Paul) Annaeus Seneca to Paul Greeting: I suppose, Paul, you have been informed of that conversation which passed yesterday between me and my Lucilius, ... concerning hypocrisy and other subjects; for there were some of your disciples in company with us; We were much delighted with your book of many Epistles, which you have wrote to some cities and chief towns of provinces, and contain wonderful instructions for moral conduct: Such sentiments as I suppose you were not the author of but only the instrument of conveying, though sometimes both the author and the instrument. For such is the sublimity of those doctrines, and their grandeur, that I suppose the age of a man is scarce sufficient to be instructed and perfected in the knowledge of them. I wish your welfare, my brother Farewell,

***********Reference Column***********

Nero's torture

(Nero puts the blame on the Christians for the Great Fire: Tacitus, Book 15,44) Therefore, to scotch the rumor, Nero substituted as culprits, and punished with the utmost refinements of cruelty, a class of men, loathed for their vices, whom the crowd styled Christians. Christus, the founder of the name, had undergone the death penalty in the reign of Tiberius, by sentence of the procurator Pontius Pilate, ... vast numbers were convicted, not so much on the count of arson as for hatred of the human race. And derision accompanied their end: they were covered with wild beasts' skins and torn to death by dogs; or they were fastened on crosses, and, when daylight failed were burned to serve as lamps by night. Nero had offered his Gardens for the spectacle, and gave an exhibition in his Circus, mixing with the crowd in the habit of a charioteer...

Peter and Paul's energy and dedication were an inspiration to all. However, even though Peter was Pope of the Christian Church, Paul appears to have wielded more influence than Peter due to his Epistles. These Epistles have certainly modified and enhanced Jesus' teachings to the point that many would say that Christianity resembles more of Paul's teachings than those of Jesus.

The unifying factor behind these anomalies is that Jesus in the flesh was behind what Paul wrote. In fact, in the 'Letters of Paul and Seneca', it is clear that Seneca is aware of the collaboration between Jesus and Paul.

Without Paul's Epistles, there would have been no structure to the Church. Those who think that my father Paul distorted Jesus' teachings should understand that my father Paul was acting and writing under my grandfather Jesus' instruction! In fact, what is thought of as being the unadulterated teachings of Jesus such as the 'Sermon on the Mount' were really composed by other teachers before him, such as Hilliel. Thus Christianity was developed over time and did not appear suddenly and is still evolving today.

And now I must once again bring up the pain of Nero's actions. No ruler can be worse than the Emperor Nero who would be remembered for the murder of his own mother, the fire at Rome, and most of all for his savage treatment of the Christians which included the deaths of Peter and Paul in AD 64. With rulers who have absolute power, the only solution is to assassinate them. In Nero's case it happened too late to save my father and Peter and so many Christians.

After my father's execution, we fled from Rome to Lugdunum Convenarum. It was such a scary time and we were crying and crying and missing our dear sweet Paul. But we had copies of his Epistles to remind us of his greatness and kindness.

After settling down in Lugdunum Convenarum, and after our grief had subsided, things were quiet for us. Phoebe would leave from time to time for Rome, but mostly we would attend Church and I especially loved singing the hymns.

Then on Christmas AD 71, my grandfather Jesus asked me to write the true story of the Resurrection. This gave my life purpose as a writer, like my father Paul and my grandfather Jesus, as a contributing member to the Church and to God.

Lugdunum Convenarum, Paulina's home town

PE-Chi-Rho(Pesher of Christ)

Chapter 3 The Inner Circle

"If I speak the languages of men and of angels, but have not Love, I am merely a resounding brass, or a clanging cymbal. If I can see the future and understand all mysteries and knowledge, and have faith that can move mountains, but have not Love, yet I am nothing. If I give up all my belongings and surrender my body to the flames, but have not Love, I have gained nothing. Love is impartial, Love is kind, Love is not jealous, Love is not boastful, is not conceited, is not self-seeking, is not given to anger, does not hold grudges, takes joy in truth and justice, surrenders all, has faith in all, has hope in all, endures all." (Paul Hymn to Agape-Love: 1Corinthians 13:1-7).

***********Reference Column***********
Two kinds of love: agape & philo

(Feed my sheep: John 21:15-17) So when they had dined, Jesus saith to Simon Peter, son of John, Lovest (agape) thou me more than these? He saith unto him, Yea, Lord; thou knowest that I love (philo) thee. He saith unto him, Feed my lambs (initiates).

He saith to him again the second time, Simon, son of Jonah, Lovest (agape) thou me? He saith unto him, Yea, Lord; thou knowest that I love (philo) thee. He saith unto him, Shepherd my sheep (congregation).

He saith unto him the third time, Simon, son of John, lovest (philo) thou me? Peter was grieved because he said unto him the third time, Lovest (philo) thou me? And he said unto him, Lord, thou knowest all things; thou knowest that I love (philo) thee. Jesus saith unto him, Feed my sheep (congregation).

John Mark, head of the monastery

(Not to die is to be inside the monastery: John 21:20-22) Peter turned round and noticed the disciple, whom Jesus loved, following - the one who at the supper had leaned back on His breast and had asked, 'Master, who is it that is betraying you?' Peter looking at him, said to Jesus, 'Lord, and what will this man do?' If I desire him to remain till I return,' replied Jesus, 'what concern is that of yours? You, yourself, must follow me.' This word, therefore, went forth to the brethren that that disciple doth not die.

***********Reference Column***********
(Love(agape) is the greatest: 1Corinthians 13:13) And so there remain Faith, Hope, Love--these three; and of these the greatest is Love.

Paul's affirmation of agape-love in 1Corinthians 13 always brings tears to my eyes. It presents a world of peace and Love, sometimes, so far from our every day existence and it reminds me of my father's love. Grandfather Jesus would always emphasize the difference between agape-love and philo-love, but I do not think that I understood it fully until I was older. My love for Paul was philo-love which is a personal love that, of course, feels wonderful, but agape-love is a Love that transcends all boundaries and is centered in the heart, being your Spirit body that lives after your death.

When Jesus spoke to Peter at Mazin after the Resurrection, he used the word agape-love in the first and second question because the manifestation of agape-love would be to care for the initiates and the congregation. Peter, knowing that the honor of being made the head of the Church to the Diaspora and thus of the abbeys, had made him personally grateful and proud, carefully used the word philo-love because this would be the manifestation of personal love to Jesus. Peter's grief was because Jesus had phrased this anointing of Peter as three questions. He knew that Jesus was also reprimanding him for denying him thrice at the Crucifixion. On the third question Jesus finally used the word philo-love to show that he, too, had affection for Peter and forgave him.

As for John Mark-Bartholomew, the disciple Jesus loved, Jesus, after the Crucifixion, made him responsible for the monasteries and to continue to be his go-between to Mary Magdalene when he returned to conceive his next child.

After Paul's death, Jesus came up to Lugdunum Convenarum to comfort Phoebe as she was beside herself with grief. He sat us down in a circle and we held hands. We could feel Paul's presence telling us that he was full of joy for our bright futures and satisfied with all he had accomplished. He was also looking forward to the day that we would meet in the next world. There was no doubt in our hearts that we were in the presence of agape-love that could dissolve the divide between the realm of the earth and the astral plane.

The sum of all of Christianity is agape-love. As those who follow Jesus know, Love had the ability to keep each of their Spirits safe from harm and guide them to the Life after death. You cannot be a Christian until you have Love.

Spirit and Soul

(Paul's dissertation on the 'Unknown God': Acts 17:24-30) The God who made the world and all things in it, he, being Lord of heaven and earth, dwells not in temples made with hands, neither is he served by men's hands, as though he needed anything, seeing he himself gives to all life and breath, and all things. He made from one blood every nation of men to dwell on all the surface of the earth, having determined appointed seasons, and the bounds of their habitation, that they should seek the Lord, if perhaps they might reach out for him and find him, though he is not far from each one of us. For in him we live, and move, and have our being. As some of your own poets have said, 'For we are also his offspring.' Being then the offspring of God, we ought not to think that the Divine Nature is like gold, or silver, or stone, engraved by art and device of man. The times of ignorance therefore God overlooked. But now he commands that all men everywhere should repent, because he has appointed a day in which he will judge the world in righteousness by the man whom he has ordained; whereof he has given assurance to all men, in that he has raised him from the dead.'

(There are three bodies: 1Corinthians15:44,45) It is sown a natural body, it is raised a spiritual body; there is a natural body, and there is a spiritual body. The first man Adam was made into a living soul; the last Adam into a quickening spirit.

(Before the raising of Lazarus: John 11:25) Jesus said to her (Martha-Helena), 'I am the resurrection and the life. He who believes in me, though he die, yet will he live.'

The Inner and Outer circles

(Different teaching for outer and inner circle: 1Corinthians 3:1,2) My brothers, I (Paul) could not address you as spiritual men, but as men of the flesh, as babes in Christ. I fed you with milk, not solid food; for you were not ready for it; and even yet you are not ready..."

(Speaking in parables: Matthew 13:9-13) He who has ears to hear, let him hear.' The disciples came, and said to him, 'Why do you speak to them in parables?' He answered them, 'To you it is given to know the mysteries of the Kingdom of Heaven, but it is not given to them. For whoever has, to him will be given, and he will have abundance, but whoever doesn't have, from him will be taken away even that which he has. Therefore I speak to them in parables, because seeing they don't see, and hearing, they don't hear, neither do they understand.

It has been known since human beings became aware of their place in the universe that there can exist two other permanent states of stability within. These can be likened to the creation within of an emotional body and a mental body that I prefer to call a Spirit and a Soul. There are other confused meanings for these terms as some call the Soul the Spirit Body or say that it is just the spirit that is absorbed back into the Great Spirit or that a soul is nothing more than the life-force which animates a living creature.

My father Paul had three definitions, the natural Body, the Spirit, and the Quickening Spirit. He emphasized that those who do good are rewarded with an eternal Spirit and that if this Spirit is re-animated or resurrected by service to God it can be made to be eternal. This is what Jesus meant when he said "I am the resurrection and the Life'. I find that it is clearer to define the Soul as a separate body.

Obviously, those who have corrupted emotions and minds will disintegrate into nothing at the death of the physical body. The good do have their reward!

To understand the presence of these higher bodies, I like to use the analogy of those times when you were deathly ill with the flu. At first you forget what it was like to be well and then, as the flu disintegrates, you realize what it is like to be filled with the energy of life-force again. The proof of the existence of life-force is dependent on being in it! And then you take it for granted again.

When you enter into the Spirit through the act of creation of, for instance, music or art, you become enveloped by the Spirit and you know it to be real. And yet, after the physical plane reasserts itself with its many distractions, you doubt if Spirit really exists. It may even be difficult to find that place of Spirit again, until it becomes the center of your being.

It is even harder to enter into the realm of Soul, which is the kingdom of Heaven, because it must be reached from the Spirit. You must grow the wings of an angel out of your Spirit body and enter into the throne of God. It is then that God will help you to remember your purpose for being born.

These are the secrets revealed to us, the inner circle within the outer circle of Christianity. Ironically, these circles are now reversed because the inner circle has lost the knowledge and it is only by means of books like this, that the lost truths of the inner circle can be revealed from the outside.

It is necessary for all religions to maintain an inner circle and an outer circle because knowledge being a substance, according to the physics of the Greeks, can become so diluted that it will have no value. If truth were commonplace, it would not be valued!

It is for this reason that the teachings of Jesus and Paul to the masses were given in code or parables so that only the inner few would be allowed to learn the secrets. However, the masses were more likely to be impressed by miracles and simple truths than by complex dissertations. Therefore, Paul and other missionaries would carry certain pharmaceutical drugs and be trained in certain methods of reviving the sick in order to amaze the listeners. Certain symbolic rituals would be substituted like Baptism and Communion, rather than the knowledge of their purpose.

***********Reference Column**********
Use of Magic

(Simon Magus, the magician: Acts 8:9) But there was a man named Simon who had previously practiced magic in the city and amazed the nation of Samaria, saying that he himself was somebody great.

***********Reference Column**********
Martyrdom

(The Acts of Paul and Thecla) And Thecla, having been taken out of the hand of Tryphaena, was stripped, and received a girdle, and was thrown into the arena, and lions and bears and a fierce lioness were let loose upon her; and the lioness having run up to her feet, lay down; and the multitude of the women cried aloud. A bear ran upon her; but the lioness, meeting the bear, tore her to pieces. And again a lion that had been trained against men, ran upon her; and she, the lioness, encountering the lion, was killed along with him. And the women made great lamentation, since also the lioness, her protector, was dead.

***********Reference Column**********
The Resurrection of the Soul

(The Day of Reckoning: 1Corinthians 15:52) in a moment, in the twinkling of an eye, at the last trumpet. For the trumpet will sound, and the dead will be raised incorruptible, and we will be changed.

(The dead rise first: 1Thessalonians 16,17) For the Lord Himself will come down from Heaven with a loud word of command, and with an archangel's voice and the trumpet of God, and the dead in Christ will rise first. Afterwards we who are alive and are still on earth will be caught up in their company amid clouds to meet the Lord in the air.

***********Reference Column**********
Hidden Word

(The hidden Word shows the Christ within us: Gospel of Philip 29) Jesus took them all by stealth, for he did not appear as he was, but in the manner in which they would be able to see him. He appeared to them all. He appeared to the great as great. He appeared to the small as small. He appeared to the angels as an angel, and to men as a man. Because of this, his Word hid itself from everyone. Some indeed saw him, thinking that they were seeing themselves, but when he appeared to his disciples in glory on the mount, he was not small. He became great, but he made the disciples great, that they might be able to see him in his greatness.

Simon Magus, my step-great-grandfather, being trained as a magician, found that performing magic tricks would always draw a crowd as people were more likely to believe in the truth of magician's illusion than the truth about their spiritual potential. One of his most famous tricks was to pretend to fly by means of pulleys and rope. The gullible people would then believe him to be a god and listen to every word he said. However, Jesus and Paul did not condone this type of trickery as it added nothing to the person's well-being, but, since healing with medicines would, they did amaze many.

The murder of Christian martyrs became great sport for the Romans particularly because of their non-violent stance. Paul warned his Christians not to purposefully march off to be eaten by lions or burned on crosses because the preservation of life is clearly the superior method to achieve a Spirit and a Soul.

The act of martyrdom could by its extreme sacrifice ensure that one's Spirit would survive death, but the ability to advance to the higher state of Soul might not be achieved in time before the dissolution of the Spirit.

The Essene principle that one day there would be a Day of Reckoning was one of Paul's favorite themes. The people were enthralled by the concept that all the good souls would be directed to heaven and all the bad souls to hell. It helped people to be consoled from the evil that was done to them and it could prevent some people from being tempted to do evil.

My mother Phoebe would tell my sister and me not to believe Paul's elaboration of this process, saying that it was mere fantasy. She would say, "There is no such thing as a free pass to Heaven because the Resurrection of the Soul was within oneself." However, the theme did make for some wonderful paintings.

What I learned from my father Paul and my grandfather Jesus was that it was most important to especially be aware of the places where the text of the New Testament becomes exaggerated or defies the known laws of science. It was there that one would almost certainly find a hidden meaning.

This hidden meaning is a means of bridging the gap between this world of our five senses and the divine world that can be reached by our sixth sense of intuition. "Turning water into wine", "walking on water", "healing by touch or word", and "raising someone from the dead" are metaphors that are meant to shake up our reality. This is the same purpose that mythology has in the lives of all different peoples.

This process of teaching by parables was Jesus' favorite method. He would always tell me that parables help us to make that important leap from flesh and blood to the living bread and wine of Soul and Spirit. For it is in words that we communicate in our daily lives, but it is in the Word of God that our minds can transcend our physical natures and to express our true nature in the Kingdom of God.

My father Paul liked to call this method the 'Pesher of Christ' for the word 'pesher' was the method of interpretation that he, as Saul, with his associates in Damascus would use to reinterpret certain phrases in the Old Testament and apply them to the present. He had accused Jesus as the 'Wicked Priest', but this was before his conversion in Damascus.

The 'Pesher of Christ' not only reveals the true story of Jesus and the early Church, but also defines a new religious paradigm that is not based on doctrine, but of Love for all Humankind and its for God-ness.

My mother Phoebe, who was most dedicated to the Church, was quite opposed to its aggrandizement. "We must tear down the confining secular walls of endless denominations", she would say. "We must remove the idolatry of its founders and leaders. We must burn all dogma, which enslaves the masses and consolidate the power of the few." She was very much like her father Jesus. She would have overturned the tables of the moneychangers also.

As I had studied the New Testament for my Bat Mitzvah in 66 AD, I realized that the order in which we recited 'the Lord's Prayer' was different from the New Testament. Since Jesus had come up for the ceremony, I asked him why it was that in our version the 'temptation' line was just below 'Thy will be done'.

℟ Jesus started out, with a wave of his hand in disgust, saying "As long as a priest and a levite rule the Church, there will be only crumbs left for us dogs!" I recognized this as the metaphor that Helena, the Syro-Phoenician woman, used to justify her daughter's marriage.

℟ Jesus continued, "It is a little complicated, but let me get into their puffed-up heads and describe their logic. You see the Church leaders had no idea that the 'Lord's Prayer' and the 'Twenty-third Psalm' were a sequential formula and automatically assumed that, since 'daily bread' must be the Eucharist, it needed to be below 'Thy will'. As they were the ones who passed out the bread at communion, it gave them more power to be associated with the 'Will of God'. As to the temptation line with which they replaced the 'bread' line, thinking that the temptation was merely sexual attraction and the most difficult for them to control, they moved it to the bottom."

℟ Jesus explained further, "The proof that 'the trespasser line' used to be last is seen in Matthew when 'debtors' are used in the prayer and the 'trespassers' line appears after the prayer is finished. The importance of this 'trespassers' line is also indicated by the fact that it is the only line of the five that exists in Mark." Next he showed me the relationship of the lines in the 'Lord's Prayer' to the 'Twenty-third Psalm' which further confirmed the correct order.

40

1.
a. Our Father which art in heaven. Hallowed be thy name.
b. The Lord is my shepherd, I shall not want.
c. Mind (Hestos-Heaven) and Intelligence (Sophia-Earth)

2.
a. He maketh me to lie down in green pastures: He leadeth me beside the still waters. He restoreth my Soul:
b. Thy kingdom come. Thy will be done in earth as it is in heaven
c. Voice (Logos - Word)

3.
a. He leadeth me in the paths of righteousness for his name's sake. Yea though I walk through the valley of the shadow of death. I will fear no evil: for thou art with me; thy rod and thy staff they comfort me.
b. Lead us not into temptation, but deliver us from evil
c. Name - Life

4.
a. Thou prepareth a table before me
b. Give us this day our daily bread.
c. Church - Holy Table

5.
a. In the presence of mine enemies: thou anointest my head with oil
b. And forgive us our trespasses, as we forgive those who trespass against us.
c. Baptism - Grace

The correct order of the 'Lord's Prayer' in its usual wording is shown together with the 'Twenty-third Psalm' in its Old Testament order showing their similarities:

1. Our Father which art in heaven. Hallowed be thy name.
(The Lord is my shepherd, I shall not want)

2. Thy kingdom come. Thy will be done in earth as it is in heaven
(He maketh me to lie down in green pastures: He leadeth me beside the still waters. He restoreth my Soul:)

3. Lead us not into temptation, but deliver us from evil
(He leadeth me in the paths of righteousness for his name's sake. Yea though I walk through the valley of the shadow of death. I will fear no evil: for thou art with me; thy rod and thy staff they comfort me.)

4. Give us this day our daily bread.
(Thou prepareth a table before me)

5. And forgive us our trespasses, as we forgive those who trespass against us.
(In the presence of mine enemies: thou anointest my head with oil)

The relationships between the 'Lord's Prayer' to the 'Twenty-third Psalm' are quite obvious and each gives more insight into the other. It is important to first understand that their order is God to man, but we travel from man to God (5 to 1). For instance, in line 2, the 'Twenty-third Psalm' uses the word 'Soul', that God, the Shepherd, restores, showing that the Soul has the capability of being filled by 'God's Will' shown in the same line in the 'Lord's Prayer'. This is why a Soul is eternal.

In line 3 the method is given to avoid temptation using the images of a shepherd's rod pushing us forward on the 'straight and narrow path' and the shepherd's crook to change direction to avoid danger. 'Temptation' is not the trivial sense of earthly temptations, but rather these are the temptations of the 'serpent in the Garden of Eden' or the 'battle of Michael and Satan' that involve the temptation to use knowledge to gain power over others. This is the place where the 'tares' are separated from the 'wheat' in the resurrection of the dead. Sadly some foolishly use this knowledge to merely support the state of bliss in the realm of Spirit already attained, thus to eventually end their days in the oblivion of emotional dreaming until the Spirit dies.

In line 5 is the most important step if one chooses to embark on a spiritual path that very few travel upon. It is the point of impartiality. This is the act of 'turning the other cheek'. In the 'Twenty-third Psalm', the image of 'anointing ones head with oil' is linked with 'in the presence of ones enemies', which refers directly to David expressing kingly qualities to his enemies as he did in sparing Saul's life. It is a state of emotion and mind that says I am more than a body with feelings and ego, I am made of Spirit and I will act like an angel.

The correspondence between these two prayers and Simon Magus' philosophy from Jesus' Gospel of John will be shown in a later chapter.

***********Reference Column***********

Cosmic Octave

(The David's secret chord expressed in Pythagorean notation) These five levels are the descending vibrations: 'do', 'ti', 'la', 'sol', 'fa'. Human beings are made up of body, mind, and feelings ('lower do', 're', 'mi').

Then, since the distance between 'mi' and 'fa' is not proportional and therefore requires a certain energy, this energy is obtained by maintaining impartiality of feelings, such as 'turning the other cheek' or 'forgiving our trespassers'.

Building up this emotional energy moves us to 'sol' which is the emotional 'bread' that sustains our Spirit-self.

For the Spirit-self to continue to the growth of an eternal Soul, the mind must apply the principle of right and wrong: the 'rod' to go forward and not to be contented and the 'staff' to turn to the correct path as it presents itself. By following 'God's will' we pass from 'sol' to 'la' and from 'la' to 'ti'. This is where God separates the 'tares' from the 'wheat'

At 'ti' if there is sufficient 'wheat' (Soul force), the Soul live eternally in the 'Kingdom of Heaven'. The passage from 'ti' to the 'higher do' is merely an image as it not possible to be God for God to exist. Just as the Big Bang began the universe so will the Big Crunch annihilate all matter.

***********Reference Column***********

Not my will, but thine

(Jesus in the Wilderness: Matthew 4:10) Then Jesus said to him, 'Get behind me, Satan! For it is written, 'You shall worship the Lord your God, and him only shall you serve."
(Jesus in the Garden of Gethsemane: Luke 22:42) 'Father, if it be Thy will, take this cup away from me; yet not my will but Thine be done!'

These prayers are precisely the notes of the 'secret chord of David'. For the Church to have changed the order without Jesus' permission tells us a lot about the politics of the time or maybe just of their ignorance! Ironically, these changes have just about reversed the tones so the congregation are almost reciting the tones backwards like Satanic cults do!

The verses are the notes in a Cosmic Octave that can be laid out in a circle as 'do', 'ti', 'la', 'sol', 'fa', (mi, re, do - not shown), thus spiritual growth is 'fa', 'sol', 'la', 'ti', 'do'. This formula for spiritual growth is from physical form (lower do-re-mi) to the emotional body (5 & 4) and from the emotional body to the permanent soul (3 & 2) to God (1).

'Agape-love' (5), which is the first level of spiritual growth, is obtained by the use of 'impartiality, therefore 'turning the other cheek' or 'forgiving those who trespass against us' or 'expressing kingly qualities (anointed with oil) in the presence of one's enemies'. It is often thought that a cloistered existence in a monastery would create this effect, but this existence actually makes it harder because there is less confrontation. The act of forgiveness after the fact may be a tool of therapy to sever the infinite loop of emotion-mind obsession, but it is of no use unless forgiveness is applied at the moment of the event. This method is also known as the fourth way as it is living as a spiritual being in the material world instead of separating from it as a fakir, a monk, or a yogi.

The bread (4) is the emotional energy that sustains the Spirit. The wine symbolizes the blood since this energy is centered in the heart. This is the state that is sometimes referred to as the astral plane. The sustaining of this state requires a dedication to other worldly activities, such as the creation of music or art, but not limited to these.

The 'temptations' (3) represent the passing from Spirit to Soul. It is the Devil card in the Tarot. It is Jesus tempted in the wilderness and in the Garden of Gethsemane. It represents forgoing the bliss of Spirit for the higher cause of service to God and the need to struggle with one's ego to be prepared to accept God's Will.

To serve the Will of God (2) is to finally be connected to God (1). It is the ultimate journey that brings life eternal in the Soul body.

Lourdes where Paulina's book was found

Julia the Elder, daughter of Augustus Caesar (mother of St. James and St. John) and Julia Agrippina the Younger, mother of Nero, granddaughter of the Julia the Elder (wrote the diary)

Chapter 4 Pope Clement's Recollections.
(The Recognitions of Clement and the Clementine Homilies.)

I Clement, who was born in the city of Rome,' was from my earliest age a lover of chastity; while the bent of my mind held me bound as with chains of anxiety and sorrow. For a thought that was in me - whence originating, I cannot tell - constantly led me to think of my condition of mortality, and to discuss such questions as these: Whether there be for me any life after death, or whether I am to be wholly annihilated: whether I did not exist before I was born, and whether there shall be no remembrance of this life after death, and so the boundlessness of time shall consign all things to oblivion and silence; so that not only we shall cease to be, but there shall be no remembrance that we have ever been. This also I revolved in my mind: when the world was made, or what was before it was made, or whether it has existed from eternity. For it seemed certain, that if it had been made, it must be doomed to dissolution; and if it be dissolved, what is to be afterwards? - unless, perhaps, all things shall be buried in oblivion and silence, or something shall be, which the mind of man cannot now conceive.(Recog. Clement I.1)

In AD 95, a book written by Pope Clement called the 'Clementines', arrived at our doorstep. I knew immediately that it was sent for safe keeping as we had heard the news that Pope Clement's nephew Titus Flavius Clemens had been put to death by the Emperor Domitian and his wife sentenced to exile on the island of Pandateria on a charge of 'atheism', which always meant Christianity. His own brother, Marcus Arrecinus Clemens, had been killed only the year before.

With this island Pandateria being the same island of exile for the two Julias, who were the composite for the mother in the 'Clementines', I cannot help thinking that the Emperor Domitian had seen the 'Clementines' and was acting on the advice of the leaders of the Church. Was his choice of Pandateria his way of being ironic? It seemed a harsh punishment for Titus Flavius Clemens who was the nephew of Domitian's father, Emperor Vespasian, and Flavia Domitilla, who was, after all, his own niece.

His Flavian family of Emperor Vespasian and Emperor Titus had previously taken a great interest in the Jewish historian Titus Flavius Josephus, who had taken their family names as his first names in respect for them. He was still alive in Rome, having published his writings: 'The Wars of the Jews' and 'The Antiquities of the Jews'. (Many of my references have been from his writings.) Domitian would then have been well-versed in Jewish religion and thus of its related version, Christianity.

His brother, Emperor Titus, who died after a brief reign from AD 79 to AD 81, had proceeded Domitian to the throne. Titus had almost married Queen Bernice who was of the Church of Simon Magus and was still living and would have influence to protect Simon. That Domitian singled out the family of Pope Clemens, I believe, demonstrates that he was being influenced by the opposing factions in our own Church.

(Stephanus revenges their death: Suetonius, Lives of the Twelve Caesars: Domitian) Concerning the nature of the plot and the manner of his death, this is about all that became known. As the conspirators were deliberating when and how to attack him, whether at the bath or at dinner, Stephanus, Domitilla's steward, at the time under accusation for embezzlement, offered his aid and counsel. To avoid suspicion, he wrapped up his left arm in woollen bandages for some days, pretending that he had injured it, and concealed in them a dagger.

(Clementine Recognitions & Homilies) (R.IX:35 Revelations.) This person whom you see, O men, in this poor garb, is a citizen of the city Rome, descended of the stock of Caesar himself. His name is Faustinianus. He obtained as his wife a woman of the highest rank, Mattidia by name. By her he had three sons, two of whom were twins; and the one who was the younger, whose name was Clement. (H.XII:12 A Pleasure Trip.) When Peter had spoken thus, a certain one amongst us ventured to invite him, in the name of all, that next day, early in the morning, he should sail to Aradus, an island opposite, distant, I suppose, not quite thirty stadia, for the purpose of seeing two pillars of vine-wood that were there, and that were of very great girth. (R.VII:13 The Beggar Woman.) But when Peter had admired only the columns, being no wise ravished with the grace of the painting, he went out, and saw before the gates a poor woman asking alms of those who went in; and looking earnestly at her, he said: "Tell me, O woman, what member of your body is wanting, that you subject yourself to the indignity of asking alms, and do not rather gain your bread by laboring with your hands which God has given you" (R.IX:36 New Revelations)... she was ordered to depart from the city (Rome) with her twin sons, leaving the younger one with his father; and how on their voyage they had suffered shipwreck through the violence of a storm; and how, when they were cast upon an island called Aradus, Mattidia was thrown by a wave upon a rock, but her twin children were seized by pirates and carried to Caesarea, and there sold to a pious woman, (Justa-Luna) who treated them as sons, and brought them up, and caused them to be educated as gentlemen; and how the pirates had changed their names, and called the one Niceta and the other Aquila;

In the next year, fortunately, our fears for Pope Clement's life were allayed because Clemens' servant Stephanus had avenged his master's death by assassinating the Emperor Domitian in September AD 96 with the help of the members of the Senate. Not that my grandfather Jesus would have approved of this, but it was a relief for us.

Pope Clement wrote us then to ask that we continue to hold on to the book, as he feared that the Church leaders would try to destroy it. There was too much material in it that the leaders had striven so long and hard to suppress to allow it to be published. It is too easy to dismiss the 'Clementines' as a fantasy story because its reality flies in the face of the Church imposed story. Thus this is all the more reason that I need to support it in detail here.

The 'Clementines' were composed between AD 59, the year that Agrippina's diary was published, and AD 62, when James the Just was killed, since James is mentioned as being alive, as the bishop of Jerusalem. Pope Clement, who is his own character, Clement, in the 'Clementines', had considerable connections in real life to the emperors of Rome. These connections, which are mentioned in his book, are therefore not fictional. Thus, his nephew's servant had the access to assassinate Domitian and, prior to that, Pope Clement's father, Marcus Arrecinus Tertullus Clemens, was head of the Praetorian Guard and had helped in the assassination of Emperor Caligula and Claudius' ascent to the throne.

King Agrippa, who had also taken an active role in the making of Emperor Claudius, was a friend of Julia Livilla and would have personally rescued her from her exile on Pandateria Island. This island would be used in the 'Clementines' as a model for the island where the mother would be rescued. Julia was the granddaughter of Julia the Elder and the great-granddaughter of Augustus Caesar. Later, Julia Livilla would be accused by Messalina, the wife of Claudius, of having an affair with Seneca, who was a friend of my father Paul. This event confirms the validity of the 'Letters of Paul and Seneca' and Julia's connection with Agrippa.

The important parallels are:

1. **The real island is Pandateria Island:** The real mother, who was banished to the island of Pandateria, is Julia the Elder, the daughter of Augustus Caesar. She had an illicit affair with Jullus Antonius, who is the son of Mark Antony. He was also her step-brother from Antony's marriage to Octavia the Younger, the sister of Augustus. Julia gave birth to twins: Niceta-St James and Aquila-St. John.
   Her character is then amalgamated with Julia Livilla ('the little Livia'), her granddaughter, and the sister of Agrippina (who wrote the diary);

2. **the story island is Aradus (which is also the real island where my great-grandmother Helena-Justa-Luna was a Vestal Virgin):** The story mother is Mattidia, shipwrecked on Aradus (corresponding to my great-grandmother Helena-Justa-Luna, the real step-mother who adopted the twins: Niceta-St James and Aquila-St. John).

*********** Reference Column ***********

Connecting the Characters

(James and John: Matthew 4:21) Going on from there, he saw two other brothers, James, the son of Zebedee, and John, his brother, in the boat with Zebedee, their father, mending their nets. He called them.

(Syro-Phoenician woman: Clementine Homilies H.II:19) "There is amongst us one Justa, a Syro-Phoenician, by race a Canaanite, whose daughter was oppressed with a grievous disease. And she came to our lord, crying out, and' entreating that He would heal her daughter."

(Syro-Phoenician woman: Mark 7:26) She was a Gentile woman, a Syro-Phoenician by nation: and again and again she begged Him to expel the demon from her daughter.

(Helena-Justa is Luna the Moon: Clementine Homilies H.II:23) There was one John, a day-baptist, who was also, according to the method of combination, the forerunner of our Lord Jesus; and as the Lord had twelve apostles, bearing the number of the twelve months of the sun, so also he, John, had thirty chief men, fulfilling the monthly reckoning of the moon, in which number was a certain woman called Helena, that not even this might be without a dispensational significance. For a woman, being half a man, made up the imperfect number of the triacontad (30); as also in the case of the moon, whose revolution does not make the complete course of the month.

(Simon Magus: Acts 8:9) And a certain man, by name Simon, was before in the city using magic, and amazing the nation of Samaria, saying himself to be a certain great one,

(Bernice as the Whore of Babylon: Revelation 7:4,5) And the woman was arrayed with purple and scarlet-color, and gilded with gold, and pearls, having a golden cup in her hand full of abominations and uncleanness of her whoredom, upon her forehead was written: 'Secret, Babylon the Great, the Mother of the Whores, and the Abominations of the earth.'

(Zacchaeus as Ananus the Younger: Luke 19:2,3) And there was a man named Zacchaeus; he was a chief tax collector, and rich. And he sought to see who Jesus was, but could not, on account of the crowd, because he was small of stature.

(Matthias-Barnabas-Joses: Acts 1:26;4:46) They drew lots for them, and the lot fell on Matthias, and he was numbered with the eleven apostles. Joses, who by the apostles was surnamed Barnabas (which is, interpreted, Son of Exhortation), a Levite, a man of Cyprus by race,

Since I knew many of the facts upon which the 'Clementines' were built, I was certainly amazed at how Pope Clement had masterfully created this historical fiction.

The characters in the 'Clementines' reveal the real characters with real histories beyond their sparse identities in the New Testament.

These real life characters are brought to life when the 'Clementines' are connected with the New Testament:

1. Helena-Justa-Luna is shown as the consort of Simon Magus and foster-mother of Niceta and Aquila, thus connecting Simon Magus with Zebedee as the step-father of St. James-Niceta and St. John-Aquila.
2. Helena-Justa-Luna is shown as the Syro-Phoenician woman, quoting the New Testament story, thus connecting her natural daughter with Mary Magdalene.
3. Niceta and Aquila are related to the Emperor's family and by interpolation, illegitimate grandsons of Augustus Caesar and Mark Antony.
4. Helena-Justa-Luna is shown as a major person being the one female with 29 men for the days of a moon-month in John the Baptist's organization and that Simon Magus became its head after John the Baptist was deposed.
5. Simon Magus was a magician and thus matches the description of him in Acts. As he is a worthy adversary of Peter, he must be the unknown Simons, but excluding Simon Peter, of course, who appear in the Gospels, also the Simon who is as one of the twelve.
6. Bernice is shown as the daughter of Justa, thus Helena-Justa-Luna, was her superior. Bernice is the twin sister of Agrippa II and significantly is called the 'Scarlet Whore of Babylon' in Revelations.
7. Zacchaeus was a helper to Peter and made bishop of Caesarea connecting him with the Zacchaeus in Luke who climbed the sycamore tree to see Jesus. He being short and thus being the youngest priest (tax collector), shows that he must be Ananus the Younger.
8. Barnabas is shown as Matthias who replaced Judas Iscariot as one of the twelve, thus he is Jesus' brother Joses.

With the New Testament having been deceptively edited to disguise not only the importance of my step-great-grandfather Simon Magus in the early Church, but also of my great-grandmother Helena, and my grandmother Mary Magdalene, it is essential to have this inside information from the 'Clementines'.

The blood relationships to the Roman Emperors that are revealed in the 'Clementines' demonstrate an important reason why Christianity had so easily appeared to the world. By building on Herod's mission to the Jews abroad that had already influenced many of the Roman aristocracy and royalty, its momentum was unstoppable. These connections, which are often overlooked, explain the reason that the Jews were the only group who were exempt from recognizing the Emperor as their supreme god. This exemption would also apply to Christians, thought to be just another sect of the Jews, as long as they did not treat Christ as a deity.

Peter had been extremely influential when he came to Rome in AD 44, because the groundwork had already been established. What he brought was a Church that was similar to the Jewish faith, but not requiring conformity with Jewish customs. Thus there were many who secretly followed Christianity.

It is for these reasons that it was natural that Rome would replace Jerusalem as the central power of Christianity and even be a partner in its spread throughout the Empire.

One of these powerful families was that of Pope Clement. His aunt Pomponia Graecina had already been accused of practicing a "foreign superstition" (Christianity) and was acquitted by her husband, Aulus Plautius, the distinguished conqueror of Britain.

She walked around as a nun in black, which allowed her to extend her mourning for the murder of Julia Livilla, Drusus-Germanicus's daughter and great-granddaughter of Augustus Caesar, and to openly practice celibacy for the Church. The Empress Messalina, the wife of Emperor Claudius, had unfairly sent Julia Livilla back into exile and had her killed. (Julia Livilla is the amalgamated character used by Pope Clement for Mattidia, the mother of the twins.)

In writing the 'Clementines', Pope Clement had access to a great deal of material of dialogues pro and con on Jewish Christianity and Greek mythology and philosophy, and, since he was well-studied and understood them, he placed these in the mouths of Peter and Simon Magus.

However, I found the philosophical arguments difficult to follow, but in the other story parts I did get insight into what it felt like to become a Christian, such as the description of early Christian baptism. Of course, I was born into the Faith, but Pope Clement's search for a religion that could answer his questions showed me the path that I would have followed.

The other information contained in the 'Clementines' is invaluable and has confirmed many stories I had heard, but I had not fully verified. Their factual content is assured because of the verifiable facts upon which the story is based.

***********Reference Column***********
Baptism (continued)

Let him attend to frequent fastings, and approve himself in all things, that at the end of these three months he may be baptized on the day of the festival. But every one of you shall be baptized in ever flowing waters, the name of the Trine Beatitude being invoked over him; he being first anointed with oil sanctified by prayer, that so at length, being consecrated by these things, he may attain a perception of holy things."

***********Reference Column***********
Barnabas

(The beginning of the Clementine Story: Clementine Recognitions R.I:7) Arrival of Barnabas at Rome. Now, the man who spoke these things to the people was from the regions of the East, by nation a Hebrew, by name Barnabas, who said that he himself was one of His disciples, and that he was sent for this end, that he should declare these things to those who would hear them. When I heard these things, I began, with the rest of the multitude, to follow him, and to hear what he had to say. Truly I perceived that there was nothing of dialectic artifice in the man, but that he expounded with simplicity, and without any craft of speech, such things as he had heard from the Son of God, or had seen. For he did not confirm his assertions by the force of arguments, but produced, from the people who stood round about him, many witnesses of the sayings and marvels which he related.

***********Reference Column***********
Joses, brother of Jesus

(Barnabas-Matthias chosen to replace Judas Iscariot: Clementine Recognitions R.I:60) After him Barnabas, who also is called Matthias, who was substituted as an apostle in the place of Judas (Acts 1:23-26), began to exhort the people that they should not regard Jesus with hatred, nor speak evil of Him.

(James the Just is passed over: Acts 1:23,26) And they set two: Joseph called Barsabas, who was surnamed Justus (James, the younger brother of Jesus), and Matthias (Barnabas). They drew lots for them, and the lot fell on Matthias, and he was numbered with the eleven apostles.

(Jesus' brothers: Mark 6:3) Is not this the carpenter, Mary's son, the brother of James and Joses, Jude and Simon? ...

(Jesus' brothers: Matthew 13:55) Is not this the carpenter's son? Is not his mother called Mary? And are not his brothers, James, Joseph, Simon and Judah

Now that Pope Clement is gone, there has already been an effort by the Church leaders to label Clement's writings as heresy or, at best, pseudo-literature. It is therefore important for me to explain to you the origins of the storyline that Pope Clement wrote, so that you can know that it is all based on truth. Although I cannot answer for the philosophical side, I can certainly vouch for the history, which except for some very small artistic embellishment, is clearly based on fact. I intend to prove this to you now.

The story begins:
One day Clement hears Barnabas speaking in Rome and, being of philosophical nature and hopelessly confused by the rhetoric, he finds the sincere, simple manner of Barnabas' presentation to be the answer to his search.

The crowds turn on him and Clement comes to his rescue, putting him up at his house in Rome. The Basilica of San Clemente was built upon the foundations of his house after the great fire in Nero's reign. It was one of the two secret meeting places of the Christians; the other being the house of Pudens where I studied.

In speaking with him, Clement was intrigued by the simplicity of the religion of the Christians. Clement decides to leave his fortunes and follow Barnabas to meet St. Peter and to be baptized into the Church.

Barnabas and Paul were good friends. Barnabas was the one who had replaced Judas in the Twelve, where he is called Matthias, as revealed in the 'Clementines'. He was Jesus' third brother, called Joses, and was chosen over James the Just, his second brother, because James was demanding that the Gentiles obtain a Jewish identity with rites such as circumcision.

As is clear from the Gospel of Matthew and Mark, Jesus had four brothers: James, Joses, Jude, and Simon; with the Gospel of Mark having the correct order.

Barnabas-Joses agreed with Paul that Christianity did not have to include the Jewish customs. This was Jesus' intention for Christianity to embrace both Jews and Gentiles as equals. Clement being a Gentile also supported this concept when he was Pope.

***********Reference Column***********
Clement meets Peter

(Clement meets Peter: Clementine Recognitions R.I:13.) His Cordial Reception By Peter. But Peter most kindly, when he heard my name, immediately ran to me and kissed me. Then, having made me sit down, he said, "Thou didst well to receive as thy guest Barnabas, preacher of the truth, nothing fearing the rage of the insane people. Thou shalt be blessed. For as you have deemed an ambassador of the truth worthy of all honor, so the truth herself shall receive thee a wanderer and a stranger, and shall enroll thee a citizen of her own city; and then there shall be great joy to thee, because, imparting a small favor, thou shalt be written heir of eternal blessings."

***********Reference Column***********
The Baptism of Clement

(Clement is baptized: Clementine Recognitions R.VI:15.) Bishops, Presbyters, Deacons, And Widows Ordained At Tripolis. ... And while in this manner he was teaching the word of God for three whole months, and converting multitudes to the faith, at the last he ordered me to fast; and after the fast he conferred on me the baptism of ever-flowing water, in the fountains which adjoin the sea.

***********Reference Column***********
The Family History

(Born of Caesar: Homilies H.XII:8.) Family History. Then Peter inquired, "Are you really, then, alone in your family?" Then I (Clement) answered, " There are indeed many and great men, being of the kindred of Caesar (Augustus). Wherefore Caesar himself gave a wife of his own family to my father, who was his foster-brother; and of her three sons of us were born, two before me, who were twins and very like each other, as my father told me...

***********Reference Column***********
The Mattidia departs

(Clementine Recognitions R.IX:36.) New Revelations. She was ordered to depart from the city with her twin sons, leaving the younger one with his father; and how on their voyage they had suffered shipwreck through the violence of a storm; and how, when they were cast upon an island called Aradus, Mattidia was thrown by a wave upon a rock, but her twin children were seized by pirates and carried to Caesarea, and there sold to a pious woman, who treated them as sons, and brought them up, and caused them to be educated as gentlemen; and how the pirates had changed their names, and called the one Niceta and the other Aquila; ...

To continue the story, Peter welcomes Clement with open arms. Peter is especially grateful to him for having rescued Barnabas in Rome from the mob and taken him to his house.

Clement asks Peter many questions. About the soul, he asks 'whether the soul is mortal or immortal; and if immortal, whether it shall be brought into judgment for those things which it does here.' About creation, he asks 'whether the world was created, and why it was created, and whether it is to be dissolved, and whether it is to be renovated and made better, or whether after this there shall be no world at all.'

After discussing these things briefly, Peter invites Clement to accompany him from city to city, on his way to Rome, in order to hear his discourses.

In their travels in pursuing Simon Magus so that Peter can challenge him in oration, Clement is instructed by Peter privately with his other disciples and he hears and jots down Peter's speeches and the speeches of Simon Magus, who refutes their content, at impromptu public gatherings.

Simon Magus, being of the opposing Church, is treated as a deceptive and perhaps even an evil person. This is done as a story device to hold the readers attention as they see Peter championing over evil.

After a time, Peter decides that Clement had been properly instructed and he baptizes him as one of his disciples.

The amazing synchronicities begin to unfold:
How Clement's father, Faustus (Faustinianus), was a foster-brother of the Emperor who gave him a wife of his own family. This is not very far from reality, Julia is the daughter of Augustus and Jullus is his step-son, as we will see shortly in greater detail.

When Clement was five years old, his mother Mattidia told her husband Faustus that she had seen a vision warning her that unless she and her twin sons speedily left Rome, all must perish miserably.

The vision, which she had related, had been feigned in order to escape from the incestuous advances of her husband's brother, without causing family discord by revealing his wickedness.

Mattidia left with her twins Faustinus and Faustinianus leaving Clement, at the age of five, behind and was absent for ten years.

The boat is shipwrecked and Mattidia is marooned on an island and Faustinus and Faustinianus are captured by pirates and their names are changed to Niceta and Aquila. They are purchased as slaves by Helena (Justa-Luna), my great-grandmother, who educated them like gentlemen. With Helena, being the consort of Simon Magus, who was Zebedee, these twins would be baptized as James and John, the sons of Zebedee.

***********Reference Column***********

Justa adopts the twins

(My great-grandmother Justa adopts James and John: (Clementine Recognitions R.VII:32) He Bringeth them unto their Desired Haven. Then Niceta began to say: " On that night, O mother, when the ship was broken up, and we were being tossed upon the sea, supported on a fragment of the wreck, certain men, whose business it was to rob by sea, found us, and placed us in their boat, and overcoming the power of the waves by rowing, by various stretches brought us to Caesarea Stratonis. There they starved us, and beat us, and terrified us, that we might not disclose the truth; and having changed our names, they sold us to a certain widow, a very honorable women, named Justa. She, having bought us, treated us as sons, so that she carefully educated us in Greek literature and liberal arts. And when we grew up, we attended to philosophic studies also, that we might be able to confute the Gentiles, by supporting the doctrines of the divine religion by philosophic disputations.

***********Reference Column***********

The Memoirs for the Story

(The Memoirs of Agrippina the Younger

- One memoir was an account of her mother's life
- a second memoir was about the fortunes of her mother's family
- and the last memoir recorded the misfortunes (casus suorum) of the family of Agrippina and Germanicus.

(Mentioned by Tacitus as one of his sources: Tacitus Annals Book IV Chap. LIII)
The anecdote which is not related by historians, I have found in the memoirs of Agrippina the Younger, the mother of Nero, who left behind her a record of her own life and the fortunes of her family.

(Also mentioned by Pliny: Natural History 7 Chap 8) Moreover, Agrippina hath left in writing, That her son Nero also, late Emperor, who all the time of his reign was a very enemy to all mankind, was born with his feet forward. And in truth by the right order and course of Nature, a man is brought into the world with his head first, but is carried forth with his feet foremost.

After her departure, having received no tidings of his wife or sons, Clement's father, Faustus, leaves to search for them and disappears.

The very honorable widow, named Helena, also named Luna (the Moon in John the Baptist's group of thirty) or Justa (as female counterpart of Simon Magus under John the Baptist), having purchased Niceta and Aquila, brings them up as her own sons. The twin boys studied under Simon Magus, their step-father, for a time before joining Zacchaeus.

When Peter finds a beggar women on the island of Aradus of Phoenicia, he realizes from her sad story that Clement is her son and that his disciples Niceta and Aquila are her sons also. Peter reunites them in a tearful reunion.

The father Faustus appears and blames astrology for the situation. For a time Simon Magus turns him into his likeness, but Peter removes the magic and and shows him how faith in God can overcome fate. Both he and Mattidia are won over to Christ.

***The End.

Within this exquisitely interweaved romantic tale are the real facts that Pope Clement modeled into his story from Agrippina the Younger, who had written her memoirs. They were published after her death in March 23 AD 59 and had become quite popular.

Agrippina was the youngest child of Germanicus and Agrippina the Elder and was the great-granddaughter of the Emperor Augustus.

She was also the great-niece of the Emperor Tiberius; the sister of the Emperor Caligula and the youngest of her sisters: Julia Drusilla and Julia Livilla; and also the mother of the Emperor Nero, who later murdered her.

(Incidentally, the Roman naturalist and philosopher Pliny, who tells of Agrippina writings that she left behind, attributes Nero's evil nature to the fact that he was born feet first.)

In her memoirs Agrippina the Younger gave the story of the three separate exiled existences on the island of Pandateria of her immediate family: her grandmother Julia the Elder with her great-grandmother Scribonia by Augustus Caesar; her mother Agrippina the Elder by Tiberius; and her sister Julia Livilla, exiled with Agrippina the Younger by Caligula.

In AD 62 Claudia Octavia, Nero's first wife, would be added to the list of exiles to Pandateria island where she was put to death. Following her in AD 95 was Flavia Domitilla, the wife Pope Clement's nephew, Titus Flavius Clemens.

The island of Pandateria is one of the Pontine Islands, is 25 miles off the coast of Campania, the west coast of Italy, south of Rome in the Tyrrhenian Sea.

(Here are all the exiles to Pandateria Island by every Roman Emperor from Augustus to Nero except Titus in chronological order:

- Julia the Elder banished 2 BC - AD 4, the only natural child of Octavius (Augustus), banished for 5 years (2 BC - AD 4) by her father Augustus Caesar, accusing her of adultery.
- Agrippina the Elder, Tiberius' grandniece, banished AD 29 for undermining his authority. She perished, probably of malnutrition AD 33
- Julia Livilla (Livilla) and Agrippina the Younger, his sisters, banished by Caligula in AD 39 to the Pontine Islands for conspiring to replace him. (Livilla was on Pandateria Island and Agrippina on another of the islands.) Julia Livilla and Agrippina the Younger returned after the death of Caligula January 24, AD 41. Julia Livilla was sent back by Claudius at the instigation of his wife Messalina, charged with adultery with Seneca the Younger, who was also exiled. She was executed. (Dio Cassius Roman History Book 60)
- Claudia Octavia, Nero's first wife, banished in AD 62 by Nero and executed. The initial grounds for putting Octavia aside was the charge that she was barren because she had no children. With the connivance of Poppaea whom he then married, charges of adultery were added. Her severed head was sent to Rome.
- Flavia Domitilla, was exiled in AD 95 by the Emperor Domitian. Her husband being Titus Flavius Clemens was killed.)

(Augustus banishes his daughter Julia the Elder to Pandateria Island in 2 BC: Dio Cassius Roman History, Book LV)

Of this, however, Augustus took no account; but when he at length discovered that his daughter Julia was so dissolute in her conduct as actually to take part in revels and drinking bouts at night in the Forum and on the very rostra, he became exceedingly angry. He had surmised even before this time that she was not leading a straight life, but refused to believe it. For those who hold positions of command, it appears, are acquainted with everything else better than with their own affairs; and although their own deeds do not escape the knowledge of their associates, have no precise information regarding what the associates do.

Pope Clement replaced Pandateria Island with the island of Aradus for his story, which is north of Tripoli, two miles off the Syrian coast and was the third part of the Phoenician grouping of Tyre and Sidon. He chose this island because it was the island where Helena was a Vestal Virgin, and she in real life was the adoptive mother of Niceta and Aquila.

Clement had to disguise the island of Pandateria as Aradus and the identities of the women Julia the Elder, the real mother of the twins and daughter of Augustus, and Julia Livilla, her descendant, to guard against the possibility of being accused of defaming the Emperor's family. The identities of the women are amalgamated into the story character of Mattidia as their natural mother.

The flimsy excuse that Peter gives in H.XII:12 for going to Aradus is: 'for the purpose of seeing two pillars of vine-wood that were of very great girth'. This was quite out of character for Peter who was always on task. After all, he was supposed to be proselytizing the masses, not taking a vacation to see a pillar! Actually, even this contained a subtle metaphor that related to the fact that the original Church called themselves the Vineyard. Their rival group, that espoused war with Rome, were called the Fig Tree.

Thus before the Crucifixion, Jesus cursed the fig tree because it was unable to produce fruit (proselytes) by fighting a doomed war against Rome. Thus the two pillars in the Vineyard mission would be my step-great-grandfather Simon and my great-grandmother Helena. In the metaphor they are only made of wood, whereas Peter is 'the rock' and, together, with Paul they are the stronger pillars of the new Church.

Clearly, Pope Clement did not waste images. In fact the whole scene of the father of Niceta and Aquila turning into Simon, by his magic, is also symbolic of the fact that Simon really was their adoptive step-father.

It was Julia the Elder, the Emperor Augustus' only natural child and daughter who would be the basis for the mother Mattidia of the Clementine story. The truth of this event brings out a well-kept secret that the real twins Niceta and Aquila (St. James and St. John), were the illegitimate grandchildren of Augustus.

How this occurred is that Julia was ordered by her father Augustus to marry Tiberius because he had adopted him as heir to the throne. They had a distaste for each other and by 6 BC they had separated. Julia requested a divorce, but Augustus would not grant it.

Then Julia got involved with Jullus Antonius, the son of Mark Antony. He was also her step-brother from Antony's marriage to Octavia the Younger, the sister of Augustus, thus making Augustus Caesar his step-uncle. This would have been ignored if Julia had not become pregnant by him and delivered twins.

Julia the Elder banished (continued)

In the present instance, when Augustus learned what was going on, he gave way to a rage so violent that he could not keep the matter to himself, but went so far as to communicate it to the senate. As a result Julia was banished to the island of Pandateria, lying off Campania, and her mother Scribonia voluntarily accompanied her. Of the men who had enjoyed her favors, Jullus Antonius, on the ground that his conduct had been prompted by designs upon the monarchy, was put to death along with other prominent persons.

***********Reference Column***********
Julia Livilla banished

(Caligula banishes his sister Julia Livilla to Pandateria Island and Agrippina to another Pontian Island in AD 39: Dio Cassius Roman History, Book LIX)
Another of his victims was Lepidus, that lover and favorite of his, the husband of Drusilla, the man who had together with Gaius (Caligula) maintained improper relations with the emperor's other sisters, Agrippina and Julia, the man whom he had allowed to stand for office five years earlier than was permitted by law and whom he kept declaring he would leave as his successor to the throne. He deported his sisters to the Pontian Islands because of their relations with Lepidus, having first accused them in a communication to the senate of many impious and immoral actions.

***********Reference Column***********
(Marcus Arrecinus Tertullus Clemens collaborates with the assassination of Caligula: Josephus, Antiquities of the Jews, XIX. 1.7) Hereupon Clement openly commended Cherea's intentions, but bid him hold his tongue; for that in case his words should get out among many, and such things should be spread abroad as were fit to be concealed, the plot would come to be discovered before it was executed, and they should be brought to punishment; but that they should leave all to futurity, and the hope which thence arose, that some fortunate event would come to their assistance; that, as for himself, his age would not permit him to make any attempt in that case.

As soon as Augustus got word of this, he was furious since this illicit union would create two claimants to the throne with more credentials than Tiberius, since Tiberius was merely Augustus' stepson. Although Augustus may have defeated Mark Antony and Cleopatra, the influence of the Antony's name was still quite powerful and so was Augustus' memory of Antony's betrayal.

Augustus exiled Julia to Pandateria Island for five years in 2 BC and had the twins sold into slavery. He also had Jullus Antonius killed. The reason being "his conduct had been prompted by designs upon the monarchy." Her mother Scribonia accompanied Julia on the island. This explains the lady who cared for the mother Mattidia of the twins in the story.

The next phase of the Clementine story is fulfilled by Julia Livilla together with her sister Agrippina. They got themselves in trouble with the Emperor Caligula in a similar way as Julia the Elder, for the two sisters conspired to court Lepidus, the widower of Drusilla, their other sister, his favorite, who had died.

The three sisters of Caligula had been given special privileges like Vestal Virgins by their brother Caligula, who had an incestuous relationship with them and even minted a coin with their three figures on it. When Drusilla was alive, Caligula would have made Lepidus the next Emperor, but now he viewed the two sister's relationship with Lepidus as a threat to his life. He knew that by now he was disliked by many.

Caligula executed Lepidus and banished Julia Livilla to Pandateria Island and Agrippina on another of the Pontine Islands in AD 39. The story of their rescue corresponds to Peter's rescue of Mattidia in the Clementine story. The incest is also referred to in the 'Clementines'.

Pope Clement's connection with the Roman Emperors is evidenced by his father, Marcus Arrecinus Tertullus Clemens, who was the Prefect of the Praetorian guard and later his daughter Arrecina Tertulla who was the first wife of the Emperor Titus. He was much beloved by his troops so that years later when his son was appointed as Prefect in 70 A.D his son was hailed with joy in the camp.

In 41 A.D, Marcus Clemens was aware of the conspiracy of Cherea and others against Emperor Caligula and turned a blind eye to the assassination for, by then, very few wanted Nero alive. Claudius on becoming Emperor would always be grateful to Marcus Arrecinus Tertullus Clemens for his help and, when his son Pope Clement turned to Christianity, he would be protected during his reign.

The closeness of Clement's family to the Emperors is shown later on from the marriage of his sister to Titus. Titus' father was the Emperor Vespasian and Titus also was Emperor after him.

There can be no doubt that Marcus Arrecinus Tertullus Clemens and King Agrippa were friends because they both would have had a good relationship with the Emperor Caligula at least before he went completely mad. It would be their friendship that made the negotiations on behalf of Claudius becoming emperor possible.

Agrippa made answer, "O senators! may you be able to compass what you have a mind to; yet will I immediately tell you my thoughts, because they tend to your preservation. Take notice, then, that the army which will fight for Claudius hath been long exercised in warlike affairs; but our army will be no better than a rude multitude of raw men, and those such as have been unexpectedly made free from slavery, and ungovernable; we must then fight against those that are skillful in war, with men who know not so much as how to draw their swords. So that my opinion is, that we should send some persons to Claudius, to persuade him to lay down the government; and I am ready to be one of your ambassadors.

Agrippa rescues Julia

He (Claudius) also brought back those whom Gaius (Caligula) had unjustly exiled, including the latter's sisters Agrippina and Julia, and restored to them their property.

The latter (Valeria Messalina) became enraged at her niece Julia because she neither paid her honor nor flattered her; and she was also jealous because the girl was extremely beautiful and was often alone with Claudius. Accordingly, she secured her banishment by trumping up various charges against her, including that of adultery (for which Annaeus Seneca was also exiled), and not long afterward even compassed her death.

Agrippa was a childhood friend of the assassinated Emperor Caligula and had made friends with many influential people in Rome, but his lavish lifestyle had got himself thrown in prison by Tiberius. When Caligula came to power, he released Agrippa and gave him a golden chain and the lands of Judaea which he then took from Herod Antipas. Therefore Agrippa was in a perfect position to be the negotiator.

In the chaos that ensued after Caligula's death, Claudius was whisked away to the Praetorian camp, where the troops of Marcus Arrecinus Tertullus Clemens acknowledged him as emperor. King Agrippa, with connections in the Senate obtained an audience with the Senators where he convinced them not to risk a fight and to accept Claudius as emperor.

Since King Herod Agrippa was in Rome during and after Caligula's assassination in January AD 41, this would correspond to the time that Julia Livilla was in exile and of her release.

Peter's rescue of Julia Livilla (the Mattidia derivative in the 'Clementines') was actually fulfilled by Herod Agrippa, King of Judaea. At that time Peter and Agrippa had a cordial relationship; but later, after he threatened Peter in AD 44, Peter also plotted his assassination with Simon Magus.

Once Claudius was made emperor, King Agrippa, being a friend of Julia Livilla and Agrippina the Younger, having asked for permission from the Emperor to rescue them, brought them back from Pandateria and the other Pontine Island. In the 'Clementines', Clement gave the rescue to Peter and though he would not have been in Rome at the time, but could have been directed to perform the rescue if he was there, since King Agrippa was his superior.

Actually Claudius' wife Valeria Messalina trumped up various charges against Julia Livilla, including that of adultery with Seneca, and had her exiled again, then also had her killed.

In summation, it is clear that the 'Clementines' does have a basis in fact and thus it is safe to assume that the other facts that relate to James and John, Simon Magus, Helena, and Mary Magdalene are also true. The 'Clementines'' are clearly as important as Acts in describing the events of the Early Church.

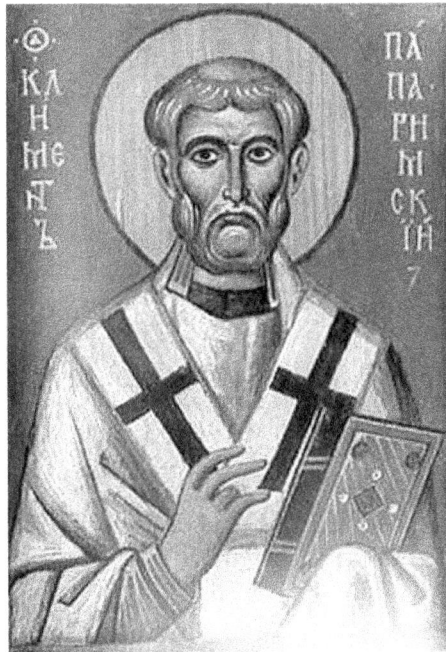

St. Clement, the first Pope after Peter

Map of Qumran area and Qumran

Chapter 5 - The Qumran, the Mirror of Jerusalem.

He who overcomes, I will make him a pillar in the temple of my God, and he will go out from there no more. I will write on him the name of my God, and the name of the city of my God, the new Jerusalem, which comes down out of heaven from my God, and my own new name. (Revelation 3:12)

Before Jesus was born in 6 BC, Herod the Great, an outsider, had maneuvered himself into the position of King of Judaea, first under Mark Antony and then Augustus Caesar, reigning from 37 BC to 4 BC. The Essenes found in him an ally to promote their new form of Judaism. Of course, Herod liked their prophecy of God creating a new order, since he envisioned this as his kingship. However, he made certain changes to their religious leadership by taking over the top priestly positions. By appointing Simon Boethus as High Priest he obtained Simon's daughter as his third wife Mariamne II, the mother of St. Thomas

Herod's innovative scheme was to require fees for the support of the Temple of Jerusalem from the circumcised Gentiles and Jews from around the world, called the Diaspora. These fees made him and his appointed priest leaders very wealthy.

When Jesus overturned the tables of the moneychangers, it was to show his dissatisfaction with the requirement of fees. It was with Christianity that these fees would be abolished and replaced with free-will offerings and with circumcision no longer required.

Herodian fee structure

(Jesus objects to the requirement of fees: John 2:14,15 (Mark 11:15; Matthew 21:12; Luke 19:45)) And he found in the temple those selling oxen (Herodian practice), and sheep (Nazarite practice), and doves (Jesus' policy of peace with Rome), and the money-changers sitting. He made a whip of cords, and threw all out of the temple, both the sheep and the oxen; and he poured out the changers' money, and overthrew their tables.

The Essenes

(Qumran: Pliny the Elder, Natural History Book 5.15 (17)) Lying on the west of the Dead Sea, sufficiently distant to escape its noxious exhalations, are the Essenes, a people that live apart from the world, and marvellous beyond all others throughout the whole earth, for they have no women among them; to sexual desire they are strangers; money they have none; the palm-trees are their only companions. Below this people was formerly the town of Ein Gedi second only to Jerusalem in the fertility of its soil and its groves of palm-trees; now, like it, it is another heap of ashes.

(Essenes: Josephus Antiquities of the Jews,18 1:4,5) The characteristic of the Essene creed is that all things are left in God's hands. They hold that souls are immortal, and that the rewards of righteousness are a prize worth a battle. Although they send dedicatory offerings to the Temple, their rites of purification when sacrificing are peculiar; they are therefore excluded from the precincts of the court of the temple and offer their sacrifices apart. In other ways they are most estimable men, whose whole energy is devoted to agriculture. It also deserves our admiration how much they exceed all other persons who addict themselves to virtue ... Their goods are in common, and the rich man enjoys no more of his possessions than he who owns nothing at all; this rule is followed by a body of men numbering over four thousand. Marriage and the keeping of slaves they abjure, ...

It is interesting to note how the requirement of circumcision for the Diaspora under Herod and also later on with early Jewish-Christianity, as can be seen in the Acts of Thomas, actually resulted in empowering the women. Since the Gentile men remained excluded because they naturally balked at this strange mutilation; the women, who were widows or desired to divorce their husbands, by merely contributing their membership coins and practicing celibacy from their uncircumcised husbands (being tired of their advances anyway), become members of the Jewish or Jewish-Christian religion and, incidentally, to save their souls.

When Herod rejected their plan for the new Temple, the Essenes left to establish their own Jerusalem on the bleak shores of the Dead Sea at Qumran. An earthquake in 31 BC, which was surely judged as a message from God, sent them away.

However, later on the Zealots who were opposing the Romans saw their chance to establish a new center for their activities and began to practice the tenets of the Essenes. Its lookout tower was well-suited for its covert purpose. Its caves could be used as hiding places for people, money, and the Scrolls.

The structure of the Community within the monastery at Qumran was to have three priests and twelve men as leaders. During the ministry of Jesus, Qumran was controlled by the Sadducees and the followers of John the Baptist. The Temple at Qumran existed in tandem with the Temple of Jerusalem, which was mostly under Pharisee control.

In the nearby towns of Ein Feshkha, Mazin, and Mird were the members of the different groups. These towns would change their names to correspond to the groups that settled there. Thus Mird was called Egypt when the Therapeuts were there; Mazin was called Galilee for the tribe of Dan; Tyre and Sidon, nearby, for Simon Magus and Judas; and Ein Feshkha was called Bethany, where the women of Asher lived.

This organization was a perfect cover for Zealots such as Theudas-Barabbas, who fought with Judas the Galilean, and Judas Iscariot, Judas' replacement, and my great-grandfather Joseph. It was a place where the Sadducees, such as the sons of Ananus, Jonathan Annas (Jacob of Alphaeus) and Matthew, his younger brother, could practice their divine priestly rulership without interference from the Pharisees. It was also a place for a disinherited Herod such as St. Thomas to have power. As for my step-great-grandfather, Simon Magus, who was their intellectual superior, it was an opportunity to scheme to become the leader of all the groups.

Since Qumran was built as the mirror image of Jerusalem, Simon Magus and Jesus cleverly referred to Qumran in the Gospel of John as 'Jerusalem' with the difference being that it was expressed grammatically in the plural form. The real Jerusalem in the other three Gospels would then use the singular form for the real Jerusalem.

When the headquarters of Christianity moved from Judaea to Antioch and finally to Rome, Qumran, which was destroyed some time before the fall of Masada in AD 73, would be viewed as an insignificant ruin near the Dead Sea. Already forgotten was its place in history as the place of Jesus' ministry, Crucifixion, and Resurrection.

Although the Temple of Jerusalem was destroyed, Jerusalem was still revered as the greatest religious city in the world. By simply ignoring the plural grammatical form of Jerusalem, Qumran would become Jerusalem. Since Qumran was Jerusalem's mirror image, all the sacred locations could be easily relocated, though their locations would continue to baffle the archeologists.

The twelve disciples were a really loose confederation of leaders outside of Qumran containing two groups of three leaders, designated as Priest, Levite, and King. The first group was made up of Jonathan Annas, Matthew Annas, and Thomas and the second, being a quasi-militarist lay group, was made up of Simon Magus, Judas, and Theudas.

Before their deaths, John the Baptist's father Zechariah was at the top position in the first group and Jesus' father Joseph was third position in the second.

At their deaths, John the Baptist would have been his father's replacement and Jesus his father's, but both John the Baptist and Jesus attempted to reform these groups. John, who called himself Elijah, originally had a group of thirty and Jesus had twelve as in the 'Clementines'.

Of these groups outside the monastery, some were celibate, some followed Nazarite principles, and some were married. Clearly, Aquila (John) and Priscilla were married as they are shown to be in Acts.

Jesus preferred the monastic center, but, fortunately for Christianity, he had to be outside of it when he was trying for a child with Mary Magdalene. It was his duty to continue the kingly line of David.

In his ministry outside the monastery, Jesus had six other disciples and was allied with the other two sets of three to form the twelve.

The Zealot organization at Qumran adopted the Essene rules but exempted themselves from 'doing no harm to others' if it was the Roman overlords. With this hypocrisy, one could be punished for 30 days for exposing oneself while urinating and yet when out of the designated holy areas, one was free to commit murder as long as it was for God and not personal gain.

In order to avoid any possibility of arousing sexual desire, the followers are taught to never be completely undressed. To say that a person is naked is to say that a man has a loin cloth and a woman a dress or girdle. This is shown in the traditional images of Jesus on the cross where it is clear that, in deference to the Jewish-Essene principles, Jesus was not stripped naked as it is usual for Roman crucifixion.

Many people still think that Joseph and Mary had to travel 600 stadia from Nazareth to Bethlehem, taking 15 hrs by donkey. To have traveled all that distance for Jesus to be born in Bethlehem near Jerusalem when Mary is almost ready to deliver seems strange, given as we will see shortly that it was not for the Roman census.

It is true that King David was born and anointed king in Bethlehem and Bethlehem had been prophesied by Micah as the place where the Messiah would be born, but the journey on a donkey could have easily brought about the birth on the way. Such a danger would not have been worth it if its only purpose of cheating on the prophecy!

(The Dwelling of the Queen (Bethlehem): The Copper Scroll 3Q15 Col VI 29) In the Dwelling of the Queen on the western side dig twelve cubits: 27 talents.

(Jesus born in Bethlehem of Judaea: Luke 2:1-7) And it came to pass in those days, there went forth a decree from Caesar Augustus, that all the world be enrolled -- This was the first enrollment made when Quirinius was governor of Syria. and all were going to be enrolled, each to his proper city,

Joseph also went up from Galilee, out of the city of Nazareth, into Judaea, to the city of David, which is called Bethlehem, because he was of the house and family of David; To be taxed with Mary his espoused wife, being great with child.

And so it was, that while they were there, the days were accomplished that she should be delivered.

And she brought forth her son -- the first-born, and wrapped him up, and laid him down in the manger, because there was not for them a place in the guest-chamber.

(Herod seeks to kill the baby Jesus: Matthew 2:1-5,7,12,13) Now when Jesus was born in Bethlehem of Judaea in the days of Herod the king, behold, wise men from the East came to Jerusalem, saying, "Where is he who has been born king of the Jews? For we have seen his star in the East, and have come to worship him."

When Herod the king heard this, he was troubled, and all Jerusalem with him; and assembling all the chief priests and scribes of the people, he inquired of them where the Christ was to be born. They told him, "In Bethlehem of Judaea; for so it is written by the prophet: ... Then Herod summoned the wise men secretly and ascertained from them what time the star appeared; ...

Being warned in a dream that they (the wise men) shouldn't return to Herod, they went back to their own country another way.

And on their having withdrawn, lo, a messenger of the Lord doth appear in a dream to Joseph, saying, 'Having risen, take the child and his mother, and flee to Egypt, and be thou there till I may speak to thee, for Herod is about to seek the child to destroy him.'

South of Qumran on the other side of the Wady is the Queen House which is listed in the Copper Scroll as one of the hiding places for the Church funds. This was a stable for the royal donkey that was ridden on Palm Sunday and the place of Jesus' birth (the mirrored location of Bethlehem).

The Gospel of Luke, by obscuring Jesus' real birth with his metaphorical "birth" at his Bar Mitzvah, makes this absurd trip seem plausible simply because it was for the taxing under Quirinius, but the taxing was definitely in AD 6 when Jesus was twelve years old!

There is a better solution to this problem, and to the other problems of Jesus' journeys if one assigns the place where Jesus lived as being at Ain Feshkha (Galilee) three hours south of Qumran (Jerusalem) and Bethlehem being at the Queen's house which is just an hour south of Qumran.

With the Queen's house having both a house and a manger, the Nativity story is actually true! Thus a king in the line of King David would appear to be born in lowly circumstances.

The 'inn' being in nearby Ain Feshkha was filled with guests who had come for the Passover.

The confusion of places and time is illustrated in King Herod the Great's 'massacre of the innocents'. Fearing that the prophesied King would take his place, Herod queried the Magian 'wise men' as to the date. They purposefully used their own calendar which was two years ahead of his. When he discovered this he would murder all the children two years and under in Bethlehem

As to Bethlehem, Herod thought it was the Bethlehem outside of Jerusalem, whereas the Bethlehem of Joseph and Mary was at the Queen's house outside of Qumran.

When Joseph and Mary hid from Herod the Great, they merely had to travel eight hours west to the vicinity of Mird. This was a place where there were many caves for Nazarites to retreat from the world and it was called the Wilderness.

This was the location where the Therapeuts of Theudas had their headquarters, although their home center was in Egypt. They would change their allegiance back and forth from Zealot to peace party. This would also be the place that Jesus would spend forty days and forty nights fasting.

The year of Jesus' Bar Mitzvah, AD 6 was an eventful year which became known as the beginning of the Period of Wrath similar to Ezekiel chapter 4 when Nebechadnezzar conquered Israel and Judah and made them slaves, but this time it was the Emperor Tiberius of Rome taking them over with taxation!

The revolt of Judas the Galilean over the taxation and the census may have failed and led to his death, but the spark that he ignited would continue after his death and become the Zealot Party. The Zealots would be a fourth group added to Pharisees, Sadducees, and Essenes.

It would be the Zealot activities that would result in Jesus' Crucifixion and his betrayer would be Judas Iscariot, the leader of the Zealots, having taken over from Judas the Galilean.

Theudas (Thaddaeus-Barabbas), the Saddok, the leader of the Therapeuts, who had joined with Judas the Galilean, did survive and was therefore a well-loved war hero, released as Barabbas at the Crucifixion. (The passage in Acts has incorrectly joined two events of Theudas: his fighting with Judas the Galilean in AD 6 and his death while leading a group of followers across the Jordan River in 44 AD on a symbolic journey as Joshua that was supposed to coincide with the expulsion of the Romans by God.)

With the failure and death of Judas the Galilean, Theudas joined the joint peace party of the Essenes (angels), Sadducees, and Therapeuts (shepherds). They would advocate peace with Rome and would also recognize Jesus' legitimacy.

Around Qumran and their wilderness hiding places, all the different groups, would use the names of the major locations of their organizations, such as Egypt for the Therapeuts, Tyre and Sidon for the Samaritans, Bethany for the tribe of Asher, etc.

This would provide Jesus with easy access to them, being merely 3-8 hour walk!

I once performed a calculation of how many stadia that Jesus would have traveled had he gone to the real locations in the New Testament and I came up with 16,719 stadia versus the distance of 1,784 stadia that Jesus actually traveled in Qumran. This is almost ten times as great!

The Annunciation (Fra Angelico)

Chapter 6 The Minor Indiscretion of my Great-Grandfather Joseph - becomes a major problem.

The circumstances of the birth of Jesus Christ were these: after his mother Mary was betrothed to Joseph, before they were united in marriage, she was found to be with child of the Holy Spirit. (Matthew 1:18)

***********Reference Column***********
John the Baptist

(The conception of John the Baptist: Luke 1:5,13,22,24) There was in the time of Herod, the king of Judaea, a priest of the name of Zechariah, belonging to the class of Abijah (A descendant of Eleazar, the son of Aaron). He had a wife who was a descendant of Aaron, and her name was Elizabeth. ... But the angel said, 'Do not be afraid, Zechariah, for your petition has been heard: and your wife Elizabeth will bear you a son, and you are to call his name John.' ... and having come out, he was not able to speak to them, and they perceived that a vision he had seen in the sanctuary ... and after those days, his wife Elisabeth conceived, and hid herself five months,

***********Reference Column***********
Trouble awaits

(The Annunciation: Matthew 1:18) The circumstances of the birth of Jesus Christ were these. After his mother Mary was betrothed to Joseph, before they were united in marriage, she was found to be with child of the Holy Spirit.

(Gabriel prepares Mary: Luke 1:26) Now in the sixth month, the angel Gabriel was sent from God to a city of Galilee, named Nazareth, to a virgin, betrothed to a man, whose name is Joseph, of the house of David, and the name of the virgin is Mary.

***********Reference Column***********
Jesus the black sheep

(Jesus does not accept Mary's criticism at the Marriage of Cana: John 2:3,4) When the wine ran out, Jesus' Mother said to him, 'They have no wine.' Jesus said to her, 'Mother, what is it to me or you? Has not my time come?'

(His mother desires to speak with him: Matthew 12:47,48) One said to him, 'Behold, your mother and your brothers stand outside, seeking to speak to you.' But he answered him who told him, 'Who is my mother? Who are my brothers?'

As seen from his father Zechariah, John the Baptist descended from the priestly Zadokite line and his mother Elizabeth, was also descended from Aaron. Shown in the Gospel of Luke in a cloaked way, Elizabeth was merely celibate, not barren, and Zechariah was not allowed to preach when they were getting together to conceive a child.

In the Gospel of Luke there was a strong attempt to associate Jesus' birth with that of John the Baptist, but John was clearly in a much higher in position. Jesus was only of the lineage of David and not of the priestly line.

The Gospel of Matthew hints at a problem with Mary and to the possible illegitimacy of Jesus as she is merely betrothed to Joseph. In Luke the problem is mapped out more clearly. Elizabeth is six months pregnant, having followed the rules of the Essenes of having sexual relations in the winter months after a betrothal in March. These were the required times for conception by the Essene rules for kings and priests who are allowed to have sexual relations only for the purpose of having a child. They are to be celibate before and after.

In looking at Mary's history of having five sons like clockwork every six years as prescribed, it is clear that Mary was super-fertile. Even one transgression would certainly come to light.

Mary always followed the rules to the letter: she was the true Virgin Mary. She favored James, her next child, because he was conceived at the correct time according to the rules for sexual relations. He was her model child, following the rules strictly, whereas Jesus flaunted the rules and even tried to change them.

Jesus does sometimes speak disrespectfully to Mother Mary, but this comes from the rivalry with his brother James, who would be exalted over him because of this 'betrothal issue'. Jesus had to be strong against any effort that would expose him to further criticism, even if it was from his mother.

In the first section of the Gospel of Luke, Mary is being told by Simeon the Essene that she will have a child. She is, of course, surprised, as they are only betrothed. It is written in a way that it would appear to be a prophecy rather than having just happened.

Since the Holy Spirit had already entered Elizabeth, she being six months pregnant, which coincided with Mary's Annunciation in June, the sixth month, it is clear that the position of Holy Spirit can be shown to be third in position in the hierarchy. Zechariah being the top priestly position, had dropped down to third position when he was 'mute' and Joseph is pretended to be at this lay third position being supposedly celibate at this time.

And thus it must be sadly revealed that Joseph, this paragon of virtue in tradition, actually 'takes her' too soon! His sin would trouble Jesus all his life. His enemies would call him the bastard son or, as in the Scrolls, 'the Son of a Lie'. It was really just a technicality since Joseph and Mary were betrothed, but to Mary it was more than that.

Mary panics and rushes to Elizabeth for comfort to the hill country of Judaea where Elizabeth has gone into seclusion since she is six months pregnant. Mary fears that if she is pregnant that she will be judged and Jesus will be declared illegitimate and put away as an orphan.

Another reason was to remove the temptation from Joseph to repeat his action.

Elizabeth consoles her by saying that John, inside her, jumped for joy because he already recognized Jesus as Lord, even if others would not. She also suggested that Mary recite 'The Magnificat' to remind her that God rewards the downtrodden. Mary was grateful for her comforting words.

Mary waits to see if she fulfills the three month trial period for ability to carry to term. She does, and meanwhile helps Elizabeth to deliver her child John.

Normally at this point, Mary would be permanently married, having proven she could carry to term, so she returns to Joseph, hoping that he will take responsibility for the problem; he rejects her.

This 'righteous man' Joseph considers putting her away secretly to hide his transgression so that, after she delivers, the child can be put up for adoption and no one would know.

(Simeon the Essene comes to their rescue: Matthew 1:20-21) But when he thought about these things, behold, an angel of the Lord appeared to him in a dream, saying, 'Joseph, you son of David, don't be afraid to take to yourself Mary, your wife, for that which is conceived in her is of the Holy Spirit. She shall bring forth a son. You shall call his name JESUS, for it is he who shall save his people from their sins.'

(The sins of the father: Ezekiel 18:20) The child will not share the guilt of the parent, nor will the parent share the guilt of the child. The righteousness of the righteous will be credited to them, and the wickedness of the wicked will be charged against them.

Joseph follows the law

(Sex after pregnancy is for the sake of the fetus: Matthew 1:25) And he (Joseph) knew her not till she brought forth her firstborn son: and he called his name JESUS.

Mary' heart is broken

(After the angels and the shepherds see Jesus: Luke 2:19) But Mary kept all these things, and pondered them in her heart.

(The angels at the manger: Luke 2:7,14) She brought forth her first-born child and wrapped him in swaddling clothes and laid him in a manger. 'Glory to God in the highest, On earth peace, good will toward men.'

(Mary as the David Queen: Revelation 12:1-6) A great sign was seen in heaven: a woman clothed with the sun, and the moon under her feet, and on her head a crown of twelve stars. and she was crying out in the pains and agony of childbirth.

(Joazar declares Jesus illegitimate: Revelation 12:1-6) Another sign was seen in heaven. Behold, a great red dragon, having seven heads and ten horns, and on his heads seven crowns. His tail was drawing after it a third part of the stars of Heaven, and it dashed them to the ground. And in front of the woman who was about to become a mother, the Dragon was standing in order to devour the child as soon as it was born. She gave birth to a son, a male child, ...

Simeon the Essene, as an angel of the Lord, having temporarily taken Zechariah's position at the top, believing that 'the sins of the father should not be visited on the son', gives his blessing to the union, declaring Jesus to be legitimate.

It was a great relief to Joseph. Later he would even be congratulated for not having sexual relations with Mary until after her delivery. Of course, this is normal to do anyway to protect the fetus.

To comfort Mary, Simeon explains that, since Joseph was acting in his position as Holy Spirit, that he was acting for God. But later it is told that Mary remembered all these things, and pondered them in her heart.

Mother Mary would remain a Virgin because all nuns are Virgins. In fact, since all the nuns were given the first name of Mary, from before Mother Mary, they all could be called Virgin Mary.

As to the definition of 'virgin', it clearly had nothing to do with the physical definition. It was a woman, who agreed to be bound by certain rules of celibacy. It was a commitment in the present with past history erased.

With my great-grandmother this definition would be pushed to the limit, as even a Vestal Virgin had rules of celibacy in spite of its later use and abuse for legalized prostitution.

There are two additional versions, besides the real birth in the Gospel of Matthew, of Mary giving birth to Jesus; these are the Gospel of Luke and Revelation. These descriptions are a metaphoric birth as they apply to Jesus' Bar Mitzvah in AD 6 when Jesus is twelve.

In the beautiful description of Mary's birth in Revelation, my great-grandmother Mary is there in all her glory as the David Queen. She is clothed by the Sun with the Moon under her feet. She has a crown of twelve stars for the representatives of the twelve tribes of Israel, who recognize her as queen. John the Baptist, just twelve and a half years old is the Sun, however, being that young, it is Elizabeth, John's mother who carries the weight of his coming stature. John and Elizabeth are the replacements for her late husband Zechariah, who was murdered by the Zealots in the previous year.

In Revelation, Mother Mary is being opposed by the High Priest Joazar Boethus (the Red Dragon). Fortunately, Joazar had advocated the acceptance of the new Roman taxation and, having lost the confidence of the people, is deposed. Ananus ben Seth, the Sadducee, is made High Priest. He would recognize Jesus' legitimacy.

When Ananus is replaced by Joseph Caiaphas, in AD 18 and throughout the rest of his ministry, Jesus had to rely on Ananus' second son Jonathan Annas to be considered legitimate.

***********Reference Column***********

Was Joseph within the Law?

(Joseph's justification: Deuteronomy 20:7) And who is the man that hath betrothed a woman, and hath not taken her? -- let him go and turn back to his house, lest he die in battle, and another man take her.

(Tamar is raped by her half-brother. Her father David took no action and her brother Absalom kills him which leads to his death also: 2Samuel 13:11-19) ... he took hold of her, and said unto her: 'Come lie with me, my sister.' And she answered him: 'Nay, my brother, do not force me; for no such thing ought to be done in Israel; do not thou this wanton deed. ... being stronger than she, he forced her, and lay with her. ... Amnon said unto her: 'Arise, be gone.' And she said unto him: 'Not so, because this great wrong in putting me forth is worse than the other that thou didst unto me.' But he would not hearken unto her. ... Tamar put ashes on her head and tore the ornate robe she was wearing. She put her hands on her head and went away, weeping aloud as she went.

(Equality in marriage: 1Corinthians 7:3,4) Let the husband render to the wife her due, and likewise also the wife to the husband. The wife hath not power of her own body, but the husband: and likewise also the husband hath not power of his own body, but the wife.

***********Reference Column***********

(Mother Mary real name Dorcas leaving the more traditional Jewish- Essenes (dying metaphorically) following James who has joined Jesus' Church: Acts 9:36-41) And in Joppa there was a certain female disciple, by name Tabitha, (which interpreted, is called Dorcas,) this woman was full of good works and kind acts that she was doing; and it came to pass in those days she, having ailed, died, ... All the widows stood by him weeping, and showing the coats and garments which Dorcas made while she was with them. Peter, however, putting every one out of the room, knelt down and prayed, and then turning to the body, he said, 'Tabitha, rise.' Dorcas at once opened her eyes, and seeing Peter, sat up. He gave her his hand, and raised her up. Calling the saints and widows, he presented her alive.

Phoebe became quite animated one day when I was young and foolishly justified the actions of my great-grandfather, her grandfather Joseph. I quoted from Deuteronomy that 'if a man is about to go off to war and is betrothed and not had sex, that he should return to do so, lest he die.' Therefore, with Joseph being a Zealot, he could be justified that his life was always in danger.

Being named after David's daughter Tamar, who was raped by her half-brother, my mother Phoebe was not very sympathetic to men who do not show the proper respect to females. She countered me by quoting from the The Tenth Commandment of 'not coveting women and cattle' and how females were associated with cattle to be preyed upon by the likes of King David and his sons and descendants!"

Phoebe had a great influence on my father Paul, who initially from his upbringing thought of females as subservient to males. Paul ended up being adored by all women for his chastity and chivalry.

P Jesus was always advocating women rites. When he began his ministry women and Gentiles were not accepted in the Church. Women were associated with Gentiles for the silly reason that they were not circumcised like Gentiles and also with the added problem of their monthly periods. This meant that as he brought Gentiles into the Church, the status of women also increased. His mother-in-law Helena made sure of that on many occasions.

Having exonerated my great-grandmother in her role as Virgin Mother. I will reveal another important phase of her life when Mother Mary was 60 years old.

Peter was aligning himself with the Church of the Herods in AD 43. James, her favorite had been persuaded to come over to this Church, lest he suffer the same fate as his father Joseph in AD 23 when Agrippa had murdered him to obtain the Church funds to clear his debts in Rome.

Mother Mary who was in charge of the widows of the convent comes also. She must therefore die to her old faith and be reborn in the new. Her real name Dorcas is used and her profession is shown as seamstress for the convent. It was Peter who 'raised her from the dead', instructing her on the new doctrine to give her the position of chief widow.

Mother Mary's house near Ephesus

Marriage at Cana (Giotto)

Chapter 7 My grandmother Mary Magdalene (maligned as a prostitute, but wife of Jesus).

And some women, who were healed of evil spirits and infirmities, Mary who is called Magdalene, from whom seven demons had gone out. (Luke 8:2)

Mary had 7 demons

(Judas as 'Demon #7' having relinquished his role of superior to Mary Magdalene: Luke 8:1-3) And it came to pass thereafter, that he (Jesus) was going through every city and village, preaching and proclaiming good news of the reign of God, and the twelve are with him, And women, some who had been healed of evil spirits and infirmities: Mary who was called Magdalene, from whom seven demons had gone out; and Joanna wife of Chuza, steward of Herod, and Susanna, and many others, who were ministering to him from their substance.

Healing of Theudas

(Demons and the Swine: Mark 5:2-20) When he (Jesus) had come out of the boat, immediately there met him out of the tombs a man with an unclean spirit, ... And when he saw Jesus in the distance, he ran and threw himself at His feet, crying out in a loud voice, 'What hast Thou to do with me, Jesus, Son of God Most High? In God's name I implore Thee not to torment me.' For he said to him, 'Come out of the man, you unclean spirit!' He asked him, 'What is your name?' He said to him, 'My name is Legion, for we are many.' He begged him much that he would not send them away out of the country. And there was there, near the mountains, a great herd of swine feeding, and all the demons did call upon him, saying, 'Send us to the swine, that into them we may enter;' and immediately Jesus gave them leave, and having come forth, the unclean spirits did enter into the swine, and the herd did rush down the steep place to the sea --- about two thousand --- they were choked in the sea ...

Jesus with Demon 7

(Judas as 'Satan' in his role of superior and protector of Mary Magdalene: Luke 4:1,2) 4:1 Then Jesus, full of the Holy Spirit, returned from the Jordan, and was led about by the Spirit in the Desert for forty days, tempted all the while by Satan. During those days He ate nothing, and at the close of them He suffered from hunger.

A discussion about my grandmother Mary Magdalene must begin first by unmasking the derogatory statement of Luke 8:1-3 concerning the women who followed Jesus. It starts off with the twelve disciples and then mentions a group of women, 'who were ministering to Jesus from their substance' and 'who had been healed of evil spirits and infirmities' and also mentions Mary Magdalene as one of these and that she had 'seven demons that had gone out of her'. This is the only mention of Mary Magdalene by her full name before the Crucifixion.

Since the feminine grammatical case is used for 'who', it applies only to the women who followed Jesus and the twelve disciples mentioned earlier in the verse had been free of 'evil spirits or infirmities'. This is an intentional omission because Theudas (Thaddaeus), who is shown as 'Legion' is one of the twelve and was healed of 'evil spirits'.

Thus the intent of these verses is to show that all females are impure and would require a special healing from Jesus and apparently for this great privilege had to give of their 'substance', which is either financial support or other services! Although it is true that Jesus did have to raise the status of women and Gentiles in order that they could be eligible to be active members of the Church, the intent of these verses is to imply that Mary Magdalene was even more impure that the other women and had 'seven demons'.

The story of Legion implies that 'demons' are Zealots and demonstrates how much Jesus detested their Zealot ways that would eventually bring destruction to Judaea. This was Theudas who had gone over to support the Roman-leaning Herods (who were swine from eating pork). He was the leader of two thousand Zealot followers.

The use of 'seven demons' with Mary Magdalene is a subtle way of referring to Judas Iscariot's Zealot title of 'Demon at level 7'. Judas Iscariot as chief levite was in charge of the female nuns and therefore the one who tested Jesus for marriage after his Nazarite vow to be 'forty days in the Wilderness' prior to marriage. By being betrothed to Mary Magdalene, Jesus would be in charge of her and thus she would be released from Judas (Demon 7)!

Suzanna is only mentioned here in Luke 8:1-3 from the whole New Testament and, by her prominent position with the two Marys, must be assumed to be name of the fourth Mary at the cross, the betrothed of James, the brother of Jesus and crown prince and thus the princess of David.

The Joanna mentioned in Luke is my great-grandmother Helena previously disguised as 'wife of Chuza, a steward of Herod'. Being one of the three major women, she has to be Helena (Mary Salome). Helena was the female in John the Baptist's organization thus 'Joanna', the feminine form of 'John'.

The story in the Gospel of John of 'The Stoning of the Prostitute', which does not tell the prostitute's name, is again a perfect opportunity for Jesus' opponents to imply that this woman was Mary Magdalene since she had been 'cured of seven devils'. This story was actually the result of Gospel-wide removal my great-grandmother Helena's name from the New Testament in all important events and replacing her name with a generic female. The accused prostitute is not Mary Magdalene but her mother Helena and has to do with Helena's legitimacy because she had served as a Vestal Virgin in her early days. What they are insinuating is that Mary Magdalene being the daughter of Vestal Virgin, whom they considered a prostitute, would make Mary Magdalene a prostitute also, which was clearly unfair.

What Jesus begins to write on the ground are the names of those who are condemning her. The issue is not that these accusers may have sinned, but rather that to accuse Helena was to accuse Herod Antipas' household and Church, of which she and Simon Magus were a part of. The memory of how John the Baptist's accusing of Herod for his illegal marriage had lead to his death would still be fresh in their minds. In addition to bending marriage rules such as marriage to first cousins, the Herods encouraged members of their Church to use sex as a tool to achieve power. Helena had danced provocatively for Herod to depose John the Baptist and, later, Helena's student Bernice, the twin sister of Agrippa II almost surpassed Cleopatra when she initiated an affair with Titus, who was to be Emperor of Rome. For this she would be called, by John in Revelation, the "Harlot of Babylon" (Babylon being Rome.) The accusers of Helena decided that they would not risk their lives after all. (The issue of the legitimacy of Helena within the Church will be covered in the chapter on Helena.)

The strict Essene principle is that women are evil and it is they who are the cause of men's sexual desire, like Eve's apple. As a consequence women were excluded from the Community and are labeled as outsiders like Gentles. Jesus attempted to reform this policy by raising their levels within the Church.

However, even at present with the Church, being ruled by men who fear the sexual power that women have over them, continues to exclude females from positions of power. They are obviously titillated by the opposing sexual opposites of Virgin Mary and reformed Prostitute Mary Magdalene and prefer to exalt them as female icons.

Also, it seems to be an almost universal religious principle that menstruating women are impure, thus they are not allowed to be in sacred spaces during these times. Thus only when pregnant or as a widow, having gone through their change of life, are they considered pure.

This is why Mary Magdalene was allowed to be the gate keeper for Peter in his thrice denial after the Crucifixion and again as Rhoda with Peter after the Schism of the Churches.

***********Reference Column***********
The Syro-Phoenician woman

(Syro-Phoenician woman entreats Jesus to remove the unclean spirit from her daughter: Mark 7:24-30) And from thence he arose, and went into the borders of Tyre and Sidon, and entered into a house, and would have no man know it: but he could not be hid. For a woman, whose little daughter had an unclean spirit, having heard of him, came and fell down at his feet. She was a Gentile woman, a Syro-Phoenician by nation: and again and again she begged Him to expel the demon from her daughter.

But Jesus said to her, 'Let the children be filled first, for it is not appropriate to take the children's bread and throw it to the dogs.'

But she answered him, 'Yes, Lord. For even the dogs under the table eat the children's crumbs.'

'For those words of yours, go home,' He replied; 'the demon has gone out of your daughter.'

So she went home, and found the child lying on the bed, and the demon gone.

***********Reference Column***********
The Canaanite woman

(The Canaanite woman entreats Jesus to remove the demon from her daughter: (Matthew 15:22-28,39) Behold, a Canaanite woman came out from those borders, and cried, saying, 'Have mercy on me, Lord, you son of David. My daughter is grievously vexed with a demon.'

But He answered her not a word. Then the disciples interposed, and begged Him, saying, 'Send her away because she keeps crying behind us.'

'I have only been sent to the lost sheep of the house of Israel,' He replied.

Then she came and threw herself at His feet and entreated Him, 'O Sir, help me!'

He replied, 'It is not right to take the children's bread and throw it to the dogs.'

But she said, 'Yes, Lord, but even the dogs eat the crumbs which fall from their masters' table.'

'O woman,' replied Jesus, 'great is your faith: be it done to you as you desire.'

And from that moment her daughter was restored to health. ...He sent away the multitudes, and entered into the boat, and came into the borders of Magdala.

***********Reference Column***********
Mission to Jews and Gentiles

(The Centurion's Gentile servant: (Luke 7:1-10) A certain centurion's servant, ... was sick and at the point of death ... (Jesus) said unto the people that followed him, ... I have not found so great faith, no, not in Israel. ... the servant ... was well.

There are two stories in the Gospels that are clearly related to each other: the Syro-Phoenician woman in the seventh chapter of Mark and the Canaanite woman in the fifteenth chapter of Matthew. They describe a woman who asks Jesus to remove an 'unclean spirit'/'demon' from her daughter.

Previously, it was established from Luke 8:1-3 that the concept of being under the control of a demon/unclean spirit was merely a way of saying that Mary Magdalene was under Judas Iscariot, 'Demon 7' where demon refers to his zealot activities. The Syro-Phoenician/Canaanite woman shown as Justa (Helena) in a matching story from the Clementines similar to it, being the consort of Simon Magus whose other name was "Simon the Zealot", would also be under the control of a demon.

Each of the versions has the strange reply, 'Let the children be filled first, for it is not appropriate to take the children's bread and throw it to the dogs.' In addition, the Canaanite women version begins with Jesus saying, 'I have only been sent to the lost sheep of the house of Israel.'

The healing in of the Syro-Phoenician/Canaanite women's daughter in Mark and Matthew with its strange words and images actually disguises one of the major turning points in Jesus' career where he agrees to give Gentiles and women a higher standing in the Church. As with other meetings that Jesus had with unnamed women like the Samaritan Women, all of whom are Helena, it can be seen that there is an underlying respect, humor, and endearment between them.

If it were a healing, the replies of Jesus would be extremely strange as he appears to only minister to the 'children of Israel' or the 'lost sheep of Israel' even when requested. This contradicts the Gospel of John: "God so loved the world he gave his only begotten son, so that whoever shall believe in him shall not perish, but have everlasting life" and his 'Healing of the Centurion's Servant'.

***********Reference Column**********
The Lost Sheep

(Parable of the lost sheep: (Luke 15:3-15:7) 'What man of you having a hundred sheep, and having lost one out of them, doth not leave behind the ninety-nine in the wilderness, and go on after the lost one, till he may find it?

(Sending forth the twelve: (Matthew 10:5,6) Jesus sent these twelve forth, and charged them, saying, 'Do not go among the Gentiles, and don't enter into any city of the Samaritans. Rather, go to the lost sheep of the house of Israel.

***********Reference Column**********
Helena is a Lost Sheep

(How Simon met Helena: Hippolytus: Refutations of All Heresies Book VI Chap. XIV) Simon ... said, however, that this Helen was the lost sheep.

***********Reference Column**********
The Syro-Phoenician-Canaanite woman

(Helena entreats Jesus to marry her daughter: (Clementine Homilies H.II:19) Justa, a Proselyte. "There is amongst us one Justa, a Syro-Phoenician, by race a Canaanite, whose daughter was oppressed with a grievous disease. And she came to our lord, crying out, and' entreating that He would heal her daughter.

But He, being asked also by us, said, 'It is not lawful to heal the Gentiles, who are like to dogs on account of their using various meats and practices, while the table in the kingdom has been given to the sons of Israel.

But she, hearing this, and begging to partake like a dog of the crumbs that fall from this table, having changed what she was, by living like the sons of the kingdom, she obtained healing for her daughter, as she asked.

For she being a Gentile, and remaining in the same course of life, he would not have healed had she remained a Gentile, on account of it not being lawful to heal her as a Gentile.

***********Reference Column**********
(Simon Magus as Lazarus: (Luke 16:20-22) While at his outer door there lay a beggar, Lazarus by name, covered with sores and longing to make a full meal off the scraps flung on the floor from the rich man's table. Nay, the dogs, too, used to come and lick his sores. It happened that the beggar died, and that he was carried away by the angels to Abraham's bosom.

Strangely, when Jesus sends out the twelve, he said, "Do not go among the Gentiles, and do not enter into any city of the Samaritans, but rather, go to the lost sheep of the house of Israel". Apparently, he is sending them out only to members of the Jewish-Essene Community.

Helena herself is called by Simon Magus, a lost sheep. Apparently, Jesus seems to be humorously implying that she is part of Simon's lost sheep and not his.

The Clementine Homilies has a similar story. It equates "the Syro-Phoenician woman" with the "Canaanite woman" and implies that she was now living as "like sons of the kingdom" which equates with "the lost sheep of the house of Israel" in the Canaanite woman version. Apparently she has undergone some conversion.

The primary excuse that Jesus gives for not doing the previous healing is 'Let the children be filled first, for it is not appropriate to take the children's bread and throw it to the dogs'. This metaphor was already used by Jesus in his parable about Lazarus, the beggar, eating scraps that had fallen from the rich man's table. The rich man had gone to Hell and Lazarus had gone to Heaven. Simon Magus used the name Lazarus when he was deposed as Pope and raised by Jesus. Helena's humorous reply is to say, 'Let me eat the scraps from the table like a beggar and I will get to Heaven and you will go to Hell.'

The crumbs that the mother referred to were collected from the holy table and distributed to those outside of the monastic section of the Church; but they were not distributed to women. She is suggesting that surely females should be allowed to partake of these crumbs like dogs do at tables from the floor. Jesus agrees that he will change this, but there is more to it as we will see.

Pope Clement, the composer of the 'Clementines', was not about to reveal this next secret easily, which was more significant than the raising of the status of Gentiles and women, for this secret had been violently suppressed and was, even when he wrote it, too dangerous to reveal.

Contained in the next paragraph in the Clementine Homilies titled "Divorced for the Faith" is a key statement which says, 'But she (Justa-Helena), being faithful to her engagements, and being in affluent circumstances, remained a widow herself, but gave her daughter in marriage to a certain man who was attached to the true faith, and who was poor.'

We, then, have before us two qualifications of this husband: 'poor' and 'attached to the true faith'. Obviously the 'true faith' is the Church of Jesus. As for 'poor' this is a name for the members of the Essenes as they give all their worldly goods to the Church and live frugally. The 'poor in spirit' appear in the Beatitudes and the Scrolls. So this means that that the daughter's husband is also of the same Church.

Since the mother of the daughter is Helena-Justa-Luna and her adopted sons are James and John, who are called "the sons of Zebedee" (the step-sons of Simon Magus) and with her association with Simon Magus herself, this natural daughter of hers is in important company. Given the choices of whom her mother would want as a husband for her daughter, it would certainly be Jesus himself, not only because of his stature, but also to cement a bond between Jesus and Simon Magus. Thus the mystery is revealed that her natural daughter is Mary Magdalene!

This request for healing was, therefore, more that just a healing, but rather a proposal of marriage that would make Helena-Justa-Luna his mother-in-law and Simon Magus, "the father of all heresy', his step-father-in-law.

Mary Magdalene's Bat Mitzvah

(Helena-12 year issue of blood and Mary Magdalene's coming of age shown as the raising of Jairus' daughter: Matthew 9:20-25) And lo, a woman having an issue of blood twelve years, having come to him behind, did touch the fringe of his garments, for she said within herself, 'If only I may touch his garment, I shall be saved.' And Jesus having turned about, and having seen her, said, 'Be of good courage, daughter, thy faith hath saved thee,' and the woman was saved from that hour. And Jesus having come to the house of the ruler, ... said, 'Go out of the room; the little girl is not dead, but asleep.' And they laughed at Him. ... Jesus went in, and on His taking the little girl by the hand, she rose up.

(Helena-12 year issue of blood and Mary Magdalene's coming of age shown as the raising of Jairus' daughter: Mark 5:25-43) A certain woman, who had an issue of blood for twelve years....for she said, 'If I but touch His clothes, I shall be cured.' In a moment the flow of her blood ceased, and she felt in herself that her complaint was cured... While he was yet speaking, there came from the ruler of the synagogue's house certain who said, Thy daughter is dead: why troublest thou the Master any further? ... Instantly the little girl rises to her feet and begins to walk (for she was twelve years old)...

(Helena-12 year issue of blood and Mary Magdalene-raising of Jairus' daughter: Luke 8:41-44-56) Behold, there came a man named Jairus, and he was a ruler of the synagogue. He fell down at Jesus' feet, and begged him to come into his house, for he had an only daughter, about twelve years old, and she was dying. And as He went, the dense throng crowded on Him. A woman who had a flow of blood for twelve years, who had spent all her living on physicians, and could not be healed by any, came behind him, and touched the fringe of his cloak, and immediately the flow of her blood stopped. While he still spoke, one from the ruler of the synagogue's house came, saying to him, 'Your daughter is dead. Don't trouble the Teacher.' ... When he came to the house, he didn't allow anyone to enter in, except Peter, John, James, the father of the girl, and her mother ... he said, 'She isn't dead, but sleeping.' But he put them all outside, and taking her by the hand, he called, saying, 'Little girl, arise!' Her spirit returned, and she rose up immediately. He commanded that something be given to her to eat. And her parents were amazed, but he charged them to say to no one what was come to pass.

The two intertwined healings by Jesus of "the twelve year issue of blood" and "healing of Jairus' daughter" both have to do with a mother and daughter and are similar to "the healing of the Syro-Phoenician woman" thus they must be about Helena and Mary Magdalene. These healings have in common the situation of a menstruating woman being unclean.

With the Essene view that the flow of blood is "impure", it follows from this that females would never be allowed in the congregation for fear that they might start their monthly cycle unexpectedly. Jesus would therefore have to 'heal' them. The occurrence of so many healings on this subject shows how hard it was to support Jesus' changes to doctrine on this issue as they would obviously be viewed as heresy.

The irony of this, of course, is that menstruation would be normal for a virgin and for a girl entering puberty. Helena explains to Jesus that she has remained a virgin since the birth of her child, thus in her analogy she would have had a flow of blood for twelve years at the time of her daughter's Bat Mitzvah. What Helena, "the Menstruous Woman", is advocating is equal rights for women who abstain from sex, in spite of their periods of 'uncleanliness'.

Jesus accepts this change to allow females practicing virginity and, except when they are menstruating, to be included with men. The others ridicule Jesus for allowing this. Jesus, knowing that this is a major change, asks the parents to keep it quiet for now. You will note that the disciples that he took in with him in the Gospel of Luke are Peter, his second in command, John and James the step-brothers of Mary Magdalene, the father-in-law of the girl (Simon Magus), and her mother (Helena-Justa-Luna-Joanna-Salome)

By symbolically raising Mary Magdalene from the dead, Jesus was giving females the right to be active members in the Church, having been previously assigned only to convents outside of the Church and thus 'dead'. This change would retroactively make her Bat Mitzvah at age 12 as an entry into the Church.

Although this change of status of females was accomplished by Jesus at the beginning of his ministry in AD 29, Mary Magdalene's coming of age would obviously have been prior to this as she was 26 in AD 29. From the 'Clementines', we can calculate her age from the time of banishment of Julia, the daughter of Augustus Caesar.

Since Julia was banished in 2 BC, this would be the birth year of the twins James and John. She returned in AD 4 after a five year exile. On returning, Julia would have searched out the location of her sons and seen to it that they were adopted by Helena, having given her money for their support.

With her daughter Mary Magdalene being born before the purchase and adoption of the James and John, it is possible to date Mary Magdalene's birth to AD 3 which also agrees with other sources that rely on the Magian calendar. Thus her age of 26 in AD 29 was older than usual, but this is due to her 'untouchability' because of her mother's history. The twins James and John, who would have been purchased by Helena when they were five or six years old, would be 30 years old and would become Jesus' disciples. Simon Magus joined up with Helena at this time, converting her to the Faith.

Symbolism of Marriage

(The wedding of a David king is shown by spikenard: Song of Solomon Cant 1:12; 4:12,13) While the king was on his couch, my spikenard gave forth its fragrance.

You are a garden locked up, my sister, my bride; you are a spring enclosed, a sealed fountain. Your plants are an orchard of pomegranates with choice fruits, with henna and spikenard,

The Betrothal of Mary Magdalene

(The issue of dowry: Luke 7:36-50) And one of the Pharisees desired him that he would eat with him. And he went into the Pharisee's house, and sat down at table.

Behold, a woman in the city who was a sinner, when she knew that he was reclining in the Pharisee's house, she brought an alabaster jar of ointment.

Standing behind at his feet weeping, she began to wet his feet with her tears, and she wiped them with the hair of her head, kissed his feet, and anointed them with the ointment.

Now when the Pharisee who had invited him saw it, he said to himself,

'This man, if he were a prophet, would have perceived who and what kind of woman this is who touches him, that she is a sinner.'

Jesus answered him,

'Simon, I have something to tell you.'

He said, 'Teacher, say on.'

'A certain lender had two debtors. The one owed five hundred denarii, and the other fifty. When they couldn't pay, he forgave them both. Which of them therefore will love him most?'

Simon answered, 'He, I suppose, to whom he forgave the most.'

He said to him, 'You have judged correctly.'

Turning to the woman, he said to Simon, 'Do you see this woman? I entered into your house, and you gave me no water for my feet, but she has wet my feet with her tears, and wiped them with the hair of her head. You gave me no kiss, but she, since the time I came in, has not ceased to kiss my feet. You didn't anoint my head with oil, but she has anointed my feet with ointment.

Therefore I tell you, her sins, which are many, are forgiven, for she loved much. But to whom little is forgiven, the same loves little.' He said to her, 'Your sins are forgiven.'

Those who sat at the table with him began to say to themselves, 'Who is this who even forgives sins?'

He said to the woman, 'Your faith has saved you. Go in peace.'

There was, however, a still larger issue that remained and this concerned Mary Magdalene's conception by a Vestal Virgin (Helena) and an 'anonymous male-temple-worshiper'. You can understand that this was precisely what endeared Jesus to Mary Magdalene as both had been born of Virgins who were technically defiled.

The reasons why Jesus initially balked at this 'healing of the Syro-Phoenician-Caananite women's daughter' must now be clear because it was a quite a bit more than 'dogs eating crumbs from the table' and the raising of status of women. This proposal of marriage to Mary Magdalene would be the most difficult, but Jesus was not one to shun controversy.

Although Simon Magus and Jesus would often have differences of opinion, his proposed marriage to Mary Magdalene would make Helena-Justa-Luna, his mother-in-law and Simon Magus, his step-father-in-law. This marital alliance would also have its pros and cons as Simon Magus, who would later to be known as 'the father of all heresy', was actually the most influential person at that time. He would work with Jesus to gain his acceptance and that of Mary Magdalene.

On the pro side, Simon and Helena with her temple dancing would successfully convince Herod Antipas to have John the Baptist removed. This was important because John had refused to baptize Jesus because he considered him illegitimate. Simon Magus would take John's place and make Jesus his alternate third in command with Theudas. On the con side, it would unjustly place Jesus on the cross with him.

The symbolism of spikenard in Matthew 26, Mark 14, Luke 7, and John 12 is to show that Jesus and Mary Magdalene, having completed the three month trial, were married like Solomon as the David king and queen just before the Crucifixion. Luke, as he did with Jesus' Bar Mitzvah, which he disguised as the Nativity, used this same event for their betrothal three years earlier.

Mary Magdalene is portrayed as a 'sinner' in the Luke story, but not in other versions that appear in Matthew, Mark, and John because this story is to illustrate the discussion between Simon Magus and Jesus concerning the problems of Mary Magdalene's birth. Simon is explaining to Jesus that it would be difficult for him to be given the third position in his order as 'Prophet', if Jesus chooses to marry Mary Magdalene. He also discusses the issue that Mary Magdalene has little dowry to give. Jesus says that he will forgive the dowry.

Jesus' and Simon's discussion is actually quite friendly for Jesus is not complaining about Simon Magus' hospitality, but, rather, he is saying that he would prefer the love of Mary Magdalene over the position that Simon offers him as Prophet-King. Jesus is content that Simon recognizes his legitimacy as David-King without needing to hold the position under him as he has decided to remain under Jonathan Annas who also recognizes his legitimacy. Mary Magdalene, of course, is once again forgiven of her sins. Also, Jesus adds that her entry into the Faith has saved her, which relates to the Clementine passages discussed earlier.

***********Reference Column***********
Fishers of Men

(The Noah Mission to Gentiles: John 1:16-20)
Passing along by the sea of Galilee, he saw Simon and Andrew, the brother of Simon, casting a net in the sea, for they were fishermen. 'Come and follow me,' said Jesus, 'and I will make you fishers for men.' Immediately they left their nets, and followed him.

And when he had gone a little further thence, he saw James the son of Zebedee, and John his brother, who also were in the boat mending their nets. Immediately he called them, and they left their father, Zebedee, in the boat with the hired servants, and went after him.

Steps of Initiation

(Entry into the Essene Church: Josephus, Jewish War: 2.8.7) But now if any one hath a mind to come over to their sect, he is not immediately admitted, but he is prescribed the same method of living which they use for a year, while he continues excluded; and they give him also a small hatchet, and the fore-mentioned girdle, and the white garment.

And when he hath given evidence, during that time, that he can observe their continence, he approaches nearer to their way of living, and is made a partaker of the waters of purification; yet is he not even now admitted to live with them; for after this demonstration of his fortitude, his temper is tried two more years; and if he appear to be worthy, they then admit him into their society.

And before he is allowed to touch their common food, he is obliged to take tremendous oaths that, ... and that he will neither conceal any thing from those of his own sect, nor discover any of their doctrines to others, no, not though anyone should compel him so to do at the hazard of his life.

Moreover, he swears to communicate their doctrines to no one any otherwise than as he received them himself; that he will abstain from robbery, and will equally preserve the books belonging to their sect, and the names of the angels.

***********Reference Column***********
Eligibility for the Holy Table

(Qumran-Manual of Discipline: 6:20-23) Of Communal Duties. When they set the table for a meal or prepare wine to drink, the priest is first to put forth his hand to invoke a blessing on the first portion of the bread and wine.

As part of the exclusion of Gentiles, a special mission was set up based on Noah symbolism. The Gentiles could then have membership in name only with the main Church that was based on the covenant of Abraham. Those who wished to be part of this mission of Shem, Ham, and Japheth, representing the sons of Noah, would be baptized in salt water. Jesus said in the Sermon on the Mount to the Gentiles (Matthew 5:13) 'Ye are the salt of the land, but if the salt may lose savour, in what shall it be salted? for nothing is it good henceforth, except to be cast without, and to be trodden down by men." Thus he was suggesting that the Noah mission was better than being just an ordinary human.

Peter and Andrew and James and John would help those baptized in the Dead Sea at Mazin back into to their boats, fishing them out in a net. These converts would then be baptized by a priest on the jetty, who in the morning fog, would appear to be 'walking on water'. These disciples were not fishermen, but truly 'fishers of men' as they assisted in the salt water baptism and were leaders of the Gentile groups.

The historian Josephus wrote of the initiation process for membership into the Essene monastery. In the first year ' the initiate is prescribed the same method of living which they use for a year, while he continues excluded; and they give him also a small hatchet (for disposal of feces), a loin cloth, and a white garment.'

When the initiate has proven that he can observe 'continence' (ability to control his bowels), he is baptized in fresh water ('the waters of purification') and then the initiate has another trial period of two years. If he appear to be 'worthy', they then admit him into their society.

The final process requires a vow to follow the rules and to not reveal their doctrines or the names of the angels (their leaders) even on pain of death. The non-revealing of names of the angels explains the common practice of having multiple names within and outside of the Church.

The Qumran Manual of Discipline states, 'When they set the table for a meal or prepare wine to drink, the priest is first to put forth his hand to invoke a blessing on the first portion of the bread and wine.' Clearly, to be present at the Holy Table was the goal of all Jewish initiates, but this privilege would be denied to the Gentiles.

***********Reference Column***********

Jesus out in the world

(Jesus leaves his monastic existence to be in the world to conceive a child to carry on the David kingly line: John 1:14) And the Word came in the flesh, and lived for a time in our midst, so that we saw His glory--the glory as of the Father's only Son, sent from His presence, full of grace and truth.

***********Reference Column***********

Betrothal in Cana

(The betrothal of Jesus and Mary Magdalene: John 2:1-10) The third day, there was a marriage in Cana of Galilee. Jesus' mother was there and also Jesus was called, and his disciples, to the marriage;
When the wine ran out, Jesus' Mother said to him, 'They have no wine.'
'Leave the matter in my hands,' He replied; 'the time for me to act has not yet come.'
His mother said to the servants, 'Whatever he says to you, do it.'
Now there were six stone jars standing there (in accordance with the Jewish regulations for purification), each large enough to hold twenty gallons or more.
Jesus saith to them, Fill the waterpots with water. And they filled them to the brim. He said to them, 'Now draw some out, and take it to the ruler of the feast.' They took it.
When the ruler of the feast tasted the water now become wine, and didn't know where it came from (but the servants who had drawn the water knew), the ruler of the feast called the bridegroom,
and said to him, 'Everyone serves the good wine first, and when the guests have drunk freely, then that which is worse. You have kept the good wine until now!'

***********Reference Column***********

The Marriage of Mary Magdalene

(Marriage is now permanent: Matthew 26:6-12) Now when Jesus was in Bethany, in the house of Simon the leper, a woman came to Him with a jar of very costly, sweet-scented ointment, which she poured over His head as He reclined at table. But when his disciples saw it, they were indignant, saying, 'Why this waste? For this ointment might have been sold for much, and given to the poor.' But Jesus heard it, and said to them, 'Why are you vexing her? For she has done a most gracious act towards me. For you always have the poor with you; but you don't always have me. For in that she poured this ointment on my body, she did it to prepare me for burial.

Jesus had left his monastic existence in AD 29 at the age of thirty-five, having been born in 7 BC, to be in the world to conceive a child for the purpose of carrying on the David kingly line.

Adjusting to the outside world may have been difficult, but by choosing Mary Magdalene, Jesus would have to make many changes to the religious structure including having to raise the status of the Gentiles and women.

The episode of the 'Syro-Phoenician woman' is shown to have been in June AD 32, but the issues that were addressed there had been already set in motion with Cana in AD 29 where Jesus would perform his first miracle of 'changing water into wine'. Although this miracle appeared to be no more than a magic trick that Simon Magus might have performed, it had a deeper significance.

Since by Church law Gentiles were excluded from the Holy Table and therefore could not drink the wine or eat the bread, Jesus' first miracle of changing 'water into wine' was a metaphor for allowing the Gentiles to proceed to the next baptism in fresh water which would make them eligible to be part of the Church and eventually to be eligible to be at the Holy Table where they could have wine.

The 'ruler of the feast' is Simon Magus, the Pope. He would be the one that would have final say on whether Jesus would be allowed to implement this change. Clearly, he has agreed to the changes for he merely makes a remark about 'keeping the good wine until last'.

The curious statement that Jesus says to his mother that has been translated as "What have I to do with thee" really should read, "What business is it for you, my mother, to say my hour has not yet come!"

Having been brought up in the convent of Dan, the tribe of Israel which was designated for Gentiles and being from Phoenicia in the north, thus the greater part of Israel, my grandmother would be called Mary of (greek: Megas) Dan or shortened to Magdala or Magdalene. With the level of Gentiles raised, Mary Magdalene, a Gentile, would be eligible to be his queen.

Mary's anointing ceremony relates to their marriage. In the Gospel of Matthew, Mark, and John before the Crucifixion, the justification for the ointment is 'to prepare Jesus for burial', which has to be an addition because at this point Jesus' Crucifixion might have been suspected, but certainly it was not a fact yet, and it could not have been known by the woman. Jesus' callous remark that 'there will always be the poor and therefore this waste of ointment was perfectly justified to be spent on him, since he was soon to die', was equally absurd. Of course, 'the poor' meant the Church, which was rich enough to spare a few drops of ointment.

***********Reference Column**********

The Marriage of Mary Magdalene

(Marriage is now permanent: Mark 14:3-9)
While he was at <u>Bethany, in the house of Simon the leper</u>, as he sat at the table, there came <u>a woman</u> having an alabaster jar of ointment of pure spikenard -- very costly. She broke the jar, and poured it over his head. But there were some who said indignantly among themselves, 'Why has the ointment been thus wasted? For this might have been sold for more than three hundred denarii, and given to the poor.' They grumbled against her. And Jesus said, Let her alone; why trouble ye her? she hath wrought a good work on me. for the poor always ye have with you, and whenever ye may will ye are able to do them good, but me ye have not always; She has done what she could. She has anointed my body beforehand for the burying. Most assuredly I tell you, wherever this gospel may be preached throughout the whole world, that also which this woman has done will be spoken of for a memorial of her.'

***********Reference Column**********

The Gospel of Mary Magdalene

(Peter contends with Mary Magdalene: Nag Hammadi Library) When Mary had said this, she fell silent, ... Peter answered ... "Did He really speak with a woman without our knowledge (and) not openly? Are we to turn about and all listen to her? Did He prefer her to us?" Then Mary wept and said to Peter, "My brother Peter, what do you think? Do you think that I thought this up myself in my heart, or that I am lying about the Saviour?

***********Reference Column**********

The Marriage of Mary Magdalene

(Marriage is now permanent: John 12:1-8)
Therefore six days before the Passover, Jesus came to <u>Bethany, where Lazarus was</u>, who had been dead, whom he raised from the dead. So they made him a supper there. <u>Martha served, but Lazarus was one of those who sat at the table with him</u>. <u>Mary</u>, therefore, took a pound of ointment of pure spikenard, very precious, and anointed the feet of Jesus, and wiped his feet with her hair. The house was filled with the fragrance of the ointment. Then <u>Judas Iscariot, Simon's son</u>, one of his disciples, who would betray him, said, 'Why wasn't this ointment sold for three hundred denarii, and given to the poor?' This he said, not that he cared for the poor; but because he was a thief, and had the bag, and bore what was put in it. Then said Jesus, Let her alone: against the day of my burial hath she kept this. For the poor you always have with you, but you have not me always.'

The commonality of the anointing stories of the Four Gospels can be shown because they all contain the issue of the 'waste of the ointment' and, although no location is shown in Luke, they all are located in Bethany where Mary and Martha are located. The 'waste of ointment' is a metaphor that is left over from requirement of her dowry, having been waived by Jesus in the Gospel of Luke.

With the misinterpretation of Jesus being the 'Son of God' and his mother being a 'Virgin', the Church had to suppress the marriage for obvious reasons, but the names of the persons involved can still be uncovered.

Mary Magdalene is a 'sinner' in Luke, and a 'woman' in Matthew and Mark, and Mary, the sister of Martha, in John. We have touched on the issue of being a 'sinner' because of her mother, and to associate 'the unnamed 'woman of great fame' with Mary is logical. The inventing of another Mary is not necessary once the truth of the marriage is known. Thus the sinner-woman is Mary Magdalene.

The Gospel of Mark, Matthew, and John give the same justification for it being for Jesus' burial, but in Mark the obvious cover-up of leaving out Mary Magdalene's name is revealed. Jesus says that 'what this woman has done will be spoken of a memorial to her' and yet her name seems to have escaped Peter with Mark the writer.

It is true that Peter objects to Mary Magdalene's privileged position with Jesus in 'The Gospel of Mary Magdalene', but then why would he even say that this 'woman' would be remembered.

Simon Magus is Simon in Luke, 'Simon the leper' in Matthew and Mark, and Lazarus in John. The association of Lazarus being only metaphorically dead and thus being the deposed Pope could easily associate him with other outcastes such as 'lepers', also the location of Bethany is common to the 'Simon the leper' and Lazarus. A further association with Simon is shown in the Gospel of John with Judas Iscariot being 'Simon's son', therefore a subordinate of Simon, and with Martha serving and connected with Mary the one who anoints Jesus, Martha being another name for my great-grandmother Helena, the consort of Simon Magus. Thus the house is in Bethany of Simon, a Pharisee, a leper and Lazarus and Simon the leader of Judas Iscariot and also the house where Martha-Helena served with she being Simon Magus' consort.

This marriage of Jesus and Mary Magdalene was the culmination of the changes that Jesus made to the doctrine that allowed them to consummate their marriage in the Fall and Winter of AD 32. Later in September AD 33, Mary would deliver a child who will be my mother Phoebe, naming her Tamar (Damaris).

Hierapolis of Philip and Mary Magdalene (level 4 daughter)

Healing a bleeding woman (Catacombs of Rome) and Whore of Babylon (Saint-Sever Beatus).

Chapter 8 My great-grandmother, mother-in-law of Jesus (a Vestal Virgin, consort of Simon Magus).

But Jesus said to her, 'Let the children (Jewish males) be filled first, for it is not appropriate to take the children's bread and throw it to the dogs (Gentiles & females).' But she answered him, 'Yes, Lord. For even the dogs under the table eat the children's crumbs.' (Mark 7:27,28) *(Syro-Phoenician woman, my great-grandmother Helena, asks for the healing of her daughter.)*

Obviously the differences of doctrine that led to the removal of the events and name of Simon Magus from the New Testament should also have included Helena, his consort, but, because she was so instrumental in the changes that Jesus brought about, it was almost impossible to remove her.

Thus the Church editors had to give her generic names like 'the Syro-Phoenician or Caananite Woman', 'the Menstruous Woman', 'the Woman of Samaria', 'the Prostitute that was to be stoned', and 'mother of the sons of Zebedee'. These anonymous appearances are her major debates with Jesus and some have been covered already.

In other that her importance be reduced they gave her many names such as Joanna, Martha, Salome, and Sapphira. Her student Bernice would have the names of Jezebel and 'the Whore of Babylon'.

The name 'Joanna' is derived from her position as the thirtieth to John the Baptist's organization as the half-person for the cycles of the moon, the triacontad (30th) in the Clementines and thus the only woman leader, the feminine version of the name 'John'. Her appearance at the tomb with Mother Mary and Mary Magdalene confirms her identity.

The name 'Martha' means 'mistress', the feminine of 'master', as the consort of Simon Magus (Lazarus). She is disguised as the sister of Mary and Lazarus, but this is a Church relationship such as sister nun and brother. Lazarus, the deposed Simon Magus, has been reduced to brother.

Of the three major women at the cross, Helena can be shown to be both Salome and 'the mother of the sons of Zebedee'. Since Zebedee is the father of James and John, using the Clementines, he can be assigned to Simon Magus as their adoptive father, making Helena their adoptive mother. The derivation of Salome refers to the time that Helena danced for Herod Antipas on behalf of his daughter-in-law Salome, which resulted in the deposing of John the Baptist.

The name 'Sapphira' in Acts shows Helena's position in the Church. As the second precious stone in the walls of 'Heavenly Jerusalem' in the Book of Revelation, Helena is second only to Pope Simon Magus.

My great-grandmother Helena's true identity as the mother of Mary Magdalene was suppressed because of an unfortunate event in her early teens as a Temple Virgin with the real name of Paulina. Having almost removed all references to Mary Magdalene for her divorce of Jesus and having removed Helena's name in the 'stoning of the prostitute', the Church created the myth of Magdalene as the 'repentant sinner'.

Helena's names in the Clementines

("mother of the sons of Zebedee" = Justa - adopts James and John: (Clementine Recognitions R.VII:32) "... they sold us to a certain widow, a very honorable women, named Justa. She, having bought us (James and John), treated us as sons, so that she carefully educated us in Greek literature and liberal arts.

(Simon Magus loved my great-grandmother Luna: Clementine Recognitions R.II:9) Simon Magus: His Profession. But not long after he (Simon Magus) fell in love with that woman whom they call Luna (Helena); and he confided all things to us (James and John) as his friends: how he was a magician, and how he loved Luna, and how, being desirous of glory, he was unwilling to enjoy her ingloriously, but that he was waiting patiently till he could enjoy her honorably ...

Helena as a Temple Virgin

(Simon Magus: Eusebius, Church History II 13.4) And there went around with him (Simon Magus) at that time a certain Helena who had formerly been a prostitute in Tyre of Phoenicia ; and her they call the first idea that proceeded from him.

The adoptive mother of James and John on Aradus

(Explaining to Peter how she became a beggar: Clementine Recognitions R.II:9) She confessed that she was sprung of a noble race, and was married to a no less noble husband, whose brother, 'said she, being inflamed by unlawful love towards me, desired to defile his brother's bed. This I abhorring, and yet not daring to tell my husband of so great wickedness, lest I should stir up war between the brothers. and bring disgrace upon the family, judged it better to depart from my country with my two twin sons, leaving the younger boy to be a comfort to his father. And that this might be done with an honorable appearance, I thought good to feign a dream, and to tell my husband that there stood by me in a vision a certain deity, who told me to set out from the city immediately with my two twins, and remain until he should instruct me to return.

In the two versions of the Clementines, my great-grandmother Helena is called 'Justa' in the Recognitions of Clement and in the Clementine Homilies, 'Luna'.

The name 'Justa' is the feminine of 'Justus' showing that in John the Baptist's organization, Simon Magus was second to John and and his consort Helena, a princess, 'Justa'.

The name 'Luna' has to do with Helena's relationship as the moon, Luna, in John the Baptist's group of thirty.

Helena's relationship with Simon Magus was as if married, however Simon was actually not sexually interested in the opposite sex being content to having her as his kingly consort. Helena was determined to remain a virgin sexually.

The issue of the legitimacy of Helena within the Church was of more concern because she had been a Vestal Virgin. Although these Virgins could be executed for not remaining virgins, it was a well known fact that the Temple leaders were not adverse to obtaining a large donation to give these Virgins out to clients. In the event of pregnancy they would be discharged secretly, the girl keeping quiet to avoid execution.

The story of my great-grandmother Helena, when she was a Vestal Virgin called Paulina, is told by the historian Josephus in his book 'The Antiquities of the Jews'. The story of this 'sad calamity' is bookend-ed by the abortive demonstration against Pilate's water canal which led to the killing of Roman soldiers with Simon Magus and Judas Iscariot being sought as accomplishes, resulting in the Crucifixion, and a brief story of 'a wise man' called Jesus. The opposite bookend is the scandal caused by Fulvia who, believing that her contribution would be for the Church in Jerusalem and not on Tiber Island, had complained to Tiberius, causing him to banish the Christians, as also recorded in Acts 18:2. All of these events are of great significance to Christianity and thus with this Temple incident between them, it had to be just as important.

There was a temple of Isis at Campus Martius on a low-lying plain enclosed on the west by a bend of the Tiber River near Tiber Island during Caligula's reign. Josephus has moved the true location of the Temple to Tiber Island to be of greater interest to his readers. However, one can surmise from the Clementines that the true location of this incident is the island of Aradus, one of the tri-cities of Phoenicia together with Tyre and Sidon in a temple dedicated to Artemis (Diana). It was here, in the Clementines, that the mother of Niceta and Aquila was shipwrecked. This noble woman being now reduced to a beggar, parallels the distress and desolation that was felt by Helena, the step-mother of Niceta and Aquila, after the real incident on this island of Aradus.

Helena as a Temple Virgin

(Helena (Paulina) serving at the temple of Isis: Josephus Antiquities of the Jews, 18 3.4) ... There was at Rome a woman whose name was Paulina, who, on account of the rank of her ancestors, and because of the regular conduct of a virtuous life, had a great reputation; she was also very rich, and although she was of a beautiful countenance, and in that flower of her age wherein women are the most gay, she led a life of great modesty. She was married to Saturninus, who well assorted in every way to her from his excellent character. Decius Mundus, a man very high in the equestrian order, fell in love with Paulina, and as she was of too great rank to be caught by presents, ... Now, Mundus had a freedwoman, ... She went to some of Isis' priests, ... And they were induced to promise to do so by the large sum of gold ... So the oldest of them went immediately to Paulina, ... he told her that he was sent by the god Anubis, who had fallen in love with her, and bade her visit him. And she took the message very kindly, and ... told her husband, that she had a message sent her, and was to sup and sleep with Anubis. And he agreed to her acceptance of the offer, being fully satisfied of the chastity of his wife. Accordingly, she went to the temple, and after she had supped there, and it was the hour to go to sleep, the priest shut the doors of the temple, when the lights were also put out in the inner sanctuary. Then did Mundus leap out, (for he was hidden there,) and did not fail to enjoy her, and she was at his service all the night long, supposing he was the god; and when he had gone away, which was before the priests who knew not of this stratagem were stirring, Paulina went home early in the morning to her husband, and told him how the god Anubis had appeared to her, and also boasted about the matter to her lady friends. And they partly disbelieved the thing when they reflected on its nature, and partly were amazed at it, but had no pretext for not believing it, when they considered her modesty and merit. But on the third day after what had been done, Mundus met Paulina, and said, "Truly, Paulina, thou hast saved me two hundred thousand drachmae, which sum thou mightest have given thine own family; ... I care not about names; but I rejoice myself the name of Anubis." When he had said this, he went his way, but she rent her garments, now first knowing what she had done, and told her husband of this wicked and black contrivance, prayed him not to neglect to assist her.

My great-grandmother Paulina served honorably as a Vestal Virgin there and apparently was most beautiful. She fully expected that her virginity would be protected by the priests as she, perhaps naively, thought she was there to serve the goddess.

The historian Josephus pretends outrage at the practice of prostitution at these temples, but it was quite common, although technically a capital crime punishable by death. If enough money were offered for the service, 'the virgin' would be persuaded into performing her duty as a goddess to her god. The man would disguise himself as a god and thus this sexual union would not be prostitution, but union with a god, also allowing for his anonymity. Her priest would be called her husband. In this story the client was foolish enough to reveal himself thus leading to the deaths of the priests involved and his exile. She had become pregnant and was secretly discharged. Note how well his exile resembles the Clementine mother's exile from Rome.

The difficulty of establishing Helena's legitimacy in the Church was due to the problem that, although according to the standards of the Gentile world, serving as a Vestal Virgin was one of the highest honors, unfortunately, its reputation as brothel for the elite would play into the hands of her enemies in the Church, especially when they applied it to her daughter, Mary Magdalene.

83

Putting the incident behind her, Helena remained a virgin throughout the rest of her life. Giving birth to a daughter from this deception, she treasured Mary Magdalene, treating her as a gift of Isis, conceived by a god. Ironically, it would be Jesus' birth that would be made into being born of God.

It was at this time that Julia, the daughter of Augustus Caesar, had returned from exile. Having learned the location of her two illegitimate sons who were now five years old and the story of the Vestal Virgin Paulina, she traveled to Caesarea and approached my great-grandmother with an offer to have her adopt the two twins in return for a lavish payment to be used for their support.

Helena-Paulina goes down to the docks and buys the twins named Niceta and Aquila. These boys, having been exiled at birth, were captured by pirates and turned into slaves.

The money was greatly appreciated to support her and her daughter, Mary Magdalene. Helena-Paulina spared no expense on their education and breeding as the children were the grandchildren of Augustus Caesar and Mark Antony, later to become St. James and St. John.

The activities of Simon Magus on Tiber Island resulted in the banishment of the Jewish Christians from Rome in AD 49. Fulvia, a lady of rank and a proselyte to Judaism, mistakenly believed that her contribution of a purple and gold cloth was to go to the Temple in Jerusalem.

She did not understand that the Jewish Christians were at odds with the Pharisees at the Temple and had actually requested it for their own church on Tiber Island.

When she complained to the Emperor Tiberius, he banished the whole colony on Tiber Island which were made up of Jews and Christians.

Christians expelled from Rome

(Parable of the Vineyard and the husbandmen: Mark 12:6-8) Therefore he had yet one, a beloved son, he sent him last to them, saying, 'They will respect my son.' But those husbandmen said among themselves, This is the heir; come, let us kill him, and the inheritance will be ours. They took him, killed him, and cast him forth out of the vineyard.

John & Priscilla are banished

(Christians are banished from Rome: Acts 18:1,2) And after these things, Paul having departed out of Athens, came to Corinth, Here he found a Jew, a native of Pontus, of the name of Aquila. He and his wife Priscilla had recently come from Italy because of Claudius's edict expelling all the Jews from Rome. So Paul paid them a visit;

Tiberius banishes Cults

(Christian and Egyptian Cults are banished from Rome: Suetonius on Tiberius p. 36) He (Tiberius) abolished foreign cults, especially the Egyptian and the Jewish rites, compelling all who were addicted to such superstitions to burn their religious vestments and all their paraphernalia. Those of the Jews who were of military age he assigned to provinces of less healthy climate, ostensibly to serve in the army. Others of the same race or of similar beliefs he banished from the city, on pain of slavery for life if they did not obey. He banished the astrologers as well, but pardoned such as begged for indulgence and promised to give up their art.

Simon Magus on Tiber Island

(Simon Magus power, Lightning: Matthew 10:18) 10:18 And he said unto them, I beheld Satan as lightning fall from heaven.

(The statute of Simon Magus on the island of Tiber: Justin Martyr quoted by Eusebius, First Apology of Justin 26) There was a Samaritan, Simon, a native of the village called Gitto, who in the reign of Claudius Caesar, and in your royal city of Rome, did mighty acts of magic, by virtue of the art of the devils operating in him.
He was considered a god, and as statue was erected on the river Tiber, between the two bridges, and bore this inscription, in the language of Rome: "Simoni Deo Sancto," (To Simon the holy God). And almost all the Samaritans, and a few even of other nations, worship him, and acknowledge him as the first god; and a woman, Helena, who went about with him at that time, and had formerly been a prostitute, they say is the first idea generated by him.

The ejection from Tiber Island, as being a major setback to the Church, was reflected in the 'Parable of the Vineyard and the Husbandmen' where the Son is killed and cast out of the vineyard.

This is an example of a parable that does not have a moral message, but represents the history of the Church. It also gives information that the Church mission was called the 'Vineyard', thus a clue to 'the winepress' of Revelation.

The ejection also included John Aquila and his wife Priscilla. St. John was the twin brother of St. James.

Actually this banishment was not just this one event, but a complete change of policy by Tiberius, which included Egyptian cults and thus the cult of Isis and Artemis

This indicates the global reason that the temple of Isis that Josephus mentioned had been dismantled, although the incident of Fulvia's complaint and the deception of Paulina would certainly have contributed to his decision.

The Christian mission on Tiber Island was present at the time that the young Jesus was brought here by Mother Mary, due to his father Joseph's missionary work. Part of the house of Herod Antipas had been converted into a Church. The importance of Simon Magus to this organization on Tiber Island is shown by the misconception of a statue to the old Etruscan deity Semo Santus being cast into the Tiber River at the time of Tiberius' dissolution of cults.

This Etruscan deity had reputedly made lightning appear during the day. This was one of the tricks that Simon Magus used of simulating the lightening from the mountain of Moses and thus one of his nicknames was 'Lightning'. This nickname and its inscription 'Semoni Sanco', which was misinterpreted as meaning 'To Simon the holy God' ('Simoni Deo Sancto'), led to the belief that the statue was of Simon Magus.

Simon rescues Helena

(How Simon met Helena: Hippolytus: Refutations of All Heresies Book VI Chap. XIV) Simon then, after inventing these tenets, not only by evil devices interpreted the writings of Moses in whatever way he wished, but even the works of the poets. For also he fastens an allegorical meaning on the story of the wooden horse and Helen with the torch, and on very many other accounts, which he transfers to what relates to himself and to Intelligence, and thus famishes a fictitious explanation of them. He said, however, that this Helen was the lost sheep. And she, always abiding among women, confounded the powers in the world by reason of her surpassing beauty. Whence, likewise, the Trojan war arose on her account. For in the Helen born at that time resided this Intelligence; and thus, when all the powers were for claiming her for themselves, sedition and war arose, during which this chief power was manifested to nations ... But the angels and the powers below - who, he says, created the world - caused the transference from one body to another of Helen's soul; and subsequently she stood on the roof of a house in Tyre, a city of Phoenicia, and on going down thither Simon professed to have found her. For he stated that, principally for the purpose of searching after this woman, he had arrived in Tyre, in order that he might rescue her from bondage. And after having thus redeemed her, he was in the habit of conducting her about with himself, alleging that this girl was the lost sheep, and affirming himself to be the Power above all things. But the deceitful fellow, becoming enamored of this miserable woman called Helen, purchased her, and enjoyed her person. He, however, was likewise moved with shame towards his disciples, and concocted this figment to conceal his disgrace.

Simon and Helena

(Simon Magus presents Helena (Luna) as Goddess: (Clementine Recognitions R.II:12) Simon Magus and Luna. "Therefore, after the death of Dositheus, Simon took Luna to himself; and with her he still goes about, as you see, deceiving multitudes, and asserting that he himself is a certain power which is above God the Creator, while Luna, who is with him, has been brought down from the higher heavens, and that she is Wisdom, the mother of all things, for whom the Greeks and barbarians contending, were able in some measure to see an image of her; but of herself, as she is, as the dweller with the first and only God, they were wholly ignorant ...

In the 'Clementines' Pope Clement had placed Mattidia, who is the real mother of Niceta and Aquila, on the island of Aradus to represent Helena-Paulina. In the story it is Peter who rescues Mattidia, whereas in real life it was Simon Magus who rescued Paulina, changing her name to Helena.

This name Helena is not just taken frivolously, but relates to the concept of Sophia (Intelligence) who becomes entangled in the Earth and forgets her true nature as the aspect of Heaven. She transmigrates from soul to soul. When humans encounter Sophia, it kindles within them a spark of Light from the Divine God. Sophia had once been trapped in the body of Helen of Troy and all the nations had sought to own her, not realizing that it was Sophia within her that they sought.

Simon Magus saw that same goddess Sophia inside my great-grandmother Paulina and called her Helena after Helen of Troy, 'the face that launched a thousand ships'. The name stuck with her when she and Simon Magus converted Queen Helena. Significantly, Simon Magus calls her 'the lost sheep' which reminds us of the issue contained in the Syro-Phoenician/Canaanite healing.

It appears that, as part of the conscious degrading of my step-grandfather Simon Magus, some writers have wrongly associated Simon with the tragic event at the temple. They refer to him as 'the deceitful fellow, who becoming enamored of this miserable woman called Helen, purchased her, and enjoyed her person.' This, of course, was a total lie.

No one was more kind and loving towards my great-grandmother Helena than my step-great grandfather Simon Magus and he respected her wish not to have sexual relations.

(My great-grandmother converted Queen Helena to the Church: Josephus, Antiquities of the Jews, XX. 2.1,3) About this time it was that Helena, queen of Adiabene, and her son Izates, changed their course of life ... Now, during the time Izates abode at Charax-Spasini, a certain Jewish merchant, whose name was Ananias (Simon Magus see Acts 5:1-10), got among the women that belonged to the king, and taught them to worship God according to the Jewish religion. He, moreover, by their means, became known to Izates, and persuaded him, in like manner, to embrace that religion; he also, at the earnest entreaty of Izates, accompanied him when he was sent for by his father to come to Adiabene; it also happened that Helena, about the same time, was instructed by a certain other Jew and went over to them.

(The good Samaritan, Jonathan Annas: Luke 10:30-34) Jesus replied, 'A man was once on his way down from Jerusalem to Jericho when he fell among robbers, who after both stripping and beating him went away, leaving him half dead. Now a priest happened to be going down that way, and on seeing him passed by on the other side. In like manner a Levite also came to the place, and seeing him passed by on the other side. But a certain Samaritan, being on a journey, came where he lay, and seeing him was moved with pity. He went to him, and dressed his wounds with oil and wine and bound them up. Then placing him on his own mule he brought him to an inn, where he bestowed every care on him.

(Simon Magus gains entry into John the Baptist's group: Clementine Recollections II:8) Simon Magus: His History. "For after that John the Baptist was killed, as you yourself also know, when Dositheus had broached his heresy,' with thirty other chief disciples, and one woman, who was called Luna whence also these thirty appear to have been appointed with reference to the number of the days, according to the course of the moon this Simon, ambitious of evil glory, as we have said, goes to Dositheus, and pretending friendship, entreats him, that if any one of those thirty should die, he should straightway substitute him in room of the dead: ... Therefore Dositheus, being greatly urged by this man, introduced Simon when a vacancy occurred among the number.

The conversion of Izates and his mother Helena, the queen of Adiabene, was a major achievement for Church. Helena and Simon Magus, using the name Ananias, were directly responsible, but some other Church groups meddled with the situation by requiring the circumcision of Izates. Queen Helena's conversion gave legitimacy to the fledgling Christian Church, giving them financial support and, during a famine, she also sent them grain.

Simon Magus and Helena were instrumental in deposing John the Baptist. Helena-Luna was already part of his group and she schemed with Simon Magus to capitalize on the nonfulfillment of his prophecies to depose him.

Although John the Baptist's mission began with high hopes, he had taken the position that Jesus was illegitimate and thus his support of Jesus' brother James as the David King was undermining Jesus' mission. He was also meddling in political affairs as with trivial issue with Herod Antipas of Herodias' divorce and remarriage.

After a first nonfulfillment, John the Baptist began to be out of favor. In the parable of the Good Samaritan', Simon Magus, representing West Manhesseh and Judas Iscariot, East Manhesseh, passed him by. However, Jonathan Annas, using the name Dositheus, as the Sadducee priest from Samaria allied himself with John the Baptist, restoring his prestige. He would do the same for Jesus when John the Baptist was gone.

Simon Magus may have claimed to have rescued Helena, but she does not seem to have needed to be rescued. As the power behind the throne, she managed to exercise her influence over Simon Magus, Jonathan Annas, John the Baptist, Antipas Herod, and even Jesus.

We learn from the 'Clementines' that Helena was 'Luna' in the organization of John the Baptist which was based on the lunar calendar thus there were thirty members, one for each day. Since the lunar cycle is 29 1/2 days, it was therefore necessary to have one female who was Helena, known as Luna (Moon) in that capacity. The one-half is because the Jewish-Essenes valued a woman as half a man. To be the only female in John the Baptist's leadership was an honor indeed!

Clearly, Helena's seductive powers, which she had learned at the Temple, when combined with her intelligence allowed her to accomplish whatever she wanted. By visualizing the power that would be created by joining the two diametrically opposite personalities of Simon Magus and Jesus, she set the wheels in motion that would create the Church of Jesus and to expand it to all Gentiles and give equal status to women.

Early on, Helena realized the importance of adopting the two twins James and John, who were related to the Emperors of Rome, as a useful link to Rome. More important than that, she succeeded in brokering the marriage of her daughter Mary Magdalene to Jesus. The mutual bond between Simon Magus and Jesus would last well past the Crucifixion, up to the Schism of the Churches. As opposites in ideology and temperament, there was little hope of any reconciliation, once Mary Magdalene divorced Jesus.

With Helena's help, Simon had been able to convince Jonathan Annas (Dositheus) to let Simon Magus into the council of thirty when there was a vacancy. John the Baptist would be the "Voice" as the Sun and Helena the "Name" as the Moon (Luna). ('Voice' and 'Name' are the Second Force.)

The flaw in John the Baptist's character was his strong affinity to the prophet Elijah, his namesake, who stood up against the pagan god Baal and King Ahab. Thus he foolishly put himself in danger by opposing Herod Antipas for the mere technically of his illegal marriage to Herodias. The Church was dependent on Herod Antipas who became the leader of the Herodian sect of the Church, which he inherited from his father Herod the Great. He controlled the membership monies from the Jews who lived abroad (the Diaspora). These funds would then be dispersed for the support of Qumran, the "Jerusalem in exile". The Church was willing to put up with the meddling of John in the affairs of state, but when his prophesies started to fail, Simon Magus and Helena seized the opportunity to get Herod Antipas to arrest him.

Helena, being the teacher of Salome, the daughter of Herodias, would be able to dance in her place. Having been a Vestal Virgin at the Temple of Artemis, her dance for Herod was clearly sexually provocative, causing him to offer her anything. Knowing that Herodias wanted John the Baptist to be killed for tarnishing her image, Helena, of course, asked for the head of John the Baptist. Clearly this was not his actual head as has been gruesomely portrayed, but just his removal as the head of the group of thirty.

Their plan was successful and Jonathan Annas was initially made the head of the thirty. However, Jonathan Annas turned out to be as stubborn and egotistic as John the Baptist and he was easily replaced by Simon Magus.

Although mostly silent about Jesus, Josephus writes favorably about John the Baptist.

The untimely death of John the Baptist left a vacuum that would be fought for by Simon Magus, Judas Iscariot, Theudas, and Jonathan Annas, but, although the group of thirty remained, it was Jesus, who successfully recruited followers away from them.

Jesus was the one who was most liked by the disciples Peter and Andrew, James and John, and John Mark and Philip. His neutrality on Zealot issues was also an asset to protect those like Simon Magus, Judas, and Theudas, who covertly supported the Zealots.

Prior to discussing the dialogue between Helena and Jesus in "the Samaritan Woman at the Well" in the fourth chapter of John, it is necessary to cover the first chapter of John, which contains the philosophy of Simon Magus and Jesus.

Simon Magus' philosophy

(Hippolytus: Refutations of All Heresies Book VI Chap. XV) This doctrine, in point of fact, was the same with the Simonian, though Valentinus denominated under different tides: for "Nous" and "Aletheia" and "Logos" and "Zoe" and "Anthropos," and "Ecclesia," and Aeons of Valentinus,
are confessedly the six roots of Simon,
viz.,
"Mind" and " Intelligence,"
"Voice" and "Name,"
"Ratiocination" and "Reflection."

Simon Magus' philosophy explained from: John 1:1-17,23,25,26

- **First Level: (Mind-Intelligence)**
  Mind (Hestos-Nous-Heaven) and
  Intelligence (Sophia-Aletheia-Earth)

John 1:1,2 "In the beginning was the Word, and the Word was 'with God', and the Word was God. The same was in the beginning with GOD"
This phrase describes the second level of creation, but the phrase "the same was in the beginning with GOD" tells that the first level acts the same way.
Thus by swapping out the secondary emanation the "Word" with "GOD",
John 1:1 would read:
"In the beginning was GOD and GOD was with GOD" (Being "Hidden" and "Manifest" at the same time) and GOD was GOD (the emanation of GOD (Spirit) is GOD existing in all things)
John 1:5 "The light shineth in darkness, and the darkness comprehendeth it not."
GOD in the "beginning" is made of three aspects which are "the Hidden" and "the Manifest" and "the Spirit". The Spirit is what permeates the whole of creation. Thus the "Hidden" (passive force) and the "Manifest" (active force) are joined together by "Spirit" (reconciling force).
The act of Creation is when the Spirit separates the "Hidden" and "Manifest", thus giving us existence in the "Manifest" by means of "the Spirit".
This process of Creation creates three levels (higher to lower) of "Hidden"-"Manifest" pairs, each are created by the level above it by means of "the Spirit".

(Hymn of the Pearl: Acts of Thomas 9)
I remembered that I was a King's son, My rank did long for its nature. I bethought me again of the Pearl ... I began to charm him, the terrible loud-breathing Serpent ... I snatched up the Pearl, and turned to the House of my Father ... On the road I found before me, my Letter that had aroused me; as with its Voice it had roused me, so now with its Light it did lead me ... For He had received me with gladness, and I was with Him in His Kingdom.

"The first verses of John have a poetic feel to them, which after verse 14 quickly breaks down into reality. Part of this is due to the editing that was done to it to make it correspond to the Synoptic Gospels, but mainly it is due to the lack of knowledge of the 'Pesher of Christ'. Scholars like to dismiss these philosophic explosions as Gnostic, but it cannot be denied that they have been canonized!

The similarity to Simon's philosophy and the presentation of changes in doctrine as miracles by Jesus, as in Simon's magic. proves the collaboration of Simon Magus and Jesus in the writing of the Gospel of John. (Shown in the reference column.)

"In the beginning was the Word, and the Word was with God, and the Word was God" (John 1:1). This is a description of the Second Level of Creation.

In GOD's Creation, the First Level makes the Second level manifest. This Second Level consists of 'Word' and 'with GOD', its complementary force, thus the pair: Voice (Word) - Name (Life). The 'Voice' and 'Name' become GOD by means of the 'Spirit' ("the Word was GOD").

The Third Level is demonstrated in the second creation story of Genesis with Adam and Eve. Here the Second Level 'Lord God', not GOD, acts because we, on the Third Level, can only see the Second level. This 'Lord God' on the Second level is a construction of our imaginings with all the shortcomings of our 'selves'; it is not GOD. The 'Lord God' merely has the 'Voice of GOD' and the complementary force of the 'Lord God' creates a world, that is merely 'Life in Name' (what we call it - Adam names the animals). Thus we are 'naked' before the 'Lord God' meaning we are as 'soul-less' as the God we imagine.

"The same was in the beginning with God" (John 1:2). This tells us that the Second Level is the mirror of the First. Thus reflecting the Second level upward to the First Level we have the 'Mind of GOD' (Hestos-Hidden) and the 'Intelligence of GOD' (Sophia-Manifest Mind) and the 'Spirit within all of Creation'.

"The light shined in darkness; the darkness comprehended it not" (John 1:5). On this First Level, the 'Hidden' and the 'Manifest' cancel each other out and there is just empty space and all space (annihilation and fulfillment at the same time).

"Spirit of God moved upon the face of the Waters" (Genesis 1:2). Spirit creates a ripple that brings the Matter into existence.

Sophia ('Intelligence') leaves the First Level and mistakenly seeks 'Light' on the Third Level thinking it was the 'Mind of God'. She becomes entangled in the Earth, forgetting her true nature as the aspect of Heaven. When her plight is discovered the 'Mind', as in "The Hymn of the Pearl" sends her a letter (a description of 'Spirit') to remind her of her true nature. The letter leads her away from the filth and death at the bottom of the Earth, where the serpent lives, back to Heaven to regain her true nature as the 'Intelligence of God'.

We must follow her back to the root of our true nature as pure intelligence (Soul).

***********Reference Column**********
Simon Magus' philosophy explained from: John 1:1-17,23,25,26) (Continued)

- **Second Level: (Voice-Name)**
  Voice (Logos/Word/Sun) and
  Name (Zoe/Life/Moon)

"And they heard the Voice of the Lord God walking in the garden' (Genesis 3:8) and 'And Adam gave Names to all the cattle and to the fowl of the air." (Genesis 2:20)

John 1:14 "The Word became flesh, and lived among us. We saw his glory, such glory as of the only Son of the Father, full of grace and truth."

John 1:23 "He (John the Baptist) said, 'I am the Voice of one crying in the wilderness, 'Make straight the way of the Lord,' as Isaiah the prophet said.'"

John 1:4 "In him was life, and the life was the light of men."

***********Reference Column**********
Simon Magus' philosophy explained from: John 1:1-17,23,25,26) (Continued)

- **Third Level (Man-Woman)**
  Reasoning (Man/Church/Light/Truth/Adam) and
  Intuition
  (Woman/Baptism/Water/Grace/Agape-Love/Eve)

Genesis 2:7 "And the Lord God formed Man out of the dust of the ground and breathed into his nostrils the breath of life"
(Genesis 2:23, 3:20) "And Adam said ... she shall be called Woman. And Adam called his wife's name Eve because she was the mother of all living'"

John 1:6-8 "There came a man, sent from God, whose name was John. The same came as a witness, that he might testify about the light, that all might believe through him. He was not the Light, but he existed that he might give testimony concerning the Light."

Baptism according to John the Baptist: Josephus Antiquities of the Jews, 18 5,2) Baptism would be acceptable to God, if they made use of it, not in order to expiate some sins, but for the purification of the body, provided that the soul was thoroughly purified beforehand by righteousness.

"The Word became flesh, and lived among us. We saw his glory, such glory as of the only Son of the Father, full of grace and truth." (John 1:14)

The 'Voice' ("Word") was expressed through John the Baptist. However, after his death, the 'Voice (Word)' would be expressed through Jesus as the 'Christ', 'The Suffering Servant' of Isaiah 53".

"He (John the Baptist) said, 'I am the Voice of one crying in the wilderness, 'Make straight the way of the Lord,' as Isaiah the prophet said.'" (John 1:23)

"Word, Voice, and Sun" are synonymous terms, as are "Life, Name, and Moon" as the forces of the Second Level. They were created by the 'Mind' (the Hidden) and 'Intelligence' (the Manifest) on the First Level above them. The First Level is described in day 1-3 of Creation. The Second Level is day 4-5. The Third Level begins with Man on Day 6 and then God rests for Man's free will must decide if Eve came from Adam.

"In him was life, and the life was the light of men."
(John 1:4)

Within him (the masculine aspect of this level: 'Word'), is its feminine aspect: 'Life', which is 'Life in the service of God'. 'Life' on the Second Level is created by 'Intelligence' acting from the First Level above."

The Second level reflects itself downward to the Third Level giving 'Reasoning (Man/Church/Light/Truth)' and 'Intuition (Woman/Baptism/Water/Grace/Agape-Love)'.

Both John the Baptist and Jesus instituted Baptism which gives 'Intuition' on the Third Level, connecting upwards to the Second Level: 'Life' and then upwards to First Level: 'Intelligence' which is Sophia who guides the way.

We are fortunate to have the words of John the Baptist from Josephus, "Baptism would be acceptable to God, if they made use of it, not in order to expiate some sins, but for the purification of the body, provided that the soul was thoroughly purified beforehand by righteousness."

After one is Baptized and enters the Church one becomes part of 'Intuition'. Then being taught the ways of God to be part of 'Reasoning'. 'Reasoning-Church' is the complement of 'Intuition-Baptism' within the 'Reasoning-Intuition' pair in the Third Level.

"There came a man, sent from God, whose name was John. The same came as a witness, that he might testify about the light, that all might believe through him. He was not the Light, but he existed that he might give testimony concerning the Light." (John 1:6-8)

On the Third Level, 'Reasoning' is also the 'Light' which illuminates the 'Word' from the Second level and then connects to the 'Mind of God' on the First Level.

But John admitted that he was not the 'Light', not because Jesus was higher, but rather because 'Light' is the Church (the coming together of all people with Love), not just one individual alone.

***********Reference Column***********
Simon Magus' philosophy explained from: John 1:1-17,23,25,26) (Continued)
John 1:25,26 "Why baptizest thou then, if thou art not that Christ, nor Elijah, neither that prophet?" John answered them, saying,"I baptize with water: but there standeth one among you, whom ye know not;"
This is the Ahuric triad (Ahura Mazda, Mithra and Apam Napat), Tai Chi Tu (Yin-Yang), the Trimurti (Brahma-Shiva-Vishnu), and the Trinity (Father, Son, Holy Spirit)

***********Reference Column***********
Samaritan woman at the well

(The woman of Samaria (Helena) talks with Jesus at the well: John 4:5-30) He cometh, therefore, to a city of Samaria, called Sychar, near to the place that Jacob gave to Joseph his son; and there was there a well of Jacob. Jesus therefore having been weary from the journeying, was sitting thus on the well; it was as it were the sixth hour.
Presently there came a woman of Samaria to draw water. Jesus asked her to give Him some water; for His disciples were gone to the town to buy provisions.
'How is it,' replied the woman, 'that a Jew like you asks me, who am a woman and a Samaritan, for water?' (For Jews have no dealings with Samaritans.)
Jesus answered and said to her, 'If thou hadst known the gift of God, and who it is who is saying to thee, Give me to drink, thou wouldest have asked him, and he would have given thee living water.'
The woman saith to him, 'Sir, thou hast not even a vessel to draw with, and the well is deep; whence, then, hast thou the living water? Art thou greater than our father Jacob, who did give us the well, and himself out of it did drink, and his sons, and his cattle?'
Jesus answered her, 'Everyone who drinks of this water will thirst again, but whoever drinks of the water that I will give him will never thirst; but the water that I will give him will become in him a well of water springing up to eternal life.'
The woman saith unto him, 'Sir, give me this water, that I may not thirst, nor come hither to draw.'
Jesus saith to her, 'Go, call thy husband, and come hither.'
The woman answered,
I have no husband.'
Jesus said to her, 'You said well, 'I have no husband,' for five husbands thou hast had, and, now, he whom thou hast is not thy husband; this hast thou said truly.'

"I baptize with water: but there standeth one among you, whom ye know not". (John 1:25,26)
John the Baptist is not acknowledging Jesus or even Simon Magus, 'the Standing One', but rather GOD, the One who stands and will stand for all time'.

The completion of the levels within oneself is the eternal soul. The Spirit is expressed as God's eternal Love in the 'Hymn of the Pearl' or in 'Jacob's Ladder'. "Most assuredly, I tell you, hereafter you will see Heaven opened, and the angels of God ascending and descending towards the Son of Man." (Jesus: John 1:51).

With this introduction it will now be possible to understand 'the Samaritan Woman at the Well' as not the chance meeting of Jesus with a naive Samaritan woman, who flirts with him, but a serious, yet lighthearted, discussion with an intelligent, knowledgeable woman who is clearly Jesus' equal, my great-grandmother Helena, the consort of Simon Magus. Once the hidden purpose of this meeting and the metaphoric images are unraveled, it will be seen that this story truly represents the turning point of Jesus' career where he declares, "I am the Christ".

In the surface story, this woman of Samaria is portrayed as a loose woman having had five previous husbands and living out of wedlock with another man. The only miracle here is that Jesus seems to read her mind and know about her past. The most significant part of the story is at the end where, strangely, he makes his first declaration that he is the Christ to an unknown woman of a sect that is not considered truly Jewish.

This apparent chance meeting happens while the disciples have 'gone for provisions', which seems extremely suspect. When they return, they also do not berate her for bothering Jesus, as they usually do with others, especially Mary Magdalene. Clearly, Jesus must have sent them away.

If one assumes that this a serious conversation between the woman and Jesus, then one must look at the timing of this event. Since it occurs when John the Baptist is in decline, and just before Helena and Simon Magus are directly involved in the deposing (taking the head) of John the Baptist, the purpose of this meeting must have been to 'test the waters' for the establishment of new alliances. As with all temporal and spiritual leaders, it is often that a female is the real power behind the throne, therefore it is clearly Helena, acting for Simon Magus.

With that in mind, when we look closer, we begin to see the significance of Jesus asking the woman for water for he must be asking if Simon Magus would be willing to accept him in his organization. Having been rejected by John the Baptist when John refused to baptize him because of his father's sin, Jesus wants to know if he will be recognized as legitimate.

Helena tests him on his willingness to accept the differences between them. Jesus indicates that 'God's gift' (the humorous name for Jonathan Annas the stuck-up priest whose name means 'God gives') is on his side. Jesus offers her living water, which is to say that his mission is still alive, and thriving.

(The woman of Samaria (Helena) talks with Jesus at the well: John 4:5-30) *(Continued)* The woman saith to him, 'Sir, I perceive that thou art a prophet; Our forefathers worshipped on this mountain, but you Jews say that the place where people must worship is in Jerusalem.'
Jesus said to her, 'Woman, believe me, the hour comes, when neither in this mountain, nor in Jerusalem, will you worship the Father. You worship that which you don't know. We worship that which we know; for salvation is from the Jews. But the hour cometh, and now is, when the true worshipers shall worship the Father in spirit and in truth: for the Father seeketh such to worship him. God is a Spirit, and those who worship him must worship in spirit and truth.'
The woman saith to him, I know that Messiah cometh, who is called Christ; when he is come, he will tell us all things.
Jesus said to her, 'I who speak to you am he.'
Just then His disciples came, and were surprised to find Him talking with a woman. Yet not one of them asked Him, 'What is your wish?' or 'Why are you talking with her?'
So the woman left without her water pot, and went away into the city, and said to the people, 'Come,' she said, 'and see a man who has told me everything I have ever done. Can this be the Christ, do you think?' They left the town and set out to go to Him.

(Jesus is of the descent of Jacob: Numbers 24:19) Out of Jacob shall come he that shall have dominion...

(The kings and rulers shall be against the Christ: Psalm 2:2) The kings of the earth take a stand, and the rulers take counsel together, against God, and against his Anointed (Christ),

(The Christ will be killed: Daniel 9:26) After this period of sixty-two sets of seven, the Anointed One (Christ) will be killed, appearing to have accomplished nothing, and a ruler will arise whose armies will destroy the city and the Temple. The end will come with a flood, and war and its miseries are decreed from that time to the very end.

(Christ shall preach to the Gentiles: Isaiah 42:6) The nations wait on His teaching; He is the light of the Gentiles.

Helena jokes that he does not have a vessel to hold the water and that the well is deep, but in reality she is asking if he can match John with baptism. Jesus insists that he can and she indicates that an alliance can be formed.

₽ Jesus questions as to whether the alliance she is offering is agreeable to her husband, meaning Simon Magus. She takes offence at his assertion that he is her husband, meaning that she has the power to create this alliance without his approval.

Then Jesus, knowing that she and Simon are not officially married, asserts that this is true, but then humorously pretends that her previous five incarnations are husbands. Simon uses these incarnations, having assigned them to Helena, in his public demonstrations as a device to show the layers of his philosophical hierarchy.

These can be expressed as the Lord's Prayer (David's secret chord in Pythagorean notation as discussed in Chapter 3: The Inner Circle) of five levels of descending vibrations corresponding to Simon's Three Levels:

- highest 'do' (Our Father in Heaven) - 'Athena' born out of Zeus (Visible from Invisible)
- 'ti' (Thy Kingdom Come) - 'Sophia' to Hestos (Intelligence and Mind)
- 'la' (Temptation) - 'Helen of Troy' (Sophia trapped below) to Paris (her lover on the Emotional-Astral Plane)
- 'sol' (Daily Bread) - 'Luna' (Helena's Moon-Name) to John the Baptist (Sun-Voice-Word)
- 'fa' (Forgive Trespassers) - 'Vestal Virgin' of Artemis-Diana' (Initiation-Intuition) to the Temple (Church-Reasoning).

When Helena questions Jesus as to whether Jesus could fulfill the role of the Messiah-King, being a distant descendant of Jacob ("the well is deep"), Jesus affirms that he has the strength to take over the role of the 'Jacob', again using his 'living water' metaphor.

They also discuss the differences of doctrine between the Samaritans and the Jews for example the Samaritans preferring Mount Gerizim instead of Jerusalem. Jesus replies that the 'new Jerusalem' will replace both temples.

Helena, knowing that Jesus is already calling himself the Christ, humorously pretends that the Christ is yet to come. Actually, she is asking if Jesus would be willing to have this role of Christ (the Messiah-Anointed One) in Simon's proposed organization that would soon replace John the Baptist. Jesus agrees to this.

This structure would be as follows: Simon Magus as Pope (Father), Jonathan as the levite (truth: Gabriel, the voice of God), and Jesus as the Christ King (spirit: Holy Spirit). It would be primarily for the Gentiles and Samaritans, thus being free from strict Jewish-Essene customs.

Ϛignificantly, Helena leaves without her waterpot, signifying that the position is his. When Helena tells Simon's Samaritan followers, they also declare their allegiance to Jesus.

***********Reference Column***********

Adoption of James and John

(My great-grandmother Justa adopts James and John: Clementine Homilies H.XIII:7) Niceta tells what Befell Him. And Niceta, who in future is to be called Faustinus, began to speak. " On that very night when, as you know, the ship went to pieces, we were taken up by some men, who did not fear to follow the profession of robbers on the deep. They placed us in a boat, and brought us along the coast, sometimes rowing and sometimes sending for provisions, and at length took us to Caesarea Stratonis," and there tormented us by hunger, fear, and blows, that we might not recklessly disclose anything which they did not wish us to tell; and, moreover, changing our names, they succeeded in selling us. Now the woman who bought us was a proselyte of the Jews, an altogether worthy person, of the name of Justa. She adopted us as her own children, and zealously brought us up in all the learning of the Greeks ...

***********Reference Column***********

James and John to sit with Jesus

(My great-grandmother asks that James and John with royal blood sit on the right and left of Jesus: Matthew 20:20-23) Then came to him the mother of the sons of Zebedee with her sons, kneeling and asking a certain thing of him. And he said to her, What wilt thou: She saith to him, Grant that these my two sons may sit, the one on thy right hand, and the other on the left in thy kingdom. But Jesus answered, 'You don't know what you ask. Are you able to drink the cup that I am about to drink, and be baptized with the baptism that I am baptized with?' They said to him, 'We are able.' And he saith to them, 'Of my cup indeed ye shall drink, and with the baptism that I am baptized with you shall be baptized; but to sit on my right hand and on my left is not mine to give, but -- to those for whom it hath been prepared by my Father.'

Let this cup pass from me

(In the Garden of Gethsemane Jesus defers to his Father Jonathan Annas: Matthew 26:39) And he (Jesus) went a little further, and fell on his face, and prayed, saying, O my Father, if it be possible, let this cup pass from me: nevertheless not as my will, but Thine be done.

In the 'Clementines', I proved that James and John are the grandsons of the Emperor Augustus by his natural daughter Julia. They were born in 2 BC. Having been sold into slavery, they were bought and adopted by my great-grandmother, Helena.

Since Helena was as if married to Simon Magus, Simon was their stepfather. In an effort to obscure Simon's name they are called the sons of Zebedee in the New Testament. When they transferred allegiance to Jonathan Annas they were called Boanerges, or the 'Sons of Thunder.'

Comparing the nicknames of Simon and Jonathan, Simon's 'Lightning' and Jonathan's 'Thunder', quite a bit can be learned about their personalities. Simon was the one with the intellect and inspiration of Moses and yet, since thunder has the power to scare those who are wavering in their faith in God, Jonathan is not to be trifled with.

Simon Magus, being unfazed by his power, would say, "Thunder comes after lightning, so Jonathan is nothing without him."

In another situation, Helena makes a request of Jesus that only his mother-in-law would have the nerve to ask. She requests for her adopted twins James and John to sit on the right and left side of Jesus in heaven. Actually she is just asking that James and John sit on his right and left in the upper platform of the Church, with Jesus in the center. The other disciples are outraged by this presumptuous statement.

Jesus', having just recently defied the Church by removing Simon Magus' excommunication as Lazarus and with Jonathan having replaced him as Pope, prefers to rely on caution. His reply is that it is up to the 'Father' meaning that he was deferring to Jonathan Annas as his superior.

This is another example of Helena, using her tactics as she did before as 'the Samaritan Woman at the Well'. She was trying to test if Jesus was willing to seize control from Jonathan Annas, at least, until Simon could be reinstated. Helena's idea was that by using James and John, the grandsons of Caesar Augustus, their royal heritage could be used to elevate the Church in the Roman Empire.

Jesus probably rejects this because he is tired of the political maneuvering, but this had its own dangers. Father Jonathan Annas would order Jesus to take the poison even before he was crucified, thus attempting to deprive him of the glory of his Crucifixion. His mother-in-law knows best!

The death of Simon Magus (Nuremberg Chronicle, 1493)

Chapter 9 My step-great-grandfather Simon Magus (maligned as the worst heretic of all time).
The many names of Simon Magus. - The more names; the more important.

And that no man might buy or sell, save him that had the mark, or the name of the beast, or the number of his name. Here is wisdom. He who has understanding, let him calculate the number of the beast, for it is the number of a man. His number is six hundred sixty-six. (Revelation 13:17,18)

***********Reference Column***********

(Simon Magus as Beast 666: (Revelation 13:17,18) And that no man might buy or sell, save him that had the mark, or the name of the beast, or the number of his name. Here is wisdom. He who has understanding, let him calculate the number of the beast, for it is the number of a man. His number is six hundred sixty-six.

(Simon as Ananias (Acts 5:1-10) There was a man of the name of Ananias who, with his wife Sapphira, sold some property but, with her full knowledge and consent, dishonestly kept back part of the price which he received for it, though he brought the rest and gave it to the Apostles. 'Ananias,' said Peter, 'why has Satan taken possession of your heart, that you should try to deceive the Holy Spirit and dishonestly keep back part of the price paid you for this land? ... Ananias fell down dead ... Instantly she fell down dead at his feet, ... So they carried her out and buried her by her husband's side.

(Saul baptized as Paul: Acts 9:17; 13:9) So Ananias went and entered the house; and, laying his two hands upon Saul, said, 'Saul, brother, the Lord--even Jesus who appeared to you on your journey--has sent me, that you may recover your sight and be filled with the Holy Spirit.' ... But Saul, who is also called Paul, filled with the Holy Spirit, fastened his eyes on him,

***********Reference Column***********
Baptismal name

(Simon becomes Peter: Matthew 16:18) And I also say unto thee, that thou art Peter, and upon this rock I will build my church;

Considering that Simon Magus has the reputation of being the worst heretic of all time, it would not be difficult to assign to him the number '666' as the personification of all evil and the anti-Christ.

The irony of this label is that it is merely the sum of the lettered levels of Church hierarchy with their gematria numbers added together: highest level priest: Taw(X)(400)+ priest: Resh(200)+initiates: Samekh(60)+ number indicator: Waw(6) equal to 666. Simon Magus was the 'Satan-beast', like Judas, merely because he was a Zealot.

Simon's only sin apparently is the buying and selling Church memberships: "And that no man might buy or sell". This ties the Beast 666 to the strange story of Peter reprimanding Ananias and Sapphira for which sin God strikes them dead.

As to Ananias being dead, this is not possible because 'the vision of Jesus' tells the blinded Saul to go to him in order to remove his 'blindness'. The importance of Ananias is shown because it is to him that Jesus entrusts the task of teaching Saul and giving him the baptismal name of Paul.

Since previously Saul had been authorized by the High Priest to arrest all Christians, Jesus would certainly entrust the task of the conversion of my future father Paul to his most trusted associate, my step-great-grandfather Simon. With Simon's address being on 'Straight Street', he is even the most trusted!

Thus returning to the linked names of Ananias and Sapphira, it has already been shown that the sapphire is the second most important jewel on the wall of Heavenly Jerusalem, implying that these two important characters can be none other than Simon Magus, in the top position and Helena as his queen. Obviously, their death's had been merely an excommunication that lasted for less than than six months.

By now it must be clear to you that it was common practice to have at least two names, one's birth name and one's baptismal name when joining the Church as an initiate, thus Saul's name was changed to Paul and Peter's name to Simon, and Mother Mary's name from Dorcas to Mary.

Student takes the name of the teacher

(Agrippa II as the student of Paul: Acts 13:7) Who was with the deputy of the country, Sergius Paulus, a prudent man; who called for Barnabas and Saul, and desired to hear the word of God.

Teacher takes the name of the student

(Mark 6: 24,25) She (Salome) at once went out and said to her mother: 'What shall I ask for?' 'The head of John the Baptist,' she replied. She came in immediately with haste to the king, and asked, 'I want you to give me right now the head of John the Baptist on a platter.'

(Sisters of the Community were Mother Mary and Simon Magus' Helena: Gospel of Philip 36) There were three who always walked with the Lord: Mary, his mother, and her sister, and Magdalene, the one who was called his companion. His sister and his mother and his companion were each a Mary.

Simon Magus as Lightning

(Simon sits on the blocking stone: Matthew 28:2,3) Behold, there was a great earthquake, for an angel of the Lord descended from the sky, and came and rolled away the stone from the door, and sat on it. His appearance was like lightning, and his clothing white as snow.

Jonathan Annas as Thunder

(The seventy return: Mark 3:17) James the son of Zebedee; John, the brother of James, and them he surnamed Boanerges, which is, Sons of thunder;

Joseph is the Star

(Joseph and Theudas: Damascus Document 9 4-9) There shall come forth a star out of Jacob, and a scepter shall rise out of Israel.

(The Star of Bethlehem: Matthew 2:9) ... and lo, the Star, that they did see in the east, did go before them, till, having come, it stood over where the child was.

(Jonathan Annas as Stephen (Stephanos, Greek: crown) (Acts 6:8) And Stephen, full of faith and power, was doing great wonders and signs among the people,

(Jonathan Annas is deposed (Acts 6:59,60) So they stoned Stephen, while he prayed as he called on the Lord, saying, 'Lord Jesus, receive my Spirit!' He kneeled down, and cried with a loud voice, 'Lord, don't hold this sin against them!' When he had said this, he fell asleep.

Often times a student name is used for the teacher. Thus Agrippa II, the son of Herod Agrippa, was called Sergius Paulus because Paul was his teacher.

We saw that the reverse is also possible where the teacher uses the name of the student when acting for them. Thus my great-grandmother Helena used the name of Salome, Herodias daughter, when she danced for John the Baptist's head.

Another name would be a religious title such as Mary or 'Miriam' as all being spiritual sisters of 'Moses'. Thus at the cross there were three important Marys: my grandmother Magdalene, and my maternal great-grandmothers: Mother Mary and Helena shown as Mary's 'sister' or Salome, also a Mary.

A Zealot, besides being Satan, would certainly have another name to disguise his identity so as not to be captured. Thus Simon Magus is Lightening and Jonathan Annas is Thunder, although he was not usually a Zealot.

When James and John switch alliance from Simon Magus to Jonathan Annas, they change from 'sons of Zebedee' to 'sons of Thunder.'

My great-grandfather Joseph is the Star and Theudas the Scepter. This is the explanation for the Star of Bethlehem. They both could occupy the third position in the hierarchy.

There also were self-styled personas such as Jonathan Annas being called Stephen (Stephanos': Greek meaning crown) when he fancied himself as both priest and king. Thus when Jonathan prescribed the celebration of Christ-mass Day as a replacement for the Celtic mid-winter Festival on the Winter solstice, it was called the Feast of St. Stephen. The month of December was used, as this was a month with no Jewish feast, even though Jesus was really born in March.

When he was deposed as High Priest, his name Stephen is used because he was in his rulership mode. Acts deceptively shows him as the first martyr.

Apollos and Paul

(Paul on the island of Malta: Act 28:3) But when Paul had gathered a bundle of sticks and laid them on the fire, a viper came out because of the heat, and fastened on his hand.

Dragon and the Eagle

(Caiaphas and Jonathan Annas: Revelation 12:13,14) When the dragon saw that he was thrown down to the earth, he persecuted the woman who gave birth to the male child. And to the woman were given two wings of a great eagle, that she might fly into the wilderness ...

(Simon Magus as Lazarus at the anointing of Jesus: (John 12:1-3) Jesus, however, six days before the Passover, came to Bethany, where Lazarus was whom He had raised from the dead. So they made him a supper there. Martha served, but Lazarus was one of those who sat at the table with him. Mary, therefore, took a pound of ointment of pure spikenard, very precious, and anointed the feet of Jesus, and wiped his feet with her hair. The house was filled with the fragrance of the ointment.

(Simon Magus (the magician), 'the great power of God': (Acts 8:9-11) But there was a certain man, Simon by name, who had used sorcery in the city before, and amazed the people of Samaria, making himself out to be some great one, to whom they all listened, from the least to the greatest, saying, 'This man is that great power of God.' They listened to him, because for a long time he had amazed them with his sorcerers.

(Simon Magus (the magician), 'the great power of God': (Clementine Recognitions R.II:7) Simon Magus: his History. "This Simon's father was Antonius, and his mother Rachel. By nation he is a Samaritan, from a village of the Gettones; by profession a magician, yet exceedingly well trained in the Greek literature; desirous of glory, and boasting above all the human race, so that he wishes himself to be believed to be an exalted power, which is above God the Creator, and to be thought to be the Christ, and to be called the Standing One. And he uses this name as implying that he can never be dissolved, asserting that his flesh is so compacted by the power of his divinity, that it can endure to eternity. Hence, therefore, he is called the Standing One, as though he cannot fall by any corruption."

Apollos when he attacked Paul was in the shape of a viper because, as the replacement of Theudas, he was leader of the Therapeuts, who had as their symbol the scepter of Apollos which had two snakes wrapped around it. In this case he was a evil snake, a viper.

Caiaphas is shown as the dragon in Revelation trying to prevent the Bar-Mitzvah of Jesus because of his 'illegitimate birth'. Jonathan Annas, the eagle, rescues Mary and declares Jesus as legitimate.

My step-great-grandfather, Simon Magus, when he was raised from the dead by Jesus, styled himself as 'Lazarus' derived from 'El-Asar-Us', an alternate name for Osiris, the Egyptian god who rose from the dead.

My great-grandmother called herself 'Luna' when she represented the Moon in John the Baptist's organization and Helena as Sophia incarnated in Helen of Troy.

The name Simon Magus is obviously the same as Simon the Magician, shown in Acts as 'the great power of God'. He also calls himself 'the Standing One' which is derived from his philosophy, meaning the one who has existed throughout time.

Simon Magus is clearly the winner as the one with the most names, having three major titles such as Magician (Magus), 'the Standing One', and 'the Great Power of God' and over ten pseudonyms: Simon, the Canaanite (disciple: Matthew 10:4, Mark 3:18),, Simon, the Zealot (disciple: Luke 6:15, Acts 1:13), Zebedee (Matthew 4:21, Mark 1:19-20, Luke 5:8-10), Simon of Cyrene (Matthew 27:32, Mark 15:21, Luke 23:26), Lazarus (John 11:1-44, John 12:1-10, Luke 16:20-23), Simon the leper (Matthew 26:6, Mark 14:3), Simon the tanner (Acts 9:43, Acts 10:6), Ananias (Acts 5:1-5, Acts 9:10-17, Josephus Antiquities 20, 34-47), Demetrius, the silversmith (Acts 19:24), and Beast 666 (Revelation 13:18).

Needless to say, Simon Magus was the most powerful person in the New Testament. He overthrew John the Baptist, assassinated King Herod Agrippa, and challenged Peter with his overpowering intellect.

It is hard to imagine anyone else other that Simon Magus who could have could have turned the worst failure of Jesus' career of almost dying on the cross into the most popular religion of its time! My step-great-grandfather Simon Magus and my great-grandmother Helena proved to be the most important people in Jesus' life, next to my father Paul.

Continuing with Simon Magus' other titles, Ananias is the same title that Simon used before in Acts and is confirmed in Josephus in the conversion of Queen Helena of Adiabene and her son Izates, born from incest with her brother the King. Simon Magus' consort, my great-grandmother was the one who taught Queen Helena and also confirming the use of her name as Helena, being her teacher.

As Bar-Jesus, Elymas, Simon Magus is accused by Paul for his role in poisoning King Agrippa. Significantly, Simon is being referred to as the son of Jesus, meaning that he is under Jesus' direction. However, Paul is making the point to Jesus that it would be impossible to have Simon Magus be associated with him if Jesus intends to join Agrippa II because it would implicate Jesus with the killing of his father King Agrippa.

This was the turning point that led to the Schism of the Churches in AD 44 with the creation of the Christian Church, which would be separate from Simon Magus' Church.

In his role as Demetrius the silversmith, Simon was preparing icons of Mary Magdalene for her funeral, for which Paul reprimanded him. (Using the definition of silver from Judas' thirty pieces of silver standing for John the Baptist's organization of thirty, it is clear that Simon is in the leadership position again.)

Simon Magus as Zebedee has already been established. The 'Clementines' specifically shown James and John as the adopted sons of Helena, his consort, thus making Simon Magus their step-father.

Simon the Canaanite and Simon the Zealot were the names used for one of the twelve disciples. Again it must be obvious that these two titles are an attempt to mask Simon Magus' participation with Jesus. Certainly it matches his persona to be involved with Zealots and be from Canaan.

The Church, knowing how absurd it would be to have Simon Magus as a disciple, have pretended that a different person existed called 'Simon Zelotes', "who was zealous for the faith". (More on this in the chapter on the disciples.)

The Gospel of Matthew and Mark have replaced Lazarus at the table in Bethany in the Gospel of John with Simon the leper, thus emphasizing his exclusion rather than his triumph over death as , having been raised from excommunication by Jesus. However, it proves that Simon is Lazarus.

Simon 'the tanner' is a pun for those who know the Hebrew word which stands for skin, hide, and leather; which is frequently used to describe the garb of prophets including John the Baptist. It is also used as in the expression 'to skin a goat' as in to rob them.

It is clear here that Peter is still reporting to Simon Magus at this time. However, it is right around this time that Jesus, having brought Paul into the fold, begins to see the advantage of joining with the Herods because Paul is the tutor of Herod Agrippa's son, who will soon be sixteen. Thus he was also in the process of persuading Cornelius (Luke) and Peter to join him.

As to the Simon of Cyrene, it is quite possible to interpret the passages in Matthew, Mark, and Luke as Simon Magus bearing his own cross. He is 'of Cyrene' because that is the farthest mission and thus represents that Simon has been excommunicated.

As to him being the father of Alexander and Rufus, these are his disciples, namely Theudas (Thaddaeus) and Thomas, the disciples of Jesus. Theudas is the representative of the Therapeuts of Alexandria and Thomas is the deposed Herod who, like Esau, was displaced by Jacob of his father Isaac's inheritance. Esau had red hair, which is Rufus in Latin. Actually all the eleven disciples together with Jesus reported to Simon Magus not, as assumed, Simon Magus and the eleven reporting to Jesus.

The Second Treatise of the Great Seth claims that Jesus was not at the Crucifixion and that Simon was in his place. While this follows a gnostic pattern, some of the information contained here is significant. Firstly, it names Simon as being crucified, secondly it confirms that poison was given on the cross, and thirdly that Jesus survived the Crucifixion.

The Gospel of John shows in four places that Judas Iscariot is 'of Simon' and clearly this is Simon Magus. The exact form is 'Judas (of Simon) Iscariot' which is to say that Simon Magus is his superior and that 'Iscariot' is a corruption of Sicarii, the dagger men.

Obviously, when Simon Magus' name was removed from the Gospel of John, the implication that Simon Magus might have ordered Judas to betray Jesus was too good to not leave in, even though all of the eleven disciples and Jesus were technically under Simon as Pope.

(Simon Magus (the magician), 'the great power of God':) Now after a few days there was a great commotion in the midst of the church, for some said that they had seen wonderful works done by a certain man whose name was Simon, and that he was at Aricia, and they added further that he said he was a great power of God and without God he did nothing. Is not this the Christ? but we believe in him whom Paul preached unto us; for by him have we seen the dead raised, and men Delivered from divers infirmities: but this man seeketh contention, we know it (or, but what this contention is, we know not) for there is no small stir made among us. Perchance also he will now enter into Rome; for yesterday they besought him with great acclamations, saying unto him: Thou art God in Italy, thou art the saviour of the Romans: haste quickly unto Rome. But he spake to the people with a shrill voice, saying: Tomorrow about the seventh hour ye shall see me fly over the gate of the city in the form (habit) wherein ye now see me speaking unto you. Therefore, brethren, if it seem good unto you, let us go and await carefully the issue of the matter. They all therefore ran together and came unto the gate. And when it was the seventh hour, behold suddenly a dust was seen in the sky afar off, like a smoke shining with rays stretching far from it. And when he drew near to the gate, suddenly he was not seen: and thereafter he appeared, standing in the midst of the people; whom they all worshipped, and took knowledge that he was the same that was seen of them the day before.

Once the multiple names are combined into this one individual, Simon Magus, his great role and strong personality become clear. As to his knowledge of philosophy and religion, he had no peer. After the Schism of the Churches in AD 45 when Simon was involved in the poisoning of King Herod Agrippa, the Church of Peter and Paul had to strongly oppose him by labeling him a heretic.

There were really only two major differences between the Churches: Simon required a fee for membership and Jesus an offering; Simon used the fees to support the Zealots against Rome and Jesus used the fees for the poor.

The real division between the Churches was the direct result of the alliance that Paul, under Jesus' orders, had created between the Church of Peter and Paul and the Herodian Church of King Herod Agrippa II. Agrippa II held his power from Rome and therefore could not oppose Rome and, also, Agrippa II could not be aligned with the murderer of his father Agrippa I.

Simon would often use magic to sway the crowds and this Jesus absolutely abhorred. However, when he and Simon Magus were writing the Gospel of John, they saw the advantage of presenting the magic tricks and staged healings as metaphors for Jesus' efforts to promote of Gentiles and females within the Church. In this way there could be a surface meaning for those not baptized and a hidden meaning for those who were. It also spiced up a somewhat boring subject that had really required endless discussions and heated debate with the Church officials.

The great magician Simon would meet his death in Rome shortly before Peter's crucifixion and Paul's execution in AD 64 when his 'flying trick' in front of the Emperor Nero went awry and he fell broke his leg in three places. This was, of course, attributed to Peter calling out the name of Jesus Christ. Tradition says that Paul helped, although he was not there.

Thus Simon Magus did not get to disappear in the sky like Elijah in 'a chariot of fire' (2Kings 2:7-12), but then Elijah's chariot was also a fable like the Resurrection. No one gets out of here alive. Simon, the creator of Jesus' fable, died shortly after, having no one to write his story.

Artemis whom Helena served as a temple priestess

Ezekiel's Vision (Raphael) showing the Lion, the Bull, the Eagle, and the Man

Chapter 10 The Schism of the Churches and the Canonization of the Gospels.

And I wept much, for no one was found worthy to open the book, or to look in it. And one of the elders saith unto me, Weep not: behold, the Lion of the tribe of Juda, the Root of David, hath prevailed to open the book, and to loose the seven seals thereof. (Revelation 5:4,5)

The story of the Schism of the Churches and the canonization of the Gospels must begin with Herod Agrippa, the grandson of Herod the Great. Agrippa, having already caused the death of my great-grandfather Joseph and John the Baptist and his father Zechariah and made fun of Jesus at his trial, had been jailed by the Roman Emperor Tiberius for misconduct concerning his debts and conspiring against the emperor.

And yet, like the Cracken monster released from its chains by Poseidon, he emerges again, having been released by his friend from youth, the cruel and insane Caligula 'little boot'. The Emperor Caligula had come to the throne in AD 37. Caligula released him from his chains and gave him a golden chain of a weight equal to the iron one he had worn in prison. He started by giving him the tetrarchy of Lysanias, the kingdom of Herod Philip, who had died.

In AD 39, Agrippa accused Herod Antipas of treason and was given his territory of Galilee and Peraea with Herod Antipas being exiled to Lugdunum Convenarum, our home town.

Again at the assassination of Caligula in AD 41, he used his charm to negotiate with the Senate with the help of Pope Clement's father Marcus Arrecinus Tertullus Clemens and brought the Emperor Claudius to the throne. In gratitude for this service he obtained the rest of the lands that his grandfather Herod the Great had owned.

One would think that this would satisfy him, but he began to evidence the madness of his grandfather, Herod the Great. He refused to recognize the Church and imprisoned Peter and excommunicated James Zebedee. Peter is released by the 'angel' Simon Magus and James was only metaphorically killed as when Peter raised 'his sword' to Jesus' brother James in the Garden of Gethsemane.

My step great-grandfather Simon Magus in AD 44 had to set up the plot to poison King Agrippa with his servant Nicolaus-Blastus by promising his promotion as leader of the third Church of Pergamum.

Agrippa was wearing his kingly robe woven with silver that reflected the rays of the sun and, while appearing before the crowds, the poison began to take effect. 'Silver' represented the fact that he had taken over the thirty leaders of Simon that John the Baptist had formed.

In true storybook fashion, Herod Agrippa sees the owl that had been predicted to appear at his death. After five days he succumbed to the poison. "He had reigned four years under Caligula (AD 37-40), during three of them over Philip's tetrarchy, while in the fourth he took over that of Herod Antipas as well (AD 40-41); and three more years under the Emperor Claudius Caesar, having Judaea, Samaria and Caesarea added to his former realm (AD 41-44)."

Simon Magus had high hopes for the removal of Herod Agrippa, as he saw this as the end of the Herod legacy and a chance for the Zealots to easily acquire this now consolidated kingdom of the Jews before Rome could divide it up again.

Jesus, however, had different ideas. He had decided to join his Church to the Herodian Church, now under Herod Agrippa's son, Agrippa II. With Agrippa II being trained by Paul and easily molded, it would be possible to finally separate from the Zealots. There would be no problem with making Agrippa II, the top of the hierarchy, as he would not interfere with the plans of the new Church that Jesus envisioned.

Agrippa's son Agrippa II was only seventeen at the time of his father's death in AD 44 and therefore considered too young to rule. He had been given a proconsulship in Cyprus until he would become of age. The indication that he was Paul's student is shown in his name being given as 'Sergius Paulus', meaning student of Paul. Jesus, disguised as 'the Holy Spirit' broaches the idea of joining with his Church to Paul and Barnabas.

To set up this union with Agrippa were the important members of the Church in Antioch. Present at the meeting were Barnabas, Paul, and John Mark having returned from Jerusalem, Simon Peter now called Niger as his wife had died, Luke, Titus (Manaen) and Jesus (the Holy Spirit). They had sailed from Antioch to Paphos in Cyprus to meet with Agrippa II.

In front of Agrippa's son Agrippa II, Paul accuses Simon Magus as 'a son of Satan' ('Satan' being a word for Zealot as he have seen with Judas Iscariot as 'Satan') for his role in the assassination plot and declares that the 'straight paths of God' are superior'. The blindness is Simon Magus' excommunication from the Church, which would last three months ('a season').

This revelation of Simon Magus' involvement in the poison plot against Agrippa II's father would drive a wedge between Simon Magus and Jesus. After Jesus joined Agrippa II, it would be impossible to accept Simon Magus as the murderer of his father.

Shortly after this, John Mark would separate from Jesus to stay with Simon Magus. Peter would continue on to Rome to write the Gospel of Mark. The Christian Church would be founded five years later.

**********Reference Column**********

Christians in Rome

(Peter in Rome with Mark his scribe: 1Peter 5:13) The Church in Babylon (Rome), chosen like yourselves by God, sends greetings, and so does Mark my son.

Christians banished from Rome

(Christians banished: Suetonius, Life of Claudius) Since the Jews constantly made disturbances at the instigation of Chrestus, he (Claudius) expelled them from Rome.

(Christians banished: Acts 18:2) Here he found a Jew, a native of Pontus, of the name of Aquila. He and his wife Priscilla had recently come from Italy because of Claudius's edict expelling all the Jews from Rome. So Paul paid them a visit;

**********Reference Column**********

The Coronation of Agrippa II

(To the Seven Churches: Revelation 1:4,5) John to the Seven Churches that are in Asia: Grace to you, and peace, from Him who is, and who was, and who is coming, and from the Seven Spirits that are before His throne, and from Jesus Christ, who is the faithful witness, and the first-begotten of the dead, and the prince of the kings of the earth. To him that loved us, and washed us from our sins in his own blood,

**********Reference Column**********

The Chariot of the Mission

(the Human, the Lion, The Ox, and the Eagle: Ezekiel 1:10,11) As for the appearance of their faces: the four had the face of a human being, the face of a lion on the right side, the face of an ox on the left side, and the face of an eagle; ...

(the Lion, the Calf, the Man, the Lion: Revelation 4:6-8) And in front of the throne there seemed to be a sea of glass, resembling crystal. And midway between the throne and the Elders, and surrounding the throne, were four living creatures, full of eyes in front and behind. The first creature was like a lion, and the second creature like a calf, and the third creature had a face like a man, and the fourth creature was like a flying eagle and the four living creatures, having each one of them six wings, are full of eyes round about and within: and they have no rest day and night, saying, Holy, holy, holy, is the Lord God, the Almighty, who was and who is and who is to come.

The emperor Claudius was for the most part favorable to the Jewish mission, but in AD 49 he abruptly ejected the Christians from Rome in AD 49. This was due to the misunderstanding over Fulvia's gift to the Church and the corruption of the Cult Temples, already discussed.

The Christian Church back in Greece were licking their wounds and realizing that it was time for a clean break between the Church of Paul and Peter and the Church of Simon Magus.

Peter had already composed the Gospel of Mark while he was in Rome, as indicated by his salutation from Babylon (Rome). The Gospel of John had been written by Jesus and Simon Magus before that.

Jesus had been writing another gospel, with Luke's help, to become the Gospel of Luke that he thought would be more acceptable to the Church elders. Matthew, the Sadducee Priest, had been writing his own Gospel.

The Gospel of Matthew, initiated by Matthew Annas, the Sadducee priest, would incorporate the writings of Hillel with the Sermon on the Mount and the Sadducees of the Herodian-Jewish form with many attacks on the Pharisees. With Simon Magus and the Pharisee Zealots on the opposing side, the Gospel of Matthew did not hesitate to criticize the Pharisees.

On June 1, AD 49, at the coronation of Agrippa II, Jesus' oldest son, my uncle Jesus Justus (indicated as 'Grace' being the crown prince), had his Essene Bar-Mitzvah at age 12. Though our party had been ejected from Rome by Claudius, we were looking forward to the future with an alliance with the young Herod King and a permanent separation with the Zealot party of Simon Magus.

This year the Four Gospels would be canonized. The prophet Ezekiel had set out a blueprint for a chariot that would sustain the Jews in their captivity in Babylon in 500 BC. It was the beginning of the Diaspora which was made of Jews all around the world. Clearly, if the gospels were to be brought to the Diaspora, then they must follow the blueprint of the eternal chariot set out by Ezekiel.

In his vision Ezekiel used the images of the fixed cross three of which there are contained in the Sphinx, namely the Man (Woman), Ox, and Lion. The fixed cross is defined as Aquarius (Man/Woman-North), Taurus (Bull/Ox-East), Leo (Lion-South), and Scorpio (Scorpion symbolizing death with its opposite Eagle symbolizing resurrection- West).

By swapping the Lion with the Eagle, Ezekiel put the chariot in motion giving, in the angel facing view, Man-above, Lion-right, Ox-left, Eagle-below. With high priest (Man) above, his levite assistant (Ox) on his left and the King of the Israelites (Lion) on his right, and the Priest to the Diaspora (Eagle) below, the Jews would be lifted to God.

***********Reference Column***********
The Four Gospels

(Jesus the Lamb opens the first seal: Revelation 6:1) And I saw when the Lamb opened one of the seals, and I heard one of the four living creatures saying, as it were a voice of thunder, 'Come and behold!'

Father:
Matthew (Man)
forehead

Holy Spirit: Holy Spirit:
Luke (Ox)   John (Lion)
left shoulder   right shoulder

Son:
Mark (Eagle)
breast

***********Reference Column***********
(The white horse: Revelation 6:2) And I saw, and lo, a white horse, and he who is sitting upon it is having a bow, and there was given to him a crown, and he went forth overcoming, and that he may overcome.

***********Reference Column***********
(The red horse: Revelation 6:3,4) And when he opened the second seal, I heard the second living creature saying, 'Come and behold!' and there went forth another horse -- red, and to him who is sitting upon it, there was given to him to receive peace from the land, and lest they may slay one another, also there was given to him the great sword of Eden.

***********Reference Column***********
(The black horse: Revelation 6:5,6) And when he opened the third seal, I heard the third living creature saying, 'Come and behold!' and I saw, and lo, a black horse, and he who is sitting upon it is having a balance in his hand, and I heard a voice in the midst of the four living creatures saying, 'A measure of wheat for a denary, and three measures of barley for a denary,' and 'The oil and the wine thou mayest not injure.'

***********Reference Column***********
(The dun horse: Revelation 6:7,8) And when he opened the fourth seal, I heard the voice of the fourth living creature saying, 'Come and behold!' and I saw, and lo, a dun horse, and he who is sitting upon him -- his name is Death, and Hades doth follow with him, and there was given to them authority over the fourth part of the land to kill with sword, and with hunger, and with death, and with the beasts of the land.

The apostle John, the twin bother of James, loved images. He filled Revelation with these in sevens. The Four Horsemen of the Apocalypse were the first four of seven represented the canonizing of the Four Gospels in this same year AD 49. Jesus, the Lamb, was present.

These Four Gospels were assigned as follows: Matthew (Man: Matthew Ananus, high priest), Luke (Ox, dedicated by Luke with Jesus to Theophilus Ananus, levite), Mark (Eagle written by Mark for Peter), and John (Lion, written by Jesus and Simon scribed by John Mark, the beloved disciple). The colors of the horses corresponded to their status, thus white for high priest, red for cardinal, black for archbishop or presbyter, and yellow-green or dun or brown for priest the Diaspora.

And finally the assignment of the Gospels in the sign of the Cross: Father: Matthew (Man-forehead), Son: Mark (Eagle-breast), Holy Spirit: Luke (Ox-left shoulder), John (Lion-right shoulder). Jesus having directed the writing of John and the Luke was transmitting his knowledge by the Holy Spirit.

The rider of white horse as the representative of the high priest of the high church of Ephesus was portrayed as the image of Artemis, the huntress, whose temple was located there.

The rider of red horse as the representative of the levite was portrayed as keeping peace by not opposing their Roman rulers, however he, as the angel of the high priest, would have the power of the Archangel Uriel, with his flaming sword, to guard the Gate to the Garden of Eden, the holy land, from unbelievers.

The rider of black horse, as the representative of the king, was portrayed as having a balance in his hand maintaining justice and collecting fees from the new converts of wheat (Nazarites), barley (married Gentiles), and to protect the traditions of laity of ordination with oil (chrism) and using fermented wine for the Eucharist or of the monastics of not using oil and using pure wine for the Eucharist.

The rider of dun horse as the representative of the priest to the Diaspora was portrayed as having the power of Life (acceptance in the Church) or Death (being outside of the Church). He had the power (to kill with a sword) and to punish the misbehaviors with fasting (famine) or excommunication (death), and to reaffirm that the Church did not support the Zealots (beasts).

(The Gospel of John must be purged of the explicit references to Simon Magus and John Mark who are in the opposing Church: Revelation 10:4-9) And when the seven thunders uttered their voices, I was about to write: and I heard a voice from heaven saying, Seal up the things which the seven thunders uttered, and write them not. Then the angel that I saw standing on the sea and on the land, lifted his right hand toward Heaven. And in the name of Him who lives until the Ages of the Ages, the Creator of Heaven and all that is in it, of the earth and all that is in it, and of the sea and all that is in it, he solemnly declared, but in the days of the voice of the seventh angel, when he is about to sound, then the mystery of God is finished, as he declared to his servants, the prophets. Then the voice which I had heard speaking from Heaven once more addressed me. It said, 'Go and take the little book which lies open in the hand of the angel who is standing on the sea and on the land. 'I (John) went to the angel, saying, 'Give me the little book.' He said to me, 'Take it, and eat it up. It will make your belly bitter, but in your mouth it will be as sweet as honey.'

(Seven healings in the Gospel of John: John 2:1-12; 4:46-54; 5:1-18; 6:1-15; 6:16-21; 9:1-41; 11:1-53)

1. John 2:1-12 - Water made wine at Cana (raising the status of Gentiles and women)

2. John 4:46-54 - Nobleman's son cured from a distance (the promotion of Philip)

3. John 5:1-18 - Impotent man cured at Jerusalem (Jesus makes fun of his brother James and his palanquin that protects him from being defiled by the Gentiles)

4. John 6:1-15 - Jesus walks on water (the illusion is merely the pier that Jesus walks, but it is Jesus acting above his grade)

5. John 6:16-21 - Five thousand fed (the allowing of a Gentile, John Aquila and James Niceta (4,000) to the Holy Communion)

6. John 9:1-41 - Blind man cured at Jerusalem (the promotion of Joses-Barnabas over James)

7. John 11:1-53 - Lazarus raised from the dead (removing Simon Magus' excommunication)

When the gospels were about to be published to the world, an objection was raised by Matthew, the high priest, that since his Church of Peter and Paul was now separate from the Eastern Zealot wing of the Church represented by Simon Magus, the Gospel of John was giving too much credit to the friendship of Simon Magus and Jesus and to John Mark, the beloved disciple, who had left with Mary Magdalene.

The expression "Take it, and eat it up; it will make your belly bitter, but in your mouth it will be as sweet as honey" was a metaphoric instruction to John, the brother of James, to take out Simon Magus, who had poisoned King Agrippa, and leave Jesus, the Word.

Thus with with the stroke of a pen, the names of Simon Magus and John Mark were removed with Simon changed to Simon the Zealot or Simon the Canaanite or to Lazarus and John Mark's name to Bartholomew or the 'beloved disciple'. Significantly the Simon name is not deleted in reference to Judas Iscariot, who is consistently referred to as 'son of Simon' in the Gospel of John.

It is fortunate that the starting prologue of the Gospel of John: "In the beginning was the Word, and the Word was with God, and the Word was God" was retained as it one of the most powerful expressions in the Bible and it is the philosophy of Simon Magus, who co-wrote the Gospel of John with Jesus, John Mark being the scribe. (The meaning of this prologue is described in detail in Chapter 8 to explain the hidden meaning of the conversation between Jesus and the Samaritan women, Helena, my great-grandmother.) The seven healings within the Gospel were also retained. The power of seven is, of course, part of the Genesis creation or as you might say a reverse parallel to the seven angels of destruction in Revelation.

Since the Magians would heal a person first by restoring the balance of the body, mind, and spirit, it was reasonable to use the metaphor of these seven healings to represent the steps by which the Gentiles and women were raised in status to be made whole as male circumcised Jews. It was also common literary practice in those times to present a popular person as performing all sorts of miracles. Jesus would certainly be able to perform these 'miracles' if, as it was believed, he had risen from the dead.

Being the adopted son of of Simon Magus, John Aquila, although converted later by Zacchaeus (Ananus the Younger), was familiar with Simon's philosophy. He used the image of the 'seven thunders' in Revelation 10 to refer to the six powers, with the resultant power being 'He who stood, stands, and will stand' (Simon's had adopted this persona for himself).

Having been given the task of editing the Gospel of John, John Aquila had inserted 'Jesus Christ' for 'Word' in John 1:17 to disguise Simon's philosophy. By then Jesus and his sons would be known as the 'Word' in distinction from the 'Voice' of John the Baptist and to disguise the truth that he was still alive after the Crucifixion and had sons.

John Aquila's changes on the Gospel that was originally dedicated to John Mark, the beloved disciple who scribed it, will forever confuse scholars as to which John was in the title of the Gospel of John. The correct answer would be both! Actually John Mark did return to Peter and Paul and to Jesus after my grandmother Mary Magdalene died, however, with the removal of his name never restored, he will be forever confused with John, the twin brother of James. Both John's were kind and caring. John Aquila, the brother of James, and his wife Priscilla were a wonderful Great Uncle and Aunt. John Mark, the beloved disciple, was also like a Great Uncle taking care of my grandmother Mary Magdalene and my great-grandmother Mother Mary in Ephesus.

It is tempting to believe that the fifth and sixth seal are the canonizing of the Gospel of Thomas and the Gospel of Philip, but I believe that these seals were not meant to refer to specific books, but represent all the writings of the Church which includes Gospel of Thomas, the Gospel of Philip, the Gospel of Peter, the Acts of the Apostles, the Acts of Peter, the Acts of Thomas, the Acts of Barnabas, Paul's Epistles, Clement's Epistle to the Corinthians, the 'Clementines', and maybe even other prophets of Gabriel.

In them will be contained the the vindication of those who were martyred for the Faith, whether it be by the politics of empires or the Church itself. These writings represent the hope that one day there will be an end to the evils of those who abuse their power either in the Church or government for their own egotistic desires.

I also predict that the opening of sixth seal, after these lesser gospels have been found, will be the discovery of the "scrolls", found in "the dens and rocks of mountains" that were used as hiding places for the Zealots.

In them will be preserved the truth about the early Christian Church at Qumran. In these Scrolls of the Dead Sea will be the true Revelation that will shake the dogma ('figs') and the foundations of the Church ('heaven'), which "will depart as a scroll when it is rolled together".

Meanwhile the Christian Church will continue to strive as it did under Peter's leadership and, after the death of Peter and Paul, under Pope Clement's leadership, having been made Pope by St Peter. In the future there will be other great leaders of the Truth.

The mission to the Gentiles has proceeded with full force. The words carpenter, tent-maker, and passers-by are all terms for the missionaries who would stand out in the marketplaces talking to those who passed by. It was a grassroots effort that would build the Church.

All twelve disciples including Barnabas, who was the brother of Jesus after James and who replaced Judas Iscariot as Mathias, had their mission territories assigned. Of course, my father, Paul was the most successful of all, but not included in the twelve.

In Barnabas' territory of Rome the Clementines tell us he would preach, "Wherefore turn ye from evil things to good, from things temporal to things eternal. Acknowledge that there is one God, ruler of heaven and earth, in whose righteous sight ye unrighteous inhabit His world. But if ye be converted, and act according to His will, then, coming to the world to come, and being made immortal, ye shall enjoy His unimaginable blessings and rewards."

I believe that the seventh seal is the silence of astonishment and shock that will come with the discovery of my writings. Though they may be vehemently argued against, believed or discarded, these arguments will serve to raise the vibration of consciousness and plant the seed of knowledge that will become the 'Tree of Life in the Garden of Eden'.

Calling of the Apostles (Duccio)

Chapter 11 - The Twelve Disciples.

I send you out as lambs in the midst of wolves. (Luke 10:3)

List in Matthew

(List of the Twelve Disciples: Matthew 10:2-4) First, Simon (who is called Peter) and his brother Andrew; James son of Zebedee, and his brother John; Philip and Bartholomew; Thomas and Matthew the publican; Jacob of Alphaeus, and Lebbaeus, whose surname was Thaddaeus; Simon the Canaanite and Judas Iscariot, who betrayed him.

List in Mark

(List of the Twelve Disciples: Mark 3:16-19) Simon (to whom he gave the name Peter); James son of Zebedee and his brother John (to them he gave the name Boanerges, which means Sons of Thunder); Andrew, Philip, Bartholomew, Matthew, Thomas, Jacob son Alphaeus, Thaddaeus, Simon the Canaanite and Judas Iscariot, who betrayed him.

List in Luke

(List of the Twelve Disciples: Luke 6:14-16) Simon (whom he also named Peter), his brother Andrew, James and John, Philip and Bartholomew, Matthew and Thomas, Jacob of Alphaeus and Simon who was called the Zealot, Judas of Jacob, and Judas Iscariot, who became a traitor.

List in Acts

(Eleven: Acts 1:13) Those present were Peter, James, John, Andrew, Philip and Thomas, Bartholomew and Matthew; Jacob son of Alphaeus and Simon the Zealot, and Judas son of Jacob.

Order of appearance in John

(1-5: unnamed, Andrew, Peter, Philip, Nathaniel: John 1:40-46) One of the two who heard John, and followed him, was Andrew, Simon Peter's brother. He first found his own brother, Simon, and said to him, 'We have found the Messiah!' (which is, being interpreted, Christ) ... On the next day, he was determined to go forth into Galilee, and he found Philip. Jesus said to him, 'Follow me.' Now Philip was from Bethsaida, of the city of Andrew and Peter. Philip found Nathanael, and said to him, 'We have found him, of whom Moses in the law, and the prophets, wrote: Jesus of Nazareth, the son of Joseph.' Nathanael said to him, 'Can any good thing come out of Nazareth?' Philip said to him, 'Come and see.'

At the beginning of Jesus' ministry, a partnership was formed, using the Church principle of twelve plus a leader, with those who more or less advocated for peace with Rome for the sake of the Church at Qumran. Within this partnership were some who leaned toward Zealot principles, but who for the most part were content to wait peacefully for the expected day when the New Jerusalem would appear and all evil defeated.

The Gospels of Matthew, Mark and Luke and Acts have specific lists of twelve, but the Gospel of John does not. The order of the disciples before adjustment and with those in John by order of appearance are shown in Table A.

The order of appearance of the disciples in the Gospel of John are two disciples of John the Baptist (one not named and the other Andrew), Peter, Philip, Nathanael, Nicodemus, Judas Iscariot, Lazarus, Thomas, 'the disciple Jesus loved', Judas not Iscariot, and the sons of Zebedee (James and John).

With James and John only appearing in what is clearly an enhanced chapter 21 of the Gospel of John and being mentioned merely as the sons of Zebedee, leads one to suspect that another John is responsible for writing the Gospel of John and not John of Zebedee.

As there is no other person called John, besides John the Baptist, in the Gospel of John, it is conceivable that the unnamed disciple with Andrew is John, the author. Thus there is also a good possibly that John is the name of 'the disciple that Jesus loved'.

In fact, it can be shown that this John was as important as Peter and was specifically removed along with Simon Magus' name because he had left with Mary Magdalene at the Schism of the Churches. The two names of Nathanael and Nicodemus and the identity of Lazarus will be covered later.

When looking at the lists, the person called Bartholomew, who appears sixth in Matthew, Mark, Luke and Acts, but missing from John, appears to be a perfect match to John, 'the beloved disciple'.

With the simple assumption that Simon the Caananite is the same as Simon the Zealot, then Judas of Jacob must be Thaddaeus; and thus, with some easy reordering, the three gospels of Matthew, Mark, and Luke and Acts can be matched up. In John it can be assumed that 'Judas not Iscariot' is 'Judas of Jacob', leaving Nathanael, Nicodemus, Lazarus,and the 'beloved disciple' yet to be matched. This is shown in Table B.

**********Reference Column**********

Order of appearance in John (continued)

(6: Nicodemus: John 3:1) There was a man of the Pharisees named Nicodemus, a ruler of the Jews

(7: Judas Iscariot: John 6:71) Now he spoke of Judas Iscariot, the son of Simon, for it was he who would betray him, being one of the twelve.

(8: Lazarus: John 11:1; 12:2) Now a certain man was sick, Lazarus of Bethany, of the village of Mary and her sister, Martha. ... Lazarus was one of them that sat at the table with him

(9: Thomas: John 11:16) Thomas therefore, who is called Didymus, said to his fellow disciples, 'Let's go also, that we may die with him (Lazarus).'

(10: 'beloved disciple': John 13:23) One of his disciples, whom Jesus loved, was at the table, leaning against Jesus' breast.

(11: Thaddeus: John 14:22) Judas (not Iscariot) said to him, 'Lord, what will happen that you will reveal yourself to us, and not to the world?'

((12-13)James and John: John 21:1,2) After these things did Jesus manifest himself again to the disciples on the sea of Tiberias, and he did manifest himself thus: Simon Peter, Thomas named Didymus, Nathanael of Cana in Galilee, the sons of Zebedee, and two others of his disciples were all together.

Bartholomew

(Derived source for the title Bartholomew - David's wife is the daughter of Talmai, the son is Absalom who betrayed him: 2Samuel 3:2,3)

Sons were born to David ... the third, Absalom the son of Maacah daughter of Talmai king of Geshur;

**********Reference Column**********

(John Mark leaning on Jesus' bosom is a metaphor for Mary Magdalene in his heart: John 13:21-25) When Jesus had thus said, he was troubled in spirit, and testified, and said, Verily, verily, I say to you, that one of you will betray me.
There was at table one of His disciples - the one Jesus loved - reclining with his head on Jesus's bosom.
Simon Peter therefore beckoned to him, and said to him: Who is it of whom he speaketh? He therefore, leaning on the breast of Jesus, saith to him: Lord, who is it?

In fact, once it is known that Jesus and Mary Magdalene are married, the derivation of the name Bartholomaios, 'son of Talmai' becomes clear. This name is an ancient Hebrew name, borne, by the King of Gessur whose daughter was a wife of King David.

Thus with Jesus representing David and Mary Magdalene representing the daughter of Talmai, Bartholomew as Mary Magdalene's replacement at male-only events would represent the son of Talmai. There is also an added derision in this title Bartholomew since the grandson of Talmai was Absalom, David's favorite son, who betrayed him.

Table A

Matthew	Mark	Luke	Acts	John
Peter	Peter	Peter	Peter	unnamed
Andrew	JamesZeb.	Andrew	Andrew	Andrew
JamesZeb.	JohnZeb.	JamesZeb.	James	Peter
JohnZeb.	Andrew	JohnZeb.	John	Philip
Philip	Philip	Philip	Philip	Nathanael
Barth.	Barth.	Barth.	Barth.	Nicodemus
Thomas	Matthew	Matthew	Matthew	Judas Isc
Matthew	Thomas	Thomas	Thomas	Lazarus
JacobAlph	JacobAlph	JacobAlph	JacobAlph	BelovedDisc
Thadd.	Thadd.	SimonZeal	SimonZeal	JudasnotIsc
SimonCaan	SimonCaan	JudasofJacob	JudasofJacob	Thomas
Judas Isc.	Judas Isc.	Judas Isc.	empty	SonsofZeb.

Table B

Matthew	Mark	Luke	Acts	John
Peter	Peter	Peter	Peter	Peter
Andrew	Andrew	Andrew	Andrew	Andrew
JamesZeb.	JamesZeb.	JamesZeb.	JamesZeb.	JamesZeb.
JohnZeb.	JohnZeb.	JohnZeb.	JohnZeb.	JohnZeb.
Philip	Philip	Philip	Philip	Philip
Barth.	Barth.	Barth.	Barth.	unknown
Matthew	Matthew	Matthew	Matthew	unknown
Thomas	Thomas	Thomas	Thomas	Thomas
JacobAlph	JacobAlph	JacobAlph	JacobAlph	unknown
Thadd.	Thadd.	JudasofJacob	JudasofJacob	JudasnotIsc
SimonCaan	SimonCaan	SimonZeal	SimonZeal	unknown
Judas Isc.	Judas Isc.	Judas Isc.	Judas-dead	Judas Isc.

As go-between for Mary Magdalene and at male-only ceremonies such as the Last Supper and also her guardian, Bartholomew would have to be the 'beloved disciple' John.

Thus the disciple next to Jesus is not actually 'leaning on Jesus' bosom' which would be perhaps disrespectful unless it was a homosexual relationship, but rather is a metaphor for Mary Magdalene being in Jesus' heart as his wife. Being in this position next to Jesus, he would be the most important disciple of Jesus.

In fact, it would appear that John's importance is greater than Peter because, at the Last Supper, Peter poses a question to Jesus, through John.

***********Reference Column**********
(John Mark (the beloved disciple) and Peter race up to the tomb: John 20:1-6) And on the first of the Sabbaths, Mary the Magdalene doth come early (there being yet darkness) to the tomb, and she seeth the stone having been taken away out of the tomb, She ran therefore, and came to Simon Peter, and to the other disciple whom Jesus loved, and said to them, 'They have taken away the Lord out of the tomb, and we don't know where they have laid him!' Peter and the other disciple started at once to go to the tomb, both of them running, So they ran both together: and the other disciple outran Peter, and came first to the sepulcher. And he stooping down, saw the linen cloths lying; yet he went not in. Then Simon Peter came, following him, and entered into the tomb...

***********Reference Column**********
John Mark as Eutychus

(Eutychus overhears Caligula and Agrippa plot against Tiberius: Josephus Antiquities 18.6.5) Now as the friendship which Agrippa had for Gaius was come to a great height, there happened some words to pass between them, as they once were in a chariot together, concerning Tiberius; Agrippa praying [to God] (for they two sat by themselves) that Tiberius might soon go off the stage, and leave the government to Gaius, who was in every respect more worthy of it. Now Eutychus, who was Agrippa's freed-man, and drove his chariot, heard these words, and at that time said nothing of them; but when Agrippa accused him of stealing some garments of his, (which was certainly true,) he ran away from him; but when he was caught, and brought before Piso, who was governor of the city, and the man was asked why he ran away, be replied, that he had somewhat to say to Caesar, that tended to his security and preservation:

***********Reference Column**********
(Mary Magdalene as Rhoda near term with Jesus' third child: Acts 12:12-15,25) Thinking about that, he (Peter) came to the house of Mary, the mother of John whose surname was Mark, where many were gathered together and were praying. When Peter knocked at the door of the gate, a maid named Rhoda came to answer. When she recognized Peter's voice, she didn't open the gate for joy, but ran in, and reported that Peter stood before the gate. They said to her, 'You are crazy!' But she insisted that it was so. They said, 'It is his angel.' ... and Barnabas and Saul did turn back out of Jerusalem, having fulfilled the ministry, having taken also with them John, who was surnamed Mark.

Also it was the 'beloved disciple' who raced with Peter up to his tomb after the Crucifixion. This places him as almost an equal with Peter. Thus it can be seen that the 'beloved disciple' is in the center of the action with Jesus and would have to be actually the head of the other five in the top six disciples.

Apparently, people still wrongly assume that Nathanael, who appears at the beginning and the end of John and is not mentioned in the other Gospels, is Bartholomew based on the trivial issue of location in the lists next to Philip and having been introduced by Philip to Jesus.

When John Mark returned back to the Church of Peter and Paul, his real name Eutychus was used. He had been a freedman of Agrippa and had accompanied Agrippa back to Rome after the Crucifixion in AD 35. As his charioteer, he overheard a conversation between Caligula and Agrippa, against the Emperor Tiberius.

When this was eventually revealed to Tiberius, Agrippa was imprisoned awaiting trial until Caligula came to the throne and released him. It is from his association with Agrippa and as the leader of the hundred ascetic churches that he is referred to as a 'centurion' at the Crucifixion.

The 'beloved disciple', having remained faithful to Mary Magdalene, went with her when she divorced Jesus in AD 45 in the Great Schism, thus causing the removal of his name in the John Gospel. John's real name is eventually shown in Acts as John Mark.

The maid at the gate when Peter knocked is Rhoda, Mary Magdalene near term with her third child. The expression 'in the house of Mary the mother of John whose surname is Mark' means Mary, the mother (of Jesus' child), of John Mark, therefore under his care. Shortly after this she would divorce Jesus. (Her name Rhoda thus of the Island of Rhodes indicates her intent to leave.) John Mark goes with Paul and Barnabas to tell Jesus of her intent to divorce him and that he will also be leaving.

Of the top six who are direct disciples of Jesus, we have shown that Bartholomew is John Mark leaving the other five who are well-known. Of Peter and Andrew, Andrew does not have much to do in the New Testament, but does figure in the Apocrypha. Of James and John, the sons of Zebedee, they have been shown to be the illegitimate grandsons of Augustus Caesar. This John is clearly the writer of Revelation together with James and others later.

And lastly, there is Philip who is well-known in Acts as the Evangelist, the one who was head of the monastery with a Virgin daughter at level 4, which was my grandmother Mary Magdalene. He was also the author of the Gospel of Philip.

Of the last six disciples whose status was equal or higher than Jesus', I will cover them from highest to lowest beginning then at Simon Magus was the most important. We have already covered his many names and personas and how the Church erased his name from the Gospels.

Actually, these last six were neither disciples or apostles, but rather colleagues of Jesus forming two structures of three: one being Simon Magus (Leader) Judas Iscariot (Assistant), and Thaddaeus-Lebbaeus-Judas son of James-Barabbas-military leader and the other Jacob son of Alphaeus (High Priest), Matthew (Levite), and Thomas (King-dispossessed Herod prince).

I was, recently, amazed by a visiting priest at our church in Lugdunum Convenarum, who proceeded to talk about the disciple of Jesus called Simon Zelotes, who suffered Crucifixion as the Bishop of Jerusalem after he had preached the Gospel in Samaria. I marveled at how completely the Church had transformed their arch-enemy and notorious heretic into this benign insignificant person. I suppose that this invention was thought up to prevent an even worse embarrassment to Jesus than choosing Judas, namely to have Simon Magus (666) as a disciple.

Once Simon's identity is accepted it is simple to see that Simon the Caananite and Simon the Zealot are identical as he like Helena, the Caananite woman, was from Syro-Phoenicia and he was also a supporter of the Zealots. In fact the proof that Simon is a Zealot and also Jesus' superior is shown in Mark when the scribes accuse Jesus of casting out demons in association with Beelzebub the ruler of demons (Zealots).

The connection of 'the father of the sons of Zebedee' and 'the mother of the sons of Zebedee' via two of Jesus' most often mentioned disciples, James and John, has been shown previously, but its significance is great because the Clementines clearly show them to be Simon Magus and Helena.

As the adoptive parents of James and John and for their mother to be at the cross with Mary Magdalene and Mother Mary shows her importance by being at least third in the order. However, even this would not be sufficiently important to have given their mother the effrontery of requesting Jesus to put James and on John on his right and left side in heaven! Clearly, Simon Magus and Helena have to be equal or greater than Jesus in importance.

The characters of Lazarus and 'Simon the leper' can be associated with Simon using the event and place of Mary Magdalene's anointing of Jesus. In the gospels of Matthew and Mark, 'Simon the leper' is present at his house in Bethany. In the gospel of John, it is Lazarus who is at the table of the house in Bethany. Since Martha (Helena) is serving, this indicates that the house is Simon's house also.

Moving on to 'Jacob son of Alphaeus', we need to look at the most important priest throughout the New Testament, the Sadducee priest Ananus ben Seth. He was High Priest from AD 6 to AD 15 and had five sons who became High Priests. Even after Ananus was removed as High Priest, he continued to have influence over the next High Priest Joseph Caiaphas from AD 18 to AD 37 by marrying his daughter to him.

We will discuss this further, but for now it is important to see that there are two persons on the lists of Matthew, Mark, Luke, and Acts that can be tied to 'of Alphaeus'.

One is 'Jacob of Alphaeus' and the other is 'Matthew', who is on the list in the Gospel of Matthew as 'Matthew, the publican' and mentioned inside as a 'tax collector'. In Mark we find 'Levi of Alphaeus' as a tax collector and since 'Jacob of Alphaeus' is in the disciple list, he must be another son of 'of Alphaeus'. Not only did this 'Levi' follow Jesus, but he also invited him to his house, which had other tax collectors, one of whom must have been 'Jacob of Alphaeus', his brother. With both being called tax collectors, it can be assumed that this is a label of some derision: that all Sadducee priests are no more useful than tax collectors of the Church fees.

The name 'Alphaeus' would appear to be a title for the top person and therefore must be Ananus, the father of these two sons. Actually his five sons were Eleazar, Jonathan, Theophilus, Matthias, and Ananus the Younger.

Of these sons, it can be immediately seen that 'Matthias' is 'Matthew', making him Jonathan's younger brother. Then knowing that Jonathan was High Priest in AD 37 for one year after Joseph Caiaphas was removed and Pontius Pilate recalled, we can try Jonathan's name with Nathanael in the Gospel of John. It turns out to be a match as both mean 'God has given'.

Thus Jonathan Annas must be 'Jacob of Alphaeus' and Nathanael. The absence of Matthew's name in the Gospel of John can be easily explained by the fact that Matthew was Jonathan's assistant as younger brother during the ministry of Jesus, but grew to predominance when he wrote the Gospel of Matthew and oversaw the canonizing of the Synoptic Gospels.

The priest Jonathan and his Sadducee relatives are very well documented in Josephus, including his own opinion of them as being haughty and rude. The method of Jonathan's death in December 57 AD was accomplished by the procurator Felix by using the Sicarii, named after the small daggers they concealed in their clothing in public places. After stabbing their victims, they would join in the public outcry and thus escape attention. Judas Iscariot had been one of them. It was from this word that Judas Iscariot got his nickname as Judas the Sicarii.

The use of his title 'Jacob', to disguise his name in the Gospels, refers to his role as 'Jacob', being third in importance of Abraham, Isaac, and Jacob (Father-Pope, Son of God (Man), and Son of Man). This was the priestly order and Jesus would have the same role as 'Son of Man' in the lay order.

My father Paul would be suspected of Jonathan Annas' death because of the known enmity between them, even prior to Paul's conversion when he was Saul. Jonathan had been made High Priest in AD 36 replacing Caiaphas, who had been responsible for Jesus' Crucifixion. He held this position for less than a year, being replaced by his younger brother Theophilus Annas.

Acting like his father Ananus being both High Priest and king, Jonathan was referred to as the Crown (in Greek 'Stephanos'). In Acts Luke disguises him under his title 'Stephen' to make it seem as if he was the first martyr for Christ. This has an irony to it as Jesus and he were usually at odds. Luke proceeds to describe his deposing as a stoning leading to his death.

Stephen's death was metaphoric, like the death of Simon Magus as Lazarus, Jonathan, is being deposed as High Priest. It was used as a literary device by Luke to reveal background information on the mission in Jonathan's speech. He would use the same device with Paul when he defended himself in court in Jerusalem.

Before Jonathan Annas was the first son, Eleazar, who was High Priest from from AD 16 to 17.

The character of Jonathan seems to be the subject of ridicule both by Jesus and Paul. Paul referred to him as an infirmity and a "thorn in his flesh". This comment has misled many into believing that Paul's infirmity was real. Anyone of his time would have known that Paul had great physical and mental strength, although his body was full of scars from countless beatings and stonings.

P Jesus ridiculed Jonathan's priestly ways of being carried in a palanquin so as not to touch the ground of the rest of the sinners.

The top platform of the Church, where Jonathan preferred to sit, had a loose board that could be removed to let the rays of the sun shine through to amaze and 'blind' the congregation below. This metaphor was used for Paul when he was converted from Saul as being blinded.

In the story of the paralytic, Jonathan has arrived in his palanquin and Jesus insolently, tells him that his sins are forgiven as if he were infirm! It is interesting that right after this, Matthew (Levi), his brother, joined Jesus showing his openness to Jesus reforms.

These Sadducee priests were a strange breed that insisted on being called 'God'. The Sadducee priest Ananus ben Seth, who was born in 22 BC, was High Priest from AD 6 to AD 15 and had five sons who became High Priests and when one counts his control over the High Priest Caiaphas as his father-in law, he welded almost autocratic control from the start of his high priesthood in AD 6 to his death in AD 66. His second son, who was the most important and active around Jesus' time, was Jonathan Annas, referred to as Jesus' disciple 'Jacob of Alphaeus'.

The Gospel of Luke says that during the time of John the Baptist, there were two High Priest's which is not really correct, but it seemed that way because Ananus controlled Caiaphas. Even at Jesus' trial strangely Jesus is brought to to Ananus first.

When the high priest asks Jesus about his disciples, and of his teaching, Jesus replies, 'I spoke openly to the world. I always taught in synagogues, and in the temple, where the Jews always meet. I said nothing in secret.'

Ananus takes this reply as insolent and has him slapped. It is only then that he is sent to Caiaphas.

These five sons of Ananus are humorously included in Jesus' parable of the rich man and Lazarus, where the rich man calls to Father Abraham to ask him to warn the five sons of his Father least they end up in Hell like him. The rich man is clearly Caiaphas and his Father is Ananus who has five sons.

In a double metaphor, the rich man is also James, "the gardener of the Church money" that Mary Magdalene mistakes for Jesus. He was in charge of burying the money in his cave, which would be the one in which Jesus was placed after the Crucifixion, and thus he was 'rich'.

In a further metaphor, James was in charge of the toilets (going to the garden). James was always a dangerous brother, one minute accusing Jesus at Gethsemane, the next, helping to ask for Jesus' body from the cross.

P Jesus had no choice but to get along with Jonathan, mainly because he recognized the legitimacy of Jesus' birth. However, these times of ridicule would not be forgotten when, as Jesus' superior, his Father, Jonathan, ordered Jesus to take the poison before he was on the cross and thus forcing Jesus to accept that his mission had failed.

Paul had been involved in the deposing Jonathan Annas as High Priest before his conversion from Saul, but his dislike for him increased when he learned that Jonathan had ordered Jesus to take poison before he was placed on the cross.

Thus Paul continued to pay no respect to Jonathan and this was obviously dangerous considering how self-important Jonathan thought he was. This was the 'thorn' in his side. However, though they were mortal enemies, Paul never would have condoned his murder in the winter of AD 57 for which he was brought to trial in Rome and eventually executed. The procurator Felix alone was responsible for the murder of Jonathan.

After Jonathan was deposed, Theophilus Annas was made High Priest from AD 37 to 41, then Matthias Annas in 43 AD and then the youngest Ananus Annas in AD 63.

The youngest son of Ananus called Ananus the Younger, having been made High Priest in AD 62, saw his chance to kill James, Jesus' brother. Seizing the opportunity when the procurator Festus died and the new procurator Albinus had not yet arrived, Ananus convened the Sanhedrin and had him accused and stoned to death. Albinus deposed Ananus when he arrived.

The reason that Ananus had James killed may have actually been prompted by revenge for the murder of his brother Jonathan under Felix. This would show that he had evidence to prove that James was responsible and not my father Paul. Ananus departed to Rome after he was deposed and was a close associate of Paul until he returned to Jerusalem just a year before Paul's death.

Ananus the Younger was Zacchaeus, the man who climbed the sycamore tree to see Jesus. He was also the teacher of James and John (Niceta and Aquila) and an assistant to Peter and ordained as Bishop of Caesarea, which is shown in the 'Clementines'.

In Paul's last Epistle to Timothy, Paul complains that Ananus, using his nickname Demas (Greek for 'people'), was too involved in present politics.

His title of 'Demas' indicates that he thinks of himself as a leader of the people. It was this leadership that would lead to his death.

(Early in AD 68 Ananus the younger gets the people to try to remove the Zealots from the inner temple: Josephus, Jewish War 4.3.7) And now the multitude were going to rise against them (Zealots) already; for Ananus, the ancientest of the high priests, persuaded them to it. He was a very prudent man, and had perhaps saved the city if he could but have escaped the hands of those that plotted against him.

(Ananus the Younger is trapped by the Idumaeans outside and the Zealots inside: Josephus, Jewish War 4.5.2) The rage of the Idumaeans being still insatiated, ... they searched for the chief priests, ... Standing over their dead bodies, they reviled. Ananus for his benevolence to the people, ...

(Span of Theudas career 6- 44 AD: Acts 5:37,36 ... at the time of the Census, came Judas, the Galilaean, and was the leader in a revolt. He too perished ... For before these days (6 AD) rose up Theudas, saying, that himself was some one, (44 AD) to whom a number of men did join themselves, as it were four hundred, who was slain, and all, as many as were obeying him, were scattered, and came to nought.

(Death of Theudas in AD 44: Josephus Antiquities of the Jews, 20.5.1
Now it came to pass, while Fadus was procurator of Judaea, that a certain magician, whose name was Theudas, persuaded a great part of the people to take their effects with them, and follow him to the river Jordan; for he told them he was a prophet, and that he would, by his own command, divide the river, and afford them an easy passage over it; and many were deluded by his words. However, Fadus did not permit them to make any advantage of his wild attempt, but sent a troop of horsemen out against them; who, falling upon them unexpectedly, slew many of them, and took many of them alive. They also took Theudas alive, and cut off his head, and carried it to Jerusalem ...

(List of the Twelve Disciples: Matthew 10:2-4) ... Lebbaeus, whose surname was Thaddaeus ...
(Acts of Thaddeus) Lebbaeus, who also is Thaddaeus, was of the city of Edessa ... an Hebrew by race, accomplished and most learned in the divine writings.

Ananus the Younger assembled a group of citizens to help to remove the Zealots who had taken refuge in the Jerusalem Temple. He knew that, if the Zealots were not removed, the Temple would be destroyed by the Romans.

It was not known to him that the Zealots had secretly sent a messenger to the Idumaeans and convinced them that Ananus was allied with the Romans. The Idumaeans became enraged.

The Idumaeans arrived and Ananus and the people were trapped between the inner walls and the outer walls of the temple. All of them were slaughtered without a proper burial.

Thus ended the last chance to remove the temple from the arena of war, for when the Roman came, they had to destroy the temple to defeat the Zealots.

As to Thaddaeus, it is logical to assume that Thaddaeus is a variant of Theudas who is mentioned as a Zealot leader, Saddok, similar to Judas the Galilean in Acts. His long life-span puts him at the start of the Age of Wrath in AD 6 with Judas the Galilean to his fateful march to the River Jordan in AD 44 to begin the new Age as a Joshua, only to meet his death under the procurator Fadus. The event at the river Jordan shows that Theudas was part of the sect of Therapeuts and clearly their leader.

The case has already been made that Thaddaeus is 'Judas of Jacob' and therefore 'Judas (not Iscariot)' in the Gospel of John. By placing 'Judas (not Iscariot)' on the Thaddaeus row, there is only empty slot in the list in John, that Nicodemus could be placed, but the reasons why this would be 'Matthew' have already been shown. Traditions seems to say that Nicodemus was part of the Sanhedrin, but this tradition can easily be proved false, due to the important role played by Nicodemus in the Gospel of John.

In the list of the disciples in the Gospel of Matthew, there is an interesting connection made between 'Thaddaeus' and 'Lebbaeus', although this is not in the Vaticanus version, having been added later. The Acts of Thaddaeus begins the statement "Lebbaeus, who also is Thaddaeus", which links him to the follow up on the letter from King Abgar to Jesus just before the Crucifixion. Therefore Theudas may have been sent to Abgar with a reply from Jesus.

Theudas is the actual Prodigal Son in Jesus' parables of past history. His older brother in the parable is Joseph, the father of Jesus. It was the dues coming in from the Diaspora, which they divided up into sections of the world. The trouble was that Theudas was using them for illegitimate means and was cut off and had to rely on the swine (the non-Jews) for money until he reformed.

Now to determine where Nicodemus should be placed, we need to look at his character. First there is the name given for him as Nicodemus which means "people's victory", clearly a name for the leader of the Zealots.

Since we previously established the connection of 'Judas (not Iscariot)' to be Theudas-Thaddeus, it is interesting to see the questions of 'Judas (not Iscariot)' at the Last Supper and Nicodemus when he came to Jesus at night, both have as their theme his trouble with 'the unseen'. Clearly, this points to a very pragmatic person, one who would believe in action. Thus when he led his people to death at the River Jordan, he did so because the action itself of 'crossing the river Jordan' meant more to him than the symbolism.

In two places in the Gospel of John, Nicodemus is referred to as 'visiting Jesus by night' and in one of these he is referred to as 'being one of them', therefore clearly a disciple.

One of the most important clues of his stature as a disciple comes when Jesus is taken off the cross to be put into the cave. Nicodemus comes with a huge quantity, a hundred pound weight of myrrh and aloes. From its weight it is clear that Nicodemus is very fit as a Zealot would be. Also given that the Therapeuts were known as healers, it would make sense that he would bring the medicine. Another important fact is that only Jesus' most trusted disciples would be involved with the pretence to Pilate that Jesus was still alive.

As to the disciple Thomas, he appears to be quite dense and not able to size up the scenes, but extremely dedicated. When Jesus says that Lazarus is dead, he wants to go there and die, too. This clearly shows that he does not understand that Lazarus issue was just the excommunication of Simon Magus.

At the Crucifixion, he would probably have been one of them who mistook the words Jesus said in Aramaic as Elijah when he said My God, my God, why have you abandoned me" as he did not know Aramaic.

At the Resurrection, in the well-known story the 'Doubting Thomas' does not believe until he touches Jesus' wounds.

In the Acts of Thomas, Thomas travels all the way to India as this was the land that he drew by lot with the other eleven disciples. He was martyred there, but not before he recites the beautiful 'Hymn of the Pearl' in prison. The Acts of Thomas and the Acts of Thaddaeus are clearly part of the eastern mission that has been over-shadowed by the accomplishments of Peter and Paul in Rome.

(Herodias marries Thomas, the son of Herod the Great: Antiquities 18.5.1).) Now Herodias their sister married Herod, the son of Herod the Great by Mariamne the daughter of Simon the high priest. They had a daughter Salome, after whose birth Herodias, in defiance of our country's laws, married Herod, the Tetrarch of Galilee and half-brother of her husband, during the lifetime of her husband, whom she divorced. Her daughter Salome married Philip, the Tetrarch of Trachonitis and son of Herod.

(Thomas is disinherited because his mother Mariamne II knew about Antipater's poison plot: Josephus, Antiquities 17.4.2) The high priest's daughter also, who was the king's wife, was accused to have been conscious of all this, and had resolved to conceal it; for which reason Herod divorced her, and blotted her son out of his testament, wherein he had been mentioned as one that was to reign after him; and he took the high priesthood away from his father-in-law, Simeon the son of Boethus, and appointed Matthias the son of Theophilus, who was born at Jerusalem, to be high priest in his room.

(Thomas is disinherited: Josephus, Wars I.30,7) Mariamne, the high priest's daughter, was conscious of this plot; and her very brothers, when they were tortured, declared it so to be. Whereupon the king avenged this insolent attempt of the mother upon her son, and blotted Herod, whom he had by her, out of his treatment, who had been before named therein as successor to Antipater.

(Judas Iscariot as Satan tempts Jesus in the wilderness: Luke 4:1-13) And Jesus, full of the Holy Spirit, turned back from the Jordan, and was brought in the Spirit to the wilderness, tempted all the while by Satan. During those days He ate nothing, and at the close of them He suffered from hunger. Satan said to him, 'If you are the Son of God, command this stone to become bread.' Jesus answered him, saying,'It is written, 'Man will not live by bread alone, but by every word of God." The devil, leading him up on a high mountain, showed him all the kingdoms of the inhabited world in a moment of time. The devil said to him, 'I will give you all this authority, and their glory, for it has been delivered to me; and I give it to whomever I want. If therefore you do homage to me, it shall all be yours.' Jesus answered him, 'Get behind me Satan! For it is written, 'You will worship the Lord your God, and him only will you serve." ...

Thomas is actually an extremely important person being of royal blood and being able to take over the King position in the Church. His mother, Mariamne II, was one of the wives of Herod the Great. Her father, Simon Boethus, had traded his daughter, to Herod in order to become high priest. However, when Herod learned that she had knowledge of a plot to poison him and did not tell him, he banished her and disinherited Thomas.

This was the start of his name Didymus meaning twin. (He was not the twin of Jesus as some have conjectured.) He like Esau had lost his birthright to his twin Jacob. Jacob had changed his name to Israel and was the father of twelve sons who would become the twelve tribes of Israel that were represented in the Church. Thomas would have to content himself with just being the other twin.

He had married Herodias, his step-niece by another wife of Herod the Great and had a child Salome, of John the Baptist beheading fame. Herodias divorces him for Herod Antipas, another step-uncle. This is the cause of John the Baptist's imprisonment by Herod Antipas when John objects to the unlawful divorce since it is not allowed by law with Thomas still living.

Thomas did not object to the divorce as it turns out that he was a homosexual, as was Jonathan Annas. He is well loved for collecting the sayings of Jesus in the Gospel of Thomas.

The last person of the twelve is Judas Iscariot, who took over at Judas the Galilean's death as the next Judas. As a Zealot he carried the name Satan, tempting Jesus in the wilderness and controlling Mary Magdalene as Demon 7.

It is Judas who objects to Mary Magdalene's marriage to Jesus on the grounds that she is the daughter of a Vestal Virgin of Artemis, and thus by Jewish law, a temple prostitute.

It is known to everyone about his betrayal of Jesus with a kiss, but with all of his scheming he could not escape his own crucifixion and he ended up on the cross as one of the robbers, just another name for Zealots, and Simon Magus was one also.

The Gospel of Matthew says Judas hanged himself and the Gospel of Luke says 'One of the malefactors, who were hanged, railed on him, saying, "If thou art Christ, save thyself and us." With the joining of the two verses with 'hanged', this would be Judas talking.

Ironically, Jesus did save himself and the others by taking the poison. Both Judas and Simon Magus were soon put in a tomb alive with only their legs broken and their hands pierced while Jesus in the next tomb was revived with only his hands pierced, standing up. We do not know if Judas would have survived because he was hurled out of the tomb by Nicodemus to the chasm below.

In Acts, the eleven disciples picked a replacement for Judas Iscariot. There were two candidates: "Joseph called Barsabas who was surnamed Justus" and Matthias. As to the surname 'Barsabas' there are two persons in Acts who have that surname: Joseph Barsabas and Judas Barsabas, it becomes immediately clear that these are the brothers of Jesus, commonly called James and Jude.

The title 'Justus' for Joseph is clearly a title for 'crown prince', showing Jesus is still alive as the 'David king'. There you have it: Jesus' full name: Jesus Barsabas, the Christ.

As to Matthias, Acts tells us that that Joses is Barnabas. Joses was Jesus' brother after James and he would be about 25 years old at the time. The Clementines tell us that Matthias is Barnabas, therefore Joses equals Barnabas equals Matthias.

Even if we did not have that information, there is a curious verse in Acts that refers to the people declaring Barnabas to be Zeus (Jupiter) and Paul to be Hermes (Mercury) which clearly implies that they think Barnabas is a King. This would make him, a brother of Jesus of the lineage of King David.

Interestingly, in the verse giving Judas Barsabas, there are listed Paul, Barnabas, Judas Barsabas, and Silas (meaning third) thus showing three of Jesus' brothers in a row and it can be surmised that Silas is Jesus' youngest brother, Simon. The correct order as given in Mark for Jesus' brothers after James are: Joses, Jude and Simon. Simon-Silas is called Silvanus in Paul's Epistles: 2Corinthians, 1&2Thessalonians and in Peter's: 1Peter.

Simon was the fifth and last son of Joseph and Mary born in AD 22, when Mary was 46 years old. Their father Joseph, always the firebrand, was assassinated in the following year. He was an associate of Paul and Timothy.

He was martyred in AD 114. Having been born in AD 22, Simon was 92 years old.

	Matthew	Mark	Luke	Acts	John
1	Peter	Peter	Peter	Peter	Peter
2	Andrew	Andrew	Andrew	Andrew	Andrew
3	James Zebedee (James Niceta)	James Zebedee (James Niceta)	James Zebedee (James Niceta)	James Zebedee (James Niceta)	James Zebedee (James Niceta)
4	John Zebedee (John Aquila)	John Zebedee (John Aquila)	John Zebedee (John Aquila)	John Zebedee (John Aquila)	John Zebedee (John Aquila)
5	Philip	Philip	Philip	Philip	Philip
6	Bartholomew (John Mark)	Bartholomew (John Mark)	Bartholomew (John Mark)	Bartholomew (John Mark)	Beloved Disciple (John Mark)
7	Matthew Annas	Matthew Annas	Matthew Annas	Matthew Annas	Matthew Annas
8	Thomas Herod	Thomas Herod	Thomas Herod	Thomas Herod	Thomas Herod
9	Jacob of Alphaeus (Jonathan Annas)	Jacob of Alphaeus (Jonathan Annas)	Jacob of Alphaeus (Jonathan Annas)	Jacob of Alphaeus (Jonathan Annas)	Nathanael (Jonathan Annas)
10	Thaddaeus Theudas	Thaddaeus Theudas	Judas of Jacob Theudas	Judas of Jacob Theudas	Nicodemus Theudas
11	Simon the Canaanite (Simon Magus)	Simon the Canaanite (Simon Magus)	Simon the Zealot (Simon Magus)	Simon the Zealot (Simon Magus)	Lazarus (Simon Magus)
12	Judas Iscariot	Judas Iscariot	Judas Iscariot	Matthias Joses Barnabas	Judas Iscariot

Origin of twelve and three

(Order of the angels: Michael, Gabriel, Sariel, Raphael: DSS\War Scroll IX 15) They shall write on all the shields of the towers: on the first Michael, on the second Gabriel, on the third Sariel, on the fourth Raphael.

(Twelve men and three priests: Michael (Priest), Gabriel (Levite-Man), Sariel (King-Son of Man): DSS Community Rule VIII.1) In the Council of the Community, there shall be twelve men and three priests, perfectly versed in all that is revealed of the Law, whose works shall be truth, righteousness, justice, loving-kindness and humility.

Three replaced as one

(Year of Melchizedek`s favor: DSS 11QMelch) Then the "Day of Atonement" shall follow after the tenth jubilee period, when he shall atone for all the Sons of Light, and the people who are predestined to Melchizedek. (...) upon them (...) For this is the time decreed for the "Year of Melchizedek`s favor", and by his might he will judge God's holy ones and so establish a righteous kingdom, as it is written about him in the Songs of David; "A godlike being has taken his place in the council of God; in the midst of divine beings he holds judgement"

The Community Rule Scrolls of Qumran state that there are three ruling priests of twelve. The three ruling priests are represented by the patriarchs of the Jews: Abraham, Isaac, and Jacob. They are used as symbols for Father, Son, Holy Spirit thus: 'Abraham' is 'Father' or 'Pope', 'Isaac' is 'Son' or 'Man', and 'Jacob' is 'the Holy Spirit'. (The Essenes assigned these positions to angels as Michael, Gabriel, Sariel.) Another way of looking at this structure was God, Son of God, Son of Man.

It is from this structure that Jesus called himself the Son of Man, passed on from his grandfather Heli and father Joseph, who died in AD 23. In fact Jesus never said he was the 'Son of God', as many believe, he always said he was the 'Son of Man'.

This simple structure became muddled as Herod the Great combined all three functions to himself. Under him would be High Priest, Levite and King. Herod would then obtain a huge share of the fees from the Jews at home and abroad, the Diaspora, making himself quite rich.

Heli was allowed to remain Son of Man, the David King, under this structure. However, when Herod heard of a prophecy of a greater king from the Magi, he became paranoid.

(Year of Melchizedek`s favor: Hebrews 7:1-3) For this Melchizedek, king of Salem, priest of God Most High, who met Abraham returning from the slaughter of the kings and blessed him, to whom also Abraham divided a tenth part of all (being first, by interpretation, King of righteousness, and then also King of Salem, which is King of peace;) without father, without mother, without genealogy, having neither beginning of days nor end of life, and being made like to the Son of God, doth remain a priest continually.

The Transfiguration

(Jesus appears on the Day of Atonement as high priest with Jonathan and Theudas: Luke 9:28-35) It was about eight days after this that Jesus, taking with Him Peter, John, and James, went up the mountain to pray. As he was praying, the appearance of his face was altered, and his clothing became white and dazzling. Behold, two men talked with him, who were Moses and Elijah, who appeared in glory, and spoke of his departure, which he was about to accomplish at Jerusalem. Now Peter and those who were with him were heavy with sleep, but when they were fully awake, they saw his glory, and the two men who stood with him. It happened, as they were parting from him, that Peter said to Jesus, 'Master, it is good for us to be here. Let's make three tents: one for you, and one for Moses, and one for Elijah,' not knowing what he said. While he said these things, a cloud came and overshadowed them, and they were afraid as they entered into the cloud. A voice came out of the cloud, saying, 'This is my beloved Son. Listen to him!'

The Pesher of Habakkuk

(The Wicked Priest is Jesus; the Teacher of Righteousness is John the Baptist: Dead Sea Scrolls Habakkuk 1QpHab XI:2-8) "Woe to him who causes his neighbors to drink; who pours out his venom to make them drunk that he may gaze on their feasts." (Habakkuk 2:15)
Its pesher, this is the city of Ephraim, those who seek smooth things during.the last days, who walk in falsehood.
Its pesher refers to the Wicked Priest who pursued after the Teacher of Righteousness to his house of exile to confusion him with his venomous anger. At the time appointed for rest for the Day of Atonement, he appeared to them to confuse them up and to cause them to stumble on the day of fasting, the Sabbath of their rest.

☧ Jesus was intent on fulfilling the prophecy of the Magi and hoped to combine all three positions in the role of Melchizedek, thus God, Son of God, and Son of Man.

⚏hen Jesus appeared on the platform of the Church dressed in the vestments of a high priest on the Day of Atonement in the Fall of AD 32 in what is called the Transfiguration, he is shown as being in the presence of Elijah and Moses. These were merely the titles of two other major officials of the Church: Jonathan Annas, who took this name Elijah after John the Baptist's death and Theudas, technically the Joshua (Moses is used for greater effect), who lead his followers over the River Jordan and was killed by the procurator Fadus. Elijah was Jonathan the Sadducee priest, Abba Father, with whom Jesus struggled to obey in the Garden of Gethsemane. Moses was Theudas-Barabbas, the person he replaced on cross. Jesus' position should have been as King, the third position, but his vestments revealed a greater role as the High Priest.

☧ Jesus had hoped to extend his kingship into one figure that of Melchizedek and thus to remove the hierarchy of three and the influence of the hereditary priests. For this he was severely reprimanded by his step-father in-law Pope Simon Magus, 'the Cloud'.

The writers of the Scroll peshers would call him the 'Wicked Priest' and the 'Man of the Lie'. They already held him responsible for the death of John the Baptist, the Teacher of Righteousness.

⚏hen the soldiers of Caiaphas came for Jesus, they had already heard this story about how Jesus tried to make himself 'God'. It had bothered Judas so much that it led him to betray Jesus.

☧ Jesus would never make this mistake again and even decided to keep the Herodian structure with himself as the third. The Herod King, Agrippa II, was above the three. Unfortunately, Matthew Annas, acting for Jonathan Annas, was able to consolidate his power and displace even Jesus from the third position replacing him with the Magus Apollos. This gave Matthew total control over the content of the Gospels, but he was still reasonably fair to all parties.

Labeled in DaVinci's Last Supper

The Resurrection of Lazarus, Russian icon (15th century)

Chapter 12 - The Raising of Lazarus. (two weeks before the Crucifixion.)

And going from the tomb, they went to the house of the young man. For he was rich. And after six days, Jesus instructed him. And when it was late, the young man went to him. He had put a linen around his naked body, and he remained with him through that night. For Jesus taught him the mystery of the kingdom of God. (Secret Mark 3:05-3:10)

***********Reference Column***********

Event that led to the Crucifixion

(Demonstration against the water channel: Josephus, Antiquities 18.3.2) But Pilate undertook to bring a current of water to Jerusalem, and did it with the sacred money, ... the Jews were not pleased with what had been done about this water; and many ten thousands of the people got together, and made a clamor against him, and insisted that he should leave off that design. Some of them also used reproaches, and abused the man, as crowds of such people usually do. So he dressed a great number of his soldiers in their clothes, who carried daggers under their garments, and sent them to a place where they might surround them ... he gave the soldiers that signal which had been beforehand agreed on; who laid upon them much greater blows than Pilate commanded them, and equally punished those that were tumultuous, and those that were not ... since the people were unarmed, and were caught by men prepared for what they were about, there were a great number of them slain by this means, and others ran away wounded.

Jesus on Caiaphas' hit list

(After the healing of Lazarus: John 11:45-57) Many therefore of the Jews, who came to Mary and beheld that which he did (i.e. raising Lazarus from the dead), believed on him. But some of them went away to the Pharisees, and told them the things which Jesus had done. The chief priests therefore and the Pharisees gathered a council, and said, What do we? for this man doeth many signs. If we let him thus alone, all men will believe on him: and the Romans will come and take away both our place and our nation ... Jesus therefore walked no more openly among the Jews, but departed thence into the country near to the wilderness, into a city called Ephraim; and there he tarried with the disciples ... Now the chief priests and the Pharisees had given commandment, that, if any man knew where he was, he should show it, that they might take him.

The raising of Lazarus was a significant turning point in Jesus' career. Jesus had raised people from the dead before as with the daughter of Jairus and the son of the widow of Nain, but these individuals had only just died and it might be possible to believe that they only appeared to be dead. In reality, these healings were metaphoric using the knowledge that, according to the Essenes, those outside of the Church were dead. In fact these healings were actually of my grandmother Mary Magdalene and Jesus' brother James.

In the situation of Lazarus, he was in the tomb for four days, two of these days Jesus purposefully waited, as some would say, to scientifically prove beyond a doubt that he could raise the dead. As this miracle occurs just before the Crucifixion, the implication is that he would use these skills to raise himself from the dead after the Crucifixion. The question arises as to whether this test of his power was important because raising someone from the dead is quite different from raising oneself from the dead, when already dead!

Since he loved Lazarus like a brother, it would have been foolish to wait because every day would make it harder to raise him. As Martha said, after Lazarus was raised from the dead, "He stinketh". One also would wonder why Jesus did not use his 'healing from a distance' skills, since it was supposedly a day's journey away. He had used this with the nobleman's son in Cana, while complaining, "Unless ye see signs and wonders ye will not believe."

Of course, the real story of Lazarus is quite different. What happened was that Simon Magus, the Pope, had hoped to embarrass Pilate with a demonstration in December, but it got out of hand and resulted in the killing of Roman soldiers. Judas Iscariot and Theudas-Barabbas were also involved. For this, Simon was excommunicated and as Pope he was severely punished by being placed in a tomb alive to symbolize his death. If no one would vouch for him, he could die.

Jesus had hesitated, being afraid to go against the elders, but now his mother-in-law Helena was begging him to rescue his father-in-law. Jesus, having waited two days to see if others like Jonathan Annas would come to to Simon's rescue, reluctantly had to do it. With this act of defying High Priest Caiaphas, Jesus went to the top of his hit list.

My step-great-grandfather Simon would later boast to his listeners that he was Lazarus (Osiris: 'El-Asar-Us'), but his name has been removed. My great-grandmother Helena is shown as merely Martha ('mistress') and my grandmother Mary Magdalene as merely Mary ('Miriam': sister of Moses).

It is fortunate that we still have some of the earlier text that was dictated to Mark by Peter when he was in Rome in AD 44-45. I obtained these text fragments from my grandfather's library, which he left to Phoebe for safe keeping. These fragments of text now seem to be called the 'Secret Gospel of Mark', but they were originally part of the 'Gospel of Peter', of which there only exists the section on the Crucifixion and Resurrection.

It is suspicious that the 'Raising of Lazarus' only appears in the Gospel of John in its edited form with Simon Magus being called Lazarus. However, since this story is contained in 'the Secret Gospel of Mark', it must have been part of Peter's original version of the Gospel of Mark. Peter was not one to deal with metaphors and there is an important reason why the Church would have removed it.

I will show each of the fragments of text along side any corresponding verses in the Gospel of John. In this way the true writings of Peter in the Gospel of Mark and Jesus in the Gospel of John can be seen before the edits of Matthew.

In this fragment which parallels John 12:54 "he walked no more openly among the Jews, but departed thence into the country near to the wilderness, into a city called Ephraim; and there he tarried with the disciples", the Secret Gospel of Mark says "he turned to the region of the Jordan. James and John go to him, and he goes to Jericho". Here Jesus is avoiding the wrath of Caiaphas after defying him by raising Lazarus.

The most important fact, which was removed from the 'Raising of Lazarus' and is revealed in the 'Secret Gospel of Mark', is that Simon is speaking from the tomb and therefore not dead.

This proves that his death was merely symbolic and this is unequivocally shown by the Secret Gospel of Mark: "And immediately a great voice (sound) was heard from the tomb." Some scholars explain this away as just a 'death cry', but such an explanation is totally absurd, certainly banshees are a Gaelic folk tale. Peter will also treat Jesus' Resurrection in the Gospel of Peter as nothing more than a miraculous rescue of Jesus in human form. (This will be shown the next chapter.)

There are two terms 'great voice' and 'naked youth' that need to be defined. 'Great voice (great sound)' means important like the king speaking. Thus when Simon Magus spoke to Jesus from the tomb, he did as if still Pope. Jesus also spoke from the cross with a 'great voice' as Holy Spirit.

Simon Magus is shown at the Garden of Gethsemane as a youth running away naked because Jesus had only just released him from the tomb from 'being 'dead'. After being cleansed and baptized he would need to go through the steps from initiate to Pope all over again, thus being a 'naked youth' wearing a simple linen surplice.

(Simon Magus as Lazarus showing the cave in which he was placed: (Luke 16:20-31) While at his outer door there lay a beggar, Lazarus by name, covered with sores and longing to make a full meal off the scraps flung on the floor from the rich man's table. Nay, the dogs, too, used to come and lick his sores. It happened that the beggar died, and that he was carried away by the angels to Abraham's bosom. The rich man also died, and was buried. And in Hell, being in torment, he looked and saw Abraham in the far distance, and Lazarus resting in his arms. So he cried aloud, and said, "Father Abraham, take pity on me and send Lazarus to dip the tip of his finger in water and cool my tongue, for I am in agony in this flame.' ''Remember, my child,' said Abraham, 'that you had all your good things during your lifetime, and that Lazarus in like manner had his bad things. But, now and here, he is receiving consolation and you are in torment. And, besides all this, a vast chasm is immovably fixed between us and you, put there in order that those who desire to cross from this side to you may not be able, nor any be able to cross over from your side to us.' "I entreat you then, father,' said he, 'to send him to my father's house. For I have five brothers. Let him earnestly warn them, lest they also come to this place of torment.' "They have Moses and the Prophets,' replied Abraham; 'let them hear them.' "No, father Abraham,' he pleaded; 'but if some one goes to them from the dead, they will repent.' "If they are deaf to Moses and the Prophets,' replied Abraham, 'they would not be led to believe even if some one should rise from the dead."

"I believe in God, the Father almighty, creator of heaven and earth. I believe in Jesus Christ, his only Son, our Lord. He was conceived by the power of the Holy Spirit and born of the Virgin Mary. He suffered under Pontius Pilate, was crucified, died, and was buried. <u>He descended into hell.</u> On the third day he rose again. He ascended into heaven and is seated at the right hand of the Father. He will come again to judge the living and the dead. I believe in the Holy Spirit, the Holy Church, the communion of saints, the forgiveness of sins the resurrection of the body, and life everlasting. Amen."

In the Gospel of Luke, the name 'Lazarus' was used in Jesus' parable of the 'Rich Man and Lazarus', where Lazarus is in Abraham's tomb and the 'rich man' is in a tomb on the other side of a chasm. In the last line of this parable, Jesus predicts his fate and expresses the doubts he has about his mission.

The purpose of this parable is to give a geographical reference to the location of the tomb that Simon Magus was placed as Lazarus and the tomb of the 'rich man.' These caves, to the south of Qumran, were separated by a chasm and, in an analogy to Jerusalem's Gehenna, represented 'Hell.'

This place Gehenna was located in the Valley of Hinnom, one of the two principal valleys surrounding the Old City. In this loathsome valley fires were kept burning perpetually to consume the filth and cadavers thrown into it. The 'rich man's' cave would be the version of Purgatory as his tongue was merely singed by the fires of Hell below.

The label 'rich man' was a humorous term used for James, the brother of Jesus, who was in charge of collecting the Church membership fees of the Gentiles.

After the Crucifixion, James is portrayed as 'the rich man Joseph of Arimathaea' in whose cave Jesus was placed while he was being revived from the poison.

In another event, the wit of Helena, as 'the Canaanite/Syro-Phoenician woman', is shown when she compares herself to the beggar Lazarus collecting crumbs from the table.

The most ironic part of this parable is that Jesus did end up in the rich man's cave, therefore in Hell, when he was taken from the cross. Thus the Apostles Creed could add 'Hell' to his journey from the cross.

While we are looking at the Apostles Creed, it is absurd that Pontius Pilate gets to have his name associated throughout all time and not Caiaphas who manipulated Pilate into placing Jesus on the cross.

Also the issue of the third day has always caused problems because Mark 8:31 says, "And he began to teach them, that the Son of man must suffer many things, and be rejected by the elders, and the chief priests, and scribes, and be killed, and after three days rise again", but all the Gospels specifically say that Mary Magdalene came on day one of the Sabbaths, Saturday. Perhaps the insistence on three days are to prove that Jesus is really as dead as Lazarus or maybe three days are meant to be counted as Thursday-Last Supper, Friday-Crucifixion, Saturday-Resurrection. In any case, he did leave the tomb on Saturday, the Sabbath.

Six days before the Passover, Jesus goes to the house in Bethany, which we have previously shown to be the house of Simon Magus where Mary Magdalene anoints Jesus to confirm their marriage. Here the Secret Gospel connects by association the young man with Lazarus and Salome with Martha. Since this is just before the marriage ceremony of Jesus and Mary Magdalene, it is interesting that the Secret Gospel shows Mother Mary present next to Helena (Martha-Salome) and Simon Magus (the young man). In the the Secret Gospel, Mary Magdalene is shown as 'the sister of the young man' ('sister' because Simon Magus is on the level of brother), however given the presence of the Mother and Salome, the context demands that 'whom Jesus loved' must refer to Mary Magdalene and not Simon.

Mother Mary was also present at the 'Marriage at Cana', which was Jesus and Mary Magdalene's betrothal ceremony.

Next it appears that Simon Magus has gone out to public declaring himself as Lazarus (Osiris) raised from the dead. Jesus, preferring to distance himself from the whole incident, stays out of sight, thus it says in the Secret Gospel, "And Jesus did not receive them."

It is important to note that, since Caiaphas is wanting to put Lazarus to death, what he is saying is that the symbolic placing of him in the tomb as dead, is now not enough, for his physical death needs to happen. The obvious implication is that Jesus did not raise Simon Magus from physical death.

We now return back to the time that is three or four days before Jesus raises Lazarus. We find Helena (Martha) discoursing with Jesus as she did as 'the Samaritan woman at the Well'. Simon Magus (Lazarus) is her brother because of his demotion to brother.

In the Secret Gospel she calls Jesus 'the Son of David'. Since Jesus' proper title is 'Son of Man', Helena is subtly saying that Jesus should exert his authority as Melchizedek as King David did. This is what made the disciples angry as the did not want a reoccurrence of 'The Transfiguration'.

The other possibility is for Jesus to persuade Jonathan Annas (God gives) to raise Lazarus. This is Jesus' preferred solution. However, Jonathan is reluctant to go against his father Ananus and his puppet Caiaphas. Jesus cannot ignore his mother-in-law and decides to act.

(Gospel of John: John 11:23-32) Jesus saith unto her, 'Thy brother shall rise again.' Martha saith unto him, 'I know that he shall rise again in the resurrection at the last day.' Jesus said unto her, 'I am the resurrection, and the life: he that believeth on me, though he die, yet shall he live; and whosoever liveth and believeth on me shall never die. Believest thou this?' She saith unto him, 'Yes, Lord: I have believed that thou art the Christ, the Son of God, even he that cometh into the world.'
When she had said this, she went away, and called Mary, her sister, secretly, saying, 'The teacher is here, and is calling you' And she, when she heard it, arose quickly, and went unto him. (Now Jesus was not yet come into the village, but was still in the place where Martha met him.) The Jews then who were with her in the house, and were consoling her, when they saw Mary, that she rose up quickly and went out, followed her, supposing that she was going unto the tomb to weep there. Mary then, when she came to Jesus and saw Him, fell at His feet and exclaimed, 'Master, if you had been here, my brother would not have died.'

(Gospel of John: John 11:33-37,38b) When Jesus therefore saw her weeping, and the Jews also weeping who came with her, he groaned in the spirit, and was troubled, and said, 'Where have ye laid him?' They say unto him, 'Lord, come and see.' Jesus wept. The Jews therefore said, 'Behold how he loved him!' But some of them said, 'But others of them asked, 'Was this man who opened the blind man's eyes unable to prevent this man from dying?' ... Now it was a cave, and a stone lay against it.

(Clement Letter: Secret Gospel of Mark 2.26a) Jesus went with her to the garden where the tomb was.

(The garden was the place of Crucifixion and the tomb: John 19:41) and there was in the place where he was crucified a garden, and in the garden a new tomb, in which no one was yet laid;

(The gardener at the tomb: John 20:15) and there was in the place where he was crucified a garden, and in the garden a new tomb, in which no one was yet laid; Jesus saith to her, 'Woman, why dost thou weep? whom dost thou seek;' she, supposing that he is the gardener, saith to him, 'Sir, if thou didst carry him away, tell me where thou didst lay him, ...'

(Gospel of John: John 11:38a) Jesus therefore again groaning in himself cometh to the tomb.
(Clement Letter: Secret Gospel of Mark 2.26b,3.01a) And immediately a great sound was heard from the tomb, Jesus therefore again groaning in himself cometh to the tomb.

Jesus says 'Thy brother shall rise again'. Helena gets nervous and questions whether he is just referring the Last Judgement. Jesus reaffirms that he will raise Lazarus using a playful expression that he is 'the resurrection and the life.' Helena jumps for joy that Jesus has agreed to do it, and essentially says that he is a wonderful son-in-law. She now uses Peter's error of calling Jesus, the Son of God, but does so deliberately to indicate that he deserves to replace Jonathan as 'Son of God'.

Mary Magdalene arrives and falls at his feet, crying because she believes that Jesus has come too late and that Lazarus has already died from suffocation.

In the Gospel of John, the onlookers appear to state the obvious point that if Jesus can perform all sorts of miracles, why was he unable to prevent Lazarus from dying.

Actually there is a subtle point here because the example they use for the healing is a 'blind man' rather that the times that he brought others to life. In other words, if Jesus could raise the status of someone from 'blind status' (wanting to be part of the Church) to 'initiate', then he could certainly do it the same with one who was dead (separated from the Church).

As Jesus walks to the tomb, we learn its characteristics. The tomb matches the description of the caves of the Resurrection being a tomb that is in a garden. This also justifies Mary Magdalene mistaking Jesus for the gardener at the Resurrection.

The statement from the Secret Gospel, "And immediately a great sound was heard from the tomb" proves that Simon Magus was always alive. Note that the Gospel of John has been changed from 'the great sound' from within the cave to 'the groan' of Jesus!

(Clement Letter: Secret Gospel of Mark 3.01b,02a) and Jesus, going toward it rolled away the stone from the entrance to the tomb.

(Gospel of John: John 11:39-42) Jesus saith, Take ye away the stone. Martha, the sister of him that was dead, saith unto him,' Lord, by this time there is a stench; for he hath been dead four days.' Jesus saith unto her, 'Said I not unto thee, that, if thou believest, thou shouldest see the glory of God?' So they took away the stone. And Jesus lifted up his eyes, and said, 'Father, I thank thee that thou heardest me. And I knew that thou hearest me always: but because of the multitude that standeth around I said it, that they may believe that thou didst send me.'

The stone at the cave rolls from the entrance: Matthew 27:60, 28:2) He then laid it in his own new tomb which he had hewn in the solid rock, and after rolling a great stone against the door of the tomb he went home ... But to their amazement there had been a great earthquake; for an angel of the Lord had descended from Heaven, and had come and rolled back the stone, and was sitting upon it.

The stone at the cave rolls: Mark 16:3) And they (Mary Magdalene, Mother Mary, and Helena) said one to another: Who shall roll us back the stone from the door of the sepulchre?

(Clement Letter: Secret Gospel of Mark 3.02b-04a) And going in immediately where the young man was, he stretched out a hand and raised him up, holding his hand.

(Gospel of John: John 11:43-44) And when he had thus spoken, he cried with a loud voice, Lazarus, come forth. He that was dead came forth, bound hand and foot with grave-clothes; and his face was bound about with a napkin. Jesus saith unto them, Loose him, and let him go.

In the Gospel of John, Jesus attempts to explain to the crowd that he has been given the authority to raise Simon even though he had not yet received it.

The Secret Gospel reveals another similarity to the Resurrection cave in that that the stone rolls making it possible for one man outside to open the cave. However, as stated in later in Mark, it is not possible for a female to roll it.

The Secret Gospel says that Jesus went in and took Lazarus' hand. Lazarus is a young man not in age, but at the level of an initiate. This is the same young man in the Garden of Gethemane in the Gospel of Mark, who runs away naked.

In the Gospel of John, Jesus speaks in a voice of authority and orders others to take Simon out to imply that he has the authority to do it. Clearly, Simon had been in great discomfort, being bound so as not to be able to escape. At baptism it would be in a loincloth then put on the linen gown of an initiate. The Gospel of John, seemingly apprehensive about the removal of the 'voice from within' from the text, adds a napkin to Lazarus' face to make sure that he could not possibly talk.

132

***********Reference Column***********

(Clement Letter: Secret Gospel of Mark 3.04b-10a) Then, the man looked at him and loved him and he began to call him to his side, that he might be with him. And going from the tomb, they went to the house of the young man. For he was rich.

And after six days, Jesus instructed him. And when it was late, the young man went to him. He had put a linen around his naked body, and he remained with him through that night. For Jesus taught him the mystery of the kingdom of God.

(Nudity: Dead Sea Scrolls which specifies in Community Rule VII) "Whoever has gone naked before his companion, without having been obliged to do so, he shall do penance for six months."

"Whoever is so poorly dressed that during a bodily movement from beneath his garment his nakedness has been seen, he shall do penance for thirty days.'

My father Paul told me a story of how some of the higher Church members, being so proud at having gotten hold of the Secret Gospel, would tell Paul that they were very disturbed by 'the love and the nakedness throughout the night'. Some of them, who were known to be detractors of Jesus, even tried to use it against him by implying that Jesus was a homosexual. Such an idea is, of course, preposterous.

Paul would then have to explain to them that the Church does not allow nudity, in fact the Community Rule of the Scrolls specifically bans it. To be 'naked' was to wear a loin cloth and the 'linen' was a Church surplice. The night ritual was the normal practice of intense instruction and prayer, to be followed by baptism. Nicodemus had come to Jesus at night as part of his baptism.

Apparently these Church members were more ready to believe this falsity, than to believe that Jesus was married twice with four children.

Obviously, having been in a tomb for four days, Simon would first have to remove 'the stench' from his body, being initially in his loin cloth. Then he would put on his surplice to be taught through the night, which would be followed by baptism in his loincloth. He would then be allowed to be amongst his brothers and sisters again.

It is important to note that the 'young man' is rich and has a house. This ties in with what we have already covered, proving that Lazarus is Simon Magus as the deposed Pope and with his house being his Church.

Resurrection (Hans Memling)

Chapter 13 - The Crucifixion at Qumran and the Myth of Jesus' Resurrection.

And the angel answered and said unto the women, "Fear not: for I know that you seek Jesus, who was crucified. He is not here: for he is risen, as he said ... (Matthew 28:5-6)

***********Reference Column***********

A fulfillment of a prophecy

(Pentecost; Acts 2,16,19,20) Peter said: "But this is that which was spoken of by the prophet Joel: And I will show wonders in heaven above, and signs on the earth beneath; blood, and fire, and vapor of smoke. The sun will be turned into darkness, And the moon into blood, Before the great and glorious day of the Lord comes."

(Joel 2:30) And I will shew wonders in the heavens and in the earth, blood, and fire, and pillars of smoke.

***********Reference Column***********

Caiaphas chooses Jesus as scapegoat

(Gospel of John: John 11:49-53) But a certain one of them, Caiaphas, being high priest that year, said unto them, Ye know nothing at all, nor do ye take account that it is expedient for you that one man should die for the people, and that the whole nation perish not. Now this he said not of himself: but, being high priest that year, he prophesied that Jesus should die for the nation; and not for the nation only, but that he might also gather together into one the children of God that are scattered abroad. So from that day forth they took counsel that they might put him to death.

***********Reference Column***********

Judas offers his services to Caiaphas

(Judas Iscariot betrays Jesus for thirty pieces of silver - the opposing group was made up of 30 leaders for the days of the moon indicated by silver: Matthew 26:14-16) Then one of the twelve, who was called Judas Iscariot, went to the chief priests, And said, What will ye give me, and I will deliver him to you? And they covenanted with him for thirty pieces of silver (the leadership role). From that time he sought opportunity to betray him.

At 6:20 pm Friday April 3, AD 33, a darkened partial eclipsed moon rose in the east, coinciding with the start of the Jewish Sabbath and Passover day. Jesus and the two others, who had been crucified, were removed from the crosses and placed in the two caves. Jesus, who was thought to be dead, had been placed in the first cave and the other two crucified men were in the second cave, thought to be suffocating to death. Jesus would be rescued that night.

Peter later on would quote from Joel, using the pesher technique of the Dead Sea Scrolls writers, as the fulfillment of this prophecy. A total lunar eclipse turns the moon to the color of 'blood'. With the lunar calendar being three hours slow from the pure Enochian Wednesday Sun Creation calendar of the Essenes, the Pharisees had removed three hour-segments from their candle clock, thus turning the 'fire' of the sun to darkness for three hours. The 'vapor of smoke' was the cover-up to Pilate that Jesus was dead.

Prior to the Crucifixion, a demonstration in December AD 32 had turned into a riot with some Roman soldiers killed. Thus Judas with Simon Magus and Theudas were being sought for the crime of insurrection. Its failure annoyed Judas, who wanted to be the leader like Judas the Galilean of whom he was the successor known as 'Satan. He resented having little influence over the towering figure of Simon Magus and the veteran Zealot, Theudas (Bar-abbas), who had taken the name Saddok when he fought alongside Judas the Galilean.

Simon Magus had been deposed as Pope for its failure and had been symbolically placed in a tomb as Lazarus. Caiaphas was intending to turn Simon over to Pilate, but after Jesus defied Caiaphas by raising Simon Magus-Lazarus, he realized that Jesus was more of a threat. Pondering aloud, the High Priest says, "There must be a way that Jesus could be put to death for the sake of their nation", then smiling, he adds, "In fact I prophecy it!"

Attempting to save his skin by making a deal, Judas says to Caiaphas, "I can help your prophecy to come true. I am in the Levite position to Simon Magus. If you replace me with Jesus by promoting this 'Son of Man' to 'Son of God' as he wants, Pilate can crucify all three: Simon, Jesus, and Theudas." Caiaphas agrees to the plan.

In an effort to gain favor from Pilate, Judas also volunteers to be in charge of getting a message to him confirming that the leaders are present in Qumran so that Pilate could arrive there on Friday morning to put them on trial and crucify them. Judas would leave the Last Supper early to accomplish this.

***********Reference Column***********

Judas alerts Pilate

(Judas Iscariot leaves to alert Pilate: John 13:21-30) When Jesus had said this, he was troubled in the spirit, and testified, 'Most assuredly I tell you that one of you will betray me.'

The disciples looked at one another, perplexed about whom he spoke. One of his disciples, whom Jesus loved, was at the table, leaning against Jesus' breast. Simon Peter therefore beckoned to him, and said to him, 'Tell us who it is of whom he speaks.' He, leaning back, as he was, on Jesus' breast, asked him, 'Lord, who is it?' Jesus answereth, 'That one it is to whom I, having dipped this piece of bread, shall give it;' and having dipped the morsel, he giveth it to Judas Iscariot of Simon. And after the morsel, then Satan entered into him, Jesus, therefore, saith to him, 'What thou dost -- do quickly;' Now no man at the table knew why he said this to him. For some thought, because Judas had the money bag, that Jesus said to him, 'Buy what things we need for the feast,' or that he should give something to the poor. Therefore, having received that morsel, he went out immediately. It was night.

***********Reference Column***********

The Last Supper

(Jesus announces that Judas is leaving: Matthew 26:24,25) ... Woe to the 'Man' that through whom the Son of Man serves as the ideal of Him ('Son of God') and not the human that is conceived (ordinary man). Judas, still serving Him (as the 'Son of 'God'), answering said, 'Teacher you are saying to Him ('God') that you are not the True God?'

Jesus is Betrayed

(Judas comes with Caiaphas' officers: John 18:3) Judas, therefore, having taken the band and officers out of the chief priests and Pharisees, doth come thither with torches and lamps, and weapons;

(Judas tries to kiss Jesus: Luke 23: 47,48) and drew near to Jesus to kiss him. But Jesus said to him, 'Judas, do you betray the Son of Man with a kiss?'

(Jesus is arrested: John 18:3-11) Jesus asks them, 'Whom do ye seek?' They to him, 'Jesus the Nazarene had stood saying he was the 'True God' and Judas, the one serving 'God', was standing with them; When therefore he asked to them, the 'True God?', they went backward, and fell to the ground. ... Jesus asks again 'Are you saying I am the 'True God?' ... Simon Peter therefore, having a sword, drew it, and struck the high priest's servant, and cut off his right ear. The servant's name was Malchus. Then said Jesus to Peter, Put up thy sword into the sheath: ...

The calculations, based on the book of Enoch and Jubilees, predicted the Last Supper to be a celebration for the Last Judgement at midnight.

Although Simon, Theudas, and Jesus had been tipped off about Caiaphas' plan to have Pilate arrest them, there was no way that the three could slip away before midnight or they would be admitting that their predictions were wrong. If, on the other hand they turned out to be right, which is what they wished for, they would need to be around to accept the credit when God deposed of the Roman Empire single-handedly according to prophecy.

₽ Jesus had sent Judas on his way, while keeping the others in the dark for fear that there would be bloodshed if they knew why Judas left. As levite, Judas was the collector of the priestly funds and he was also Satan as a Zealot, which led to the conjecture about the reason for his leaving.

Contrary to the usual assumption at the Last Supper, Jesus does not use the word 'betray', but a word that means 'beside-giving' which was used for the subordinate, referring to the passing of the sacred loaf. Jesus does not want to alarm the disciples, but says that one of his disciples, the 'Son of God' who 'beside-gives' to 'God' is resigning. In his usual teaching manner, he reprimands Judas' behavior by saying that he is not living up to his role as 'Man', the ideal of God. Woe to the 'Son of Man', Jesus, who must 'beside-gives' such a 'Man' who is acting like an ordinary human. Judas' reply is a sarcastic, "Are you saying you are not the 'True God'?".

When the band of soldiers from Caiaphas arrive to arrest Jesus at midnight, Jesus asks them who they are looking for. They reply that they are looking for Jesus, the Nazarene. who stood up on the platform as if he were the 'True God' and Judas, who was there as in his role of 'Son of God' had witnessed it. Judas tries to kiss Jesus and Jesus again reminds him that the role of Jesus is 'Son of Man', not the 'True God'. The soldiers hear 'True God' and they fall to the ground to worship him.

₽ Jesus tries to explain that he is the 'Son of Man', but meanwhile Peter is in an argument with Malchus (derived from the Hebrew for 'king'), used for Jesus' younger brother James who will be King when Jesus dies.

When James tries to assert that Jesus is the 'Son of God' according to Judas' plan. Peter, of course, who already had declared Jesus to be the Christ, but not the 'Son of God', holding up the sword of the angel at Eden, blocking the way of heretics, says that James was not fit to even sit on the right side of 'God'. This position on either side of 'God' is sometimes called the 'Ear', thus the metaphor for 'right ear'.

(Simon Magus is also arrested: Mark 14:51,52) And there followed him a certain young man, having a linen cloth cast about his naked body; and the young men laid hold on him. but he left the linen cloth, and fled from them naked.

(Jesus is arrested: John 18:12,13) The band, therefore, and the captain, and the officers of the Jews, took hold on Jesus, and bound him, and led him to Annas first, for he was father-in-law to Caiaphas, who was high priest that year.

(Jesus is first judged by Ananus the elder. (Joseph ben Caiaphas was married to his daughter): (John 18:13,14,19-24) They then brought Him to Annas first; for Annas was the father-in-law of Caiaphas who was High Priest that year. Now it was Caiaphas who gave counsel to the Jews, that it was expedient that one man should die for the people.
The high priest therefore asked Jesus of his disciples, and of his teaching.
Jesus answered him, 'I spoke openly to the world. I always taught in synagogues, and in the temple, where the Jews always meet. I said nothing in secret. Why do you question me? Question those who heard what it was I said to them: these witnesses here know what I said.'
When he had said this, one of the officers standing by slapped Jesus with his hand, saying, 'Do you answer the high priest like that?' 'If I have spoken wrongly,' replied Jesus, 'bear witness to it as wrong; but if rightly, why that blow?' Annas then sent him bound to Caiaphas the chief priest.

The young man, Simon Magus, 'God', beginning to advance from the lowest grade, tries to escape. Caiaphas' men insist that he had no standing in the Church, therefore naked, as they do not recognize Jesus' baptism of him.

Pilate, having been alerted and seeing the opportunity of being a hero by personally arresting Simon Magus, Theudas, and Jesus, decides to travel to Qumran on the northern route from Jerusalem to Jericho and then south to Qumran, a journey of 140 stadia taking a two hours by horse. He leaves two hours before dawn in order to arrive at dawn in Qumran.

Only in the Gospel of John is Jesus brought before Ananus the Elder, a Sadducee, before being sent to Caiaphas, even though Caiaphas is the High Priest.

Ananus asks Jesus about his disciples, and of his teaching. Jesus answers him, 'I spoke openly to the world. I always taught in synagogues, and in the temple, where the Jews always meet. I said nothing in secret. Why do you question me?" (Clearly, Jesus has little respect for Ananus as he is basically saying that he would know if he attended the synagogues and temples instead of staying in his palace.)

Jesus replies, 'Question those who heard what it was I said to them: these witnesses here know what I said.' (Jesus knowing that they have nothing of substance to charge him with, suggests that they find witnesses.)

When he had said this, one of the officers standing by slapped Jesus with his hand, saying, 'Do you answer the high priest like that?' 'If I have spoken wrongly,' replied Jesus, 'bear witness to it as wrong; but if rightly, why that blow?' Annas, feeling annoyed that he is being considered as a nobody, sends him bound to Caiaphas the chief priest."

Friday, April 3 AD 33 at dawn: Pontius Pilate arrives in Qumran for the trial

Judas is rejected

(Gospel of Matthew: Matthew 27:3-6) Then Judas, who betrayed him, when he saw that he was condemned, repented himself, and brought back the thirty pieces of silver to the chief priests and elders, saying, 'I have sinned in that I betrayed innocent blood.' But they said, 'What is that to us? You see to it.' He threw down the pieces of silver in the sanctuary, and departed. He went away and hanged himself. The chief priests took the pieces of silver, and said, 'It is not lawful to put them into the treasury, since it is the price of blood.'

Meanwhile, Theudas has appealed to Caiaphas that he was well-liked by the people from the days of Judas the Galilean and asked to be exempted as one of the three scape-goats. Thus Theudas will be shown as Bar-Abbas (son of the abbot), having come over to the side of Ananus the Elder again. With Judas being mostly a disagreeable person, they see the chance of replacing Theudas with Jesus.

When Judas is told about this, he is furious; metaphorically throwing down the silver coins. Now they have placed him in the position of 'hanging himself on the cross' with the sin of having betrayed Jesus upon him. It says that the returned coins are used to buy land, but this is hint as to his fate: to be hurled out of the cave. The conviction of Simon Magus and Judas is complete by the time Pilate arrived.

(Gospel of Matthew: Matthew 27:1,2;11-14) Now when morning had come, all the chief priests and the elders of the people took counsel against Jesus to put him to death: and they bound him, and led him away, and delivered him up to Pontius Pilate, the governor ... Now Jesus stood before the governor. When he was accused by the chief priests and elders, he answered nothing. Then saith Pilate to him, Hearest thou not how many things they testify against thee? But he made no reply to a single accusation, so that the Governor was greatly astonished.

(Gospel of Mark: Mark 15:1-5) At earliest dawn, after the High Priests had held a consultation with the Elders and Scribes, they and the entire Sanhedrin bound Jesus and took Him away and handed Him over to Pilate. The chief priests accused him of many things. Pilate again and again asked Him, 'Do you make no reply? Listen to the many charges they are bringing against you.' But Jesus made no further answer: so Pilate was astonished.

(Gospel of Luke: Luke 23:1,2) Then the whole assembly rose and brought Him to Pilate, and began to accuse Him. They began to accuse him, saying, 'We found this man perverting the nation, forbidding paying taxes to Caesar, and saying that he himself is Christ, a king.'

(Gospel of John: John 18:28-32) So they brought Jesus from Caiaphas to the Praetorium. It was the early morning, and they would not enter the Praetorium themselves for fear of defilement, and in order that they might be able to eat the Passover. Pilate therefore went out to them, and said, 'What accusation do you bring against this man?' 'If the man were not a criminal,' they replied, 'we would not have handed him over to you.' Pilate therefore said to them, 'Take him yourselves, and judge him according to your law.' Therefore the Jews said to him, 'It is not lawful for us to put anyone to death,' They said this that the words might be fulfilled in which Jesus predicted the kind of death He was to die.

(Gospel of Matthew: Matthew 27:11b) And the governor asked him, saying, 'Are you the King of the Jews?' Jesus said to him, 'So you say.

(Gospel of Mark: Mark 15:2) Pilate asked him, 'Are you the King of the Jews?' He answered, 'So you say.'

Pilate was outside of the vestry church when the chief priests arrived with Jesus. This was the place were pilgrims would come and therefore the priests would not go there to remain pure for the Passover. Pilate gets the information about Jesus from their representatives. He did not expect for Jesus to have been brought in as he expected to pass judgement on Theudas for sedition which will require the punishment of crucifixion. He asks why they brought Jesus to him and they reply that he is also a criminal. The representatives of the high priest read their charges: "perverting the nation, forbidding paying taxes to Caesar, and saying that he himself is Christ, a king."

Jesus knew that these charges had no weight and did not reply. This impressed Pilate who was used to having criminals deny all charges even when they were guilty of them.

Pilate sees that none of these are capital offences and replies that the Jews should judge him according to their law. The representatives then give their first lie that it is not lawful for them to put anyone to death. By this they meant 'by crucifixion' as 'stoning' was clearly an acceptable method to them. Jesus knew then that it was their intention to have him crucified.

Pilate retires to consider this situation and when he returns, he decides that if Jesus would admit to being the 'King of the Jews' then, by doing so, Jesus would be confessing to sedition.

138

**********Reference Column**********

Pilate asks Jesus is King of the Jews (continued)

(Gospel of Luke: Luke 23:3) Pilate asked him, 'Are you the King of the Jews?' He answered him, 'So you say.' (Gospel of John: John 18:33-38a) Pilate therefore entered again into the Praetorium, called Jesus, and said to him, 'Are you the King of the Jews?'

Jesus answered him, 'From thyself dost thou say this? or did others say it to thee about me?'

Pilate answered, 'Am I a Jew? Thy own nation, and the chief priests, have delivered thee to me: What hast thou done?'

Jesus answered, 'My kingdom is not of this world. If my kingdom were of this world, then my servants would fight, that I would not be delivered to the Jews. But now my kingdom is not from here.'

Pilate, therefore, said to him, 'Art thou then a king?'

Jesus answered, 'Thou dost say it; because a king I am, I for this have been born, and for this I have come to the world, that I may testify to the truth; every one who is of the truth, doth hear my voice.'

Pilate said to him, 'What is truth?'

**********Reference Column**********

Pilate hears Jesus from Galilee

(Gospel of John: John 18:38b) When he (Pilate) had said this, he went out again to the Jews, and said to them, 'I find no basis for a charge against him.

(Gospel of Luke: Luke 23:4-7,12) And Pilate said unto the chief priests, and the multitude, 'I find no basis for a charge against this man.' and they were the more urgent, saying, 'He doth stir up the people, teaching throughout the whole of Judaea, having begun from Galilee, unto this place.

And Pilate having heard of Galilee, questioned if the man is a Galilean. and having known that he is from the jurisdiction of Herod, he sent him back unto Herod, he being also in Jerusalem in those days. And on that very day Herod and Pilate became friends again, for they had been for some time at enmity.

P Jesus questions Pilate as to whether it is a serious question or whether he is asking it as the agent of the chief priests. Pilate laughs at the concept of himself being a Jew and questions again.

P Jesus then answers him, saying that his Kingdom is not of this world and the proof is that his followers would not have given him up so easily.

Pilate, still not understanding how one could be a king without a worldly kingdom, questions further. Jesus explains that he is of the Line of David, but that his kingship is to testify to the 'Truth' and that those who are of the 'Truth' will understand him. He uses the term 'Truth' as one of the secondary manifestations of the 'Word', to represent his mission and his Church.

Although Pilate does not understand what Jesus is saying, it becomes clear to him that Jesus and his followers are merely dreamers. Thus he has no reason to charge Jesus with sedition. He sarcastically replies, "What is truth!" as he believes that all persons lie to get what they want.

After this, Pilate tells the representatives that he has no basis for charges against Jesus. The Chief Priest, Caiaphas, becomes more insistent, saying that Jesus has been teaching sedition since he came from Galilee. The location of 'Galilee' suddenly gives Pilate hope to be free from this messy situation. Seeing the chance to get rid of the whole matter by turning Jesus over to Agrippa remembering that he has a small jurisdiction in Galilee that his uncle Antipas had given to him. Pilate calls in Agrippa to take over the trial and marvels at the disrespectful way that Agrippa handles Jesus. They become friends having been at enmity previously. How this happened is important to understand because it would be Herod Antipas who would engineer the release of the Jesus, Simon Magus, and Judas from the cross; not Agrippa.

There are two reasons that Pilate had no business sending Jesus to Agrippa. Firstly, Jesus was Jesus the Nazarite, not Jesus of Nazareth. He like John the Baptist spent their forty days and nights in the wilderness (Mark 1:12; Matthew 4:1-8; Luke 4:1-13). The wilderness for John the Baptist was in Bethany beyond Jordan and thus would be in Peraea, which along with Galilee was Herod Antipas' territory.

This explains why Herod Antipas had not needed to get permission from the Roman prefect when he put John the Baptist in prison. Jesus had been careful to avoid Herod Antipas' territory after John was killed and stayed in his primary mission territory to the south and east of Qumran, which would be under the prefect Pontius Pilate.

Confusion on jurisdiction

(Agrippa's jurisdiction in Galilee: Josephus Antiquities of the Jews, 18.6.1,2) A little before the death of Herod the King, Agrippa, living at Rome, and being brought up with and very intimate with Drusus, the emperor Tiberius' son, also contracted a friendship with Antonia (the wife of the elder Drusus), who held his mother Bernice in great esteem, ... but when Berenice was dead, and he was his own master, he spent a great deal extravagantly in his daily course of living, and a great deal in the immoderate presents he made, and those chiefly to the emperor's freedmen, hoping for their support, so that in a little time he was reduced to poverty, and could not live at Rome any longer ... For these reasons he went away from Rome, and set sail for Judaea, but in evil circumstances, being dejected by the loss of the money which he once had, and because he had not wherewithal to pay his creditors, who were many in number, and gave him no chance of avoiding them; so that he knew not what to do, and in shame at the state of his affairs, retired to a certain tower at Malatha, in Idumea, and had thoughts of killing himself. But his wife Cypros perceived his intention, ... So she sent a letter to his sister Herodias, who was now the wife of Herod the tetrarch, and let her know Agrippa's present design, and the necessities that drove him to it, and desired her, as a kinswoman of his, to help him and to engage her husband to do the same, as Herodias could see how she (Cypros) alleviated her husband's troubles all she could, although she had not the means they had. And they sent for him, and allotted him Tiberias for his habitation, and assigned him some money for his maintenance, and made him a magistrate of that city, by way of honoring him ....

Herod Agrippa mocks Jesus

(Gospel of Matthew: Matthew 27:27-31) Then the soldiers of the governor took Jesus into the common hall, and gathered unto him the whole band of soldiers. And they stripped him, and put on him a scarlet robe. And when they had platted a crown of thorns, they put it upon his head, and a reed in his right hand: and they bowed the knee before him, and mocked him, saying, Hail, King of the Jews! And they spit upon him, and took the reed, and smote him on the head. And after that they had mocked him, they took the robe off from him, and put his own raiment on him, and led him away to crucify him.

Secondly, since Galilee is part of Herod Antipas' tetrarchy, it has always been assumed that Pilate sent Jesus to Herod Antipas, when he actually sent him to Agrippa. Agrippa was merely magistrate of the city of Tiberius under the Tetrarch Herod Antipas built in honor or the Emperor, it being near Galilee. Agrippa was a Herod, but he would not be a King until much later.

These two Herods are often confused in the New Testament. Herod Antipas, who married Herodias and was the son of Herod the Great, was actually only a tetrarch. Herodias was the sister of Agrippa and both she and Agrippa were grandchildren of Herod the Great.

It was Herod Antipas who incurred the censure of John the Baptist leading to John's imprisonment when he married Herodias because her previous husband Herod Thomas (the disciple) was still living.

Agrippa eventually became King Herod Agrippa when Caligula was Emperor. Therefore, Agrippa is the only Herod of the two who can have the title of King. The New Testament is inconsistent on this issue.

Agrippa became magistrate of Tiberius to help him get out of debt. He had previously built up huge debts in Rome wining and dining important people, but he was thrown out of Rome by the Emperor Tiberius because of his debts and because seeing Agrippa would remind him of his favorite son Drusus who had died.

Agrippa was so despondent that he was considering suicide. His wife Cypros intervened and begged Agrippa's sister to prevail on Herod Antipas to give him an income and a title. Since Tiberius was the major town in Galilee, Pilate assumed that Agrippa had jurisdiction.

In the Gospel of Matthew and Mark, Pilate's soldiers and a band (those of Caiaphas) dress Jesus in a robe, a crown of thorns, and a reed as a scepter. The Gospel of John is similar although the 'band' is not mentioned.

Herod Agrippa mocks Jesus

(Gospel of Mark: Mark 15:16-20) And the soldiers led him away into the hall, called Praetorium; and they call together the whole band, And they clothed him with purple, and platted a crown of thorns, and put it about his head, And began to salute him, Hail, King of the Jews! And they smote him on the head with a reed, and did spit upon him, and bowing their knees did homage to him. And when they had mocked him, they took off the purple from him, and put his own clothes on him, and led him forth, that they may crucify him.

(Gospel of John: John 19:2,3) and the soldiers having plaited a crown of thorns, did place it on his head, and a purple garment they put around him, and said, 'Hail! the king of the Jews;' and And they struck Him with the palms of their hands.

(Gospel of Luke: Luke 23:8-11) Now when Herod saw Jesus, he was exceedingly glad, for he had wanted to see him for a long time, because he had heard many things about him. He hoped to see some miracle done by him. So he put a number of questions to him, but Jesus gave him no reply. The chief priests and the scribes stood, vehemently accusing him. and Herod with his soldiers having set him at nought, and having mocked, having put around him gorgeous apparel, did send him back to Pilate,

(Gospel of Peter: Gospel of Peter 2b,5b,7-9) And then Herod the king commandeth that the Lord be taken, saying to them, 'What things soever I commanded you to do unto him, do.' And he delivered him to the people on the day before the unleavened bread, their feast. And they clothed him with purple, and set him on the seat of judgement, saying 'Judge righteously, O King of Israel.' And one of them brought a crown of thorns and put it on the head of the Lord. And others stood and spat in his eyes, and others smote his cheeks: others pricked him with a reed; and some scourged him, saying, 'With this honor let us honor the Son of God.'

Pilate is ready to release Jesus

(Gospel of Luke: Luke 23:13-16) And Pilate having called together the chief priests, and the rulers, and the people, said unto them, 'Ye brought to me this man as perverting the people, and lo, I before you having examined, found in this man no fault in those things ye bring forward against him; no, nor yet Herod, for I sent you back unto him, and lo, nothing worthy of death is having been done by him; I will therefore chastise him and release him'

However, Luke and the Gospel of Peter give more detail, imply that this dressing and ridiculing Jesus happens at the instigation of Herod Agrippa, therefore it must be concluded that he is responsible for this disrespectful act, not Pilate.

The Gospel Luke and the Gospel of Peter show this dressing and mocking of Jesus happening while he is being questioned by Herod (Agrippa) and in the Gospel of Peter, specifically at Herod the king's request. (Note also that the Gospel of Peter anachronistically refers to Agrippa as king which confirms that it is the Herod here is Agrippa who became king later on and not Antipas who was never king. Peter composed his Gospel shortly after King Herod Agrippa's death.)

Now that they have dressed him up as king, they take him to Pilate again in an obvious manipulation to show that he is a seditious king. Pilate wants nothing of this charade and refuses to crucify Jesus; opting for Theudas.

Çive us Barabbas!

Not Barabbas, but Jesus

(Gospel of John: John 18:39,40) But you have a custom, that I should release to you one at the Passover. Therefore do you desire that I release to you the King of the Jews?' Then they all cried out again, saying, 'Not this man, but Barabbas!' Now Barabbas was a robber.

(Gospel of Mark: Mark 15:6-14) Now on the festival day he was wont to release unto them one of the prisoners, whomsoever they demanded. and at this time a man named Barabbas was in prison among the insurgents - persons who in the insurrection had committed murder. So the people came crowding up, asking Pilate to grant them the usual favor. 'Shall I release for you the King of the Jews?' answered Pilate. For he knew that the chief priests had delivered him up out of envy. But the chief priests stirred up the multitude, that he should release Barabbas to them instead. And Pilate again answering, saith to them: What will you then that I do to the king of the Jews? They cried out again, 'Crucify him!' 'Why, what crime has he committed?' asked Pilate. But they vehemently shouted, 'Crucify Him!'

(Gospel of Matthew: Matthew 27:15-23) Now at the feast the governor used to release to the multitude one prisoner, whom they wanted. They had then a notable prisoner, called Barabbas. When therefore they were gathered together, Pilate said to them, 'Whom do you want me to release to you? Barabbas, or Jesus, who is called Christ?' For he knew that because of envy they had delivered him up. While he was sitting on the judgment seat, his wife sent to him, saying, 'Have nothing to do with that righteous man, for I have suffered many things this day in a dream because of him.' But the chief priests and elders persuaded the multitude that they should ask Barabbas, and destroy Jesus. So when the Governor a second time asked them, 'Which of the two shall I release to you?' --they cried, 'Barabbas!' Pilate said to them, 'What then will I do to Jesus, who is called Christ?' They all said to him, 'Let him be crucified!' 'Why, what crime has he committed?' asked Pilate. But they kept on furiously shouting, 'Let him be crucified!'

Caiaphas has one more trick up his sleeve. The gullible Pilate who is ready to believe any lie about the Jewish religion is told that it is a tradition to release one prisoner on the day before Passover. In a carefully orchestrated demonstration they ask for this prisoner to be Theudas-Barabbas which means that Jesus is back as candidate for crucifixion.

Although added for theatrical effect, Pilate's wife appeals to Pilate to stop because of a dream, which sounds suspiciously like the wife of Caesar on the Ides of March. She would not have made the journey to Qumran, but it might be possible, as tradition says, that Pilate's wife has been converted to the Church, perhaps by Herodias, the wife of Antipas Herod.

Not Barabbas, but Jesus (continued)

(Gospel of Luke: Luke 23:17-23) Now he was obliged to release unto them one upon the feast day. Then the whole multitude burst out into a shout. 'Away with this man,' they said, 'and release Barabbas to us' one who was thrown into prison for a certain revolt in the city, and for murder. But Pilate once more addressed them, desiring to release Jesus. They, however, persistently shouted, 'Crucify, crucify him!' He said to them the third time, 'Why? What evil has this man done? I have found no capital crime in him. I will therefore chastise him and release him.' And they were pressing with loud voices asking him to be crucified, and their voices, and those of the chief priests, were prevailing,

Pilate washes his hands

(Gospel of Matthew: Matthew 27:24,25) When Pilate saw that he could prevail nothing, but that rather a tumult was made, he took water, and washed his hands before the multitude, saying, I am innocent of the blood of this just person: see ye to it. Then answered all the people, and said, His blood be on us, and on our children.

(Gospel of Peter: Gospel of Peter 1,2a) But of the Jews none washed his hands, neither Herod nor any one of his judges. And when they had refused to wash them, Pilate rose up.

There is no mention of Barabbas' swap in the Gospel of Peter, but he appears in the Four Gospels.

As has been shown previously, Barabbas is Theudas, the Zealot hero from the days of Judas the Galilean. From Caiaphas' point of view, he is much more valuable for his hero status and can easily be manipulated, contrary to Jesus.

Symbolically Pilate washes his hands to absolve himself of taking innocent blood according to Matthew.

The Gospel of Peter shows that Caiaphas (the Jews), Herod Agrippa, and Ananus the Elder (the previous judge from the Gospel of John) are willing to take the blame. Later on, after the Crucifixion, they will regret the consequences of their actions when Jesus and Simon Magus are able to turn this apparent failure into the triumph of a Resurrection.

Jesus is sent to be crucified.

(Gospel of Matthew: Matthew 27:26) Then released he Barabbas unto them: and when he had scourged Jesus, he delivered him to be crucified.

(Gospel of Mark: Mark 15:15) And so Pilate, willing to content the people, released Barabbas unto them, and delivered Jesus, when he had scourged him, to be crucified.

(Gospel of John: John 19:1-16) Then, therefore, did Pilate take Jesus and scourge him, Pilate, therefore, again went forth without, and saith to them, 'Lo, I do bring him to you without, that ye may know that in him I find no fault;' (19:5-19:13 repeated section) and he saith to the Jews, 'Lo, your king!' They therefore cried out, Away with him, away with him, crucify him! Pilate saith unto them, Shall I crucify your King? The chief priests answered, We have no king but Caesar. Then delivered he him therefore unto them to be crucified. And they took Jesus, and led him away.

Although it says that Pilate delivered Jesus to the Jews, the Crucifixion would clearly be performed by the Roman soldiers according to formula. Thus, following common practice, Jesus, Simon Magus, and Judas are scourged and the crossbars of their crosses will be placed on their shoulders.

(**Gospel of Luke: Luke 23:24,25**) And Pilate gave sentence yielding to their demand. And he released unto them him that for sedition and murder was cast into prison, whom they had desired; but he delivered Jesus to their will.

Simon and Jesus carry their crosses

Jesus carries his cross

(**Gospel of John: John 19:17a**) And he bearing the cross <u>of him</u> (*auto*: genitive-singular-masculine) went forth

Simon of Cyrene carries the cross

(**Gospel of Matthew: Matthew 27:32**) And as they came out, they found a man of Cyrene, Simon by name: this one they compelled to bear the cross <u>of him</u> (*auto*: genitive-singular-masculine).

(**Gospel of Mark: Mark 15:21**) And they compel one Simon a Cyrenian, who passed by, coming out of the country, the father of Alexander and Rufus, to bear cross <u>of him</u> (*auto*: genitive-singular-masculine).

(**Gospel of Luke: Luke 23:26,27**) And as they led him away, they laid hold upon one Simon, a Cyrenian, coming out of the country, and <u>on him</u> (*auto*: dative-singular-masculine) they laid the cross, that he might bear it after Jesus. if And there followed him a great company of people, and of women, which also bewailed and lamented him.

In this part of the story, we find Simon Magus as one of the crucified. We have already encountered Simon's persona as Simon the 'leper' and Lazarus and it is not difficult to gather that Simon of Cyrene (Libya) is the equivalent with Cyrene being a far-off place that a 'leper' might be sent to.

In Mark there is a further clue for the identity of Simon as he is shown as 'the father of Alexander and Rufus'. These names disguise the real names of Father Simon's disciples, who were Theudas-Barabbas, who was the leader of the Therapeuts with headquarters in Alexandria, and Thomas, who was nicknamed Didymus as red-haired Esau, the twin brother of Jacob.

The translators of Matthew, Mark, and Luke say that Simon of Cyrene has been given the task of carrying the cross of Jesus in spite of the fact that in John it says that Jesus carried his own cross. This has led to the whole fable of Jesus' walk to the cross from stations 3-9: falling the first time, meeting his Mother, Simon of Cyrene being given the cross, Veronica wiping the face of Jesus, falling the second time, meeting the daughters of Jerusalem (an absurd addition Luke 27-31 showing Jesus taking time out to talk to the women who follow the procession in a long speech), and falling a third time. Why Jesus would fall a second and third time when they say he was no longer carrying the cross is astounding!

In Matthew, "they found a man of Cyrene, Simon by name: him they compelled to bear his cross". It is actually more logical for "the cross of him" to refer to "this one" and thus to "Simon"; and similarly in Mark and Luke, "of him" and "on him". As to the use of the phrase "they found him", it merely means that, since he was already judged, they gather him from his cell.

In Mark there is a clue in the use of 'passed by', which to those not understanding the true meaning of 'passers-by', seems to imply that Simon was 'out taking a stroll', seemingly ignoring the scene! The word 'passers-by' in the Gospel of Thomas (II 32 (42)) means to be a disciple and to spread the word to those who passed by. "Coming out of the country" in Mark and Luke was not part of his 'stroll in the country', but is merely part of the metaphor of Simon's starting back up to the hierarchy from 'leper'.

In Luke it shows that Simon bears the cross "after Jesus" therefore with Jesus in the front. This is significant as it shows that the soldiers are not following the hierarchy of the Church that would place Simon in front. The Gospel of Peter ignores this scene as being uneventful. The most logical conclusion is to have all three carrying their crossbars: first is Jesus, followed by Simon Magus, then followed by Judas Iscariot (as seen later by his sarcastic comment on the cross).

***********Reference Column***********

(Gospel of Matthew: Matthew 27:33) And when they were come unto a place called Golgotha, that is to say, a place of a skull,

(Gospel of Mark: Mark 15:22) And they bring him unto the place Golgotha, which is, being interpreted, The place of a skull.

(Gospel of Luke: Luke 23:33a) And when they were come to the place, which is called the Skull,

(Gospel of John: John 19:17b) into a place called the place of a skull, which is called in the Hebrew Golgotha;

The Essene Toilets

(Toilet location: DSS: The War Scroll: 1QM 7:6-7) Any man who is not ritually clean in respect to his genitals on the day of the battle shall not go down with them into battle, for holy angels are present with their army. There shall be a distance between all their camps and the latrine of about two thousand cubits, and no shameful nakedness shall be seen in the environs of all their camps.

(Toileting: Wars of the Jews, Josephus II.8.9) [On the Sabbath] they do not even go to stool. On other day they dig a trench a foot deep with a mattock – such is the nature of the hatchet which they present to neophytes – and wrapping their mantle about them, that they may not offend the rays of the deity, sit above it. They then replace the excavated soil in the trench. For this purpose they select the more retired spots. And though this discharge of the excrements is a natural function, they make it a rule to wash themselves after it, as if defiled.

***********Reference Column***********

(Toileting: Deuteronomy 23:12-14) You shall have a place without the camp and you shall go out to it; and you shall have a stick with your weapons; and when you sit down outside, you shall dig a hole with it, and turn back and cover up your excrement. Because the LORD your God walks in the midst of your camp, to save you and to give up your enemies before you, therefore your camp must be holy, that he may not see anything indecent among you, and turn away from you.

The Crucifixion Location

(Paul gives the location of the Crucifixion as the latrine area: Hebrews 13:12,13) Therefore Jesus also, that he might sanctify the people through his own blood, suffered outside of the gate. Let us therefore go forth unto him without the camp, taking his shame on ourselves.

2nd Hiding Place of the Money

(In the Valley of Achor at Qumran: Copper Scroll) Column I.2 In the Valley of Achor ... in the tomb of the third 100 gold bars

Next, they reached the place of the Skull which might be assumed to be a cemetery, however, there is another reason that a skull marker would be there.

There would be for the Essenes a place that was equally as defiled and to be avoided as much as possible: the place of the unwashed pilgrims and the toilet.

South of the Skull is the lower half of Qumran that ends at the two caves. It has a length of 250 cubits like the upper half which included the monastery.

Since the normal rule for the location of the toilet is 2,000 cubits south of the town or camp, you might be wondering why a distance of 250 cubits would be sufficient. You must already remember that, although the true Essenes would have certainly walked 2,000 cubits to go to the toilet, they had abandoned Qumran after the earthquake in 31 BC. The group that were now here would have to be called pseudo-Essenes.

The logic of these Essenes was like this: a city is defined as 2,000 cubits, but the complex at Qumran being 250 cubits is only one-eight the size, so the latrine distance would only have to be 2,000 cubits divided by eight or 250 cubits. Problem solved: the toilet in one of the caves at the bottom fulfills the rule exactly!

Apparently, in respect to urination, less strict rules applied, and thus the existing structure, thought to be the stables but too small for horses, being enclosed and at least 50 feet from the Holy of Holies, was acceptable. Since it straddles the unclean area, the urine would be collected in pots and emptied by the assigned person already below the area of the Skull, who would empty them at the cave at the edge of the south section.

With this background, it is now possible to figure out what my father Paul told us in his 'Epistle to the Hebrews' that, first of all, my grandfather Jesus had suffered outside the Gate and, in addition, it was 'without the camp'. The southwest point on the boundary between the two areas in Qumran, with the north section being the temple complex, was marked by the Skull. This was the mirror image of the Essene Gate in Jerusalem, through which the Essenes went to toilet into the cesspool of Hinnom Valley. 'Without the camp' was the euphemism for going to the toilet.

Being reminded that Crucifixion is not that shiny polished icon on our wall, but a gruesome and horrible experience, there is one more point to be made that Jesus, after he was taken down from the cross in the unclean area, was placed in the cave which was that very toilet!

Incidentally this was also the hiding place of the 'filthy' money amassed from the Diaspora, managed by the 'rich man' Joseph of Arimathea (James, the brother of Jesus) as the crown-prince. Its location is revealed in the Copper Scroll. The 'third' being last in Priest, Levite, King (Jesus/James).

At 9 AM Jewish Time: 12 noon Roman Time, Jesus is put on the cross. Mark has the third hour; John has the sixth hour.

***********Reference Column***********

(Gospel of Matthew: Matthew 27:34) They gave him vinegar to drink mingled with gall: and when he had tasted thereof, he would not drink.

(Gospel of Mark: Mark 15:23) And they gave him to drink wine mingled with myrrh: but he received it not.

(Gospel of Luke: Luke 23:36) And the soldiers also mocked him, coming to him, and offering him vinegar,

***********Reference Column***********
Let this cup pass from me

(In the Garden of Gethsemane Jesus defers to his Father Jonathan Annas: Mark 14:32-37) They came to a place which was named Gethsemane. He said to his disciples, 'Sit here, while I pray and he took Peter, James, and John with him, and began to be overawed and depressed. He said to them, 'My soul is exceedingly sorrowful, even to death. Stay here, and watch.' And he went forward a little, and fell on the ground and prayed: 'Is it possible the time may be passing from me?'
And he said, Abba, Father, all things are possible unto thee; take away this cup from me: nevertheless not what I will, but what thou wilt.
And he came, and saw them sleeping, and said to Peter, Simon, are you sleeping? were you not able to keep watch one hour?

There appears to be a hidden agenda here as to why Matthew would have gall (poison) being offered before being crucified and not later when Jesus was in pain. It is possible that for humanitarian reasons that the wine and myrrh of Mark could have been given to relieve the pain of the spikes in the hands and vinegar would stop infection, but it would not have much use internally. In any case, Jesus rejects these mixtures now, but accepts them just before he appears to die on the cross. The use of the word 'cup' in the Garden of Gethsemane prior to his arrest appears to be linked.

In the Garden of Gethsemane, Jesus is aware of the imminent failure at midnight of his Restoration prophecy where God will destroy the Romans and make him King. He knew that John the Baptist had been killed because of the failure of his prophecy. The rumors that Judas had alerted Pontius Pilate, who was on his way to arrest and crucify the leaders of the insurrection, indicated that his own death was likely.

Now Jonathan Annas, his superior with the title of 'Abba Father' tells him that it would be repugnant to God to be nailed to a cross and that he must take the cup of poison that he will have ready for him before the nailing. Jonathan, knowing of a possible plan to save those nailed to the cross, was not trying to save Jesus from pain, but wanting to rid himself of Jesus forever!

When Simon Magus, the deposed Pope, heard of the poison cup, he thought how perfect it would be as part of the plan he had worked out with Herod Antipas to be rescued from the cross. Jesus was not to take it before being nailed, but later at a predetermined time. Peter knows nothing of this, thus 'sleeping'.

At 9 AM Jewish Time: 12 noon Roman Time, Jesus is put on the cross. Mark has the third hour; John has the sixth hour.

***********Reference Column***********
The crucifixion at 9 AM

(Gospel of Matthew: Matthew 27:35a) And they crucified him,

(Gospel of Mark: Mark 15:25) And it was the third hour, and they crucified him.

(Gospel of Luke: Luke 23:33b) (place of the Skull), there they crucified him.

At this point, the clocks are about to be adjusted. An adjustment of days had just happened, but the clock was still three hours too slow.

The gospel of Mark shows that it is the third hour or 9 AM Jewish Time. This is the time before adjustment. Since it is the equinox, sunrise had occurred three hours before the beginning of the first hour at 6 am.

The crucifixion at 12 AM

(Gospel of John: John 19:14a,18a) and it was the preparation of the passover, and as it were the sixth hour, (Golgotha) Where they crucified him,

King of the Jews

(Gospel of Matthew: Matthew 27:37) And set up over his head his accusation written, THIS IS JESUS THE KING OF THE JEWS.

(Gospel of Mark: Mark 15:26) And the superscription of his accusation was written over, THE KING OF THE JEWS.

(Gospel of Luke: Luke 23:38) And a superscription also was written over him in letters of Greek, and Latin, and Hebrew, THIS IS THE KING OF THE JEWS.

(Gospel of Peter: Gospel of Peter 11) And when they had raised the cross, they wrote upon it, This is the King of Israel.

(Gospel of John: John 19:19-22) And Pilate wrote a title, and put it on the cross. And the writing was, JESUS OF NAZARETH THE KING OF THE JEWS. This title then read many of the Jews: for the place where Jesus was crucified was nigh to the city: and it was written in Hebrew, and Greek, and Latin. Then said the chief priests of the Jews to Pilate, Write not. The King of the Jews; but that he said, I am King of the Jews. Pilate answered, What I have written I have written.

Casting of lots

(Gospel of Matthew: Matthew 27:35b,36) and parted his garments, casting lots: that it might be fulfilled which was spoken by the prophet, They parted my garments among them, and upon my vesture did they cast lots. And sitting down they watched him there;

(Gospel of Mark: Mark 15:24) And when they had crucified him, they divided his garments, casting lots upon them, what every man should take.

(Gospel of John: John 19:23,24) Then the soldiers, when they had crucified Jesus, took his garments, and made four parts, to every soldier a part; and also his coat: now the coat was without seam, woven from the top "throughout. They said therefore among themselves. Let us not rend it, but cast lots for it, whose it shall be: that the scripture might be fulfilled, which saith. They parted my raiment among them, and for my vesture they did cast lots. These things thus the soldiers did.

The gospel of John shows the correct time after adjustment as the sixth hour or 12 noon. John did the adjustment at 6 am, the other Gospels would do it at 12 noon.

This is a fortunate occurrence because it will shorten the time on the cross by three hours, which increases the possibility of surviving. Keeping Pilate drunk and oblivious to this sleight of hand, was the first part of the plan to rescue Simon Magus and Jesus.

The writing is placed on the cross and Pilate was clearly having a laugh at the irony that, in order to get Jesus on the cross, they had to admit that he was their king and now Pilate was killing their king.

As it was written in three languages, it was merely "Jesus King of the Jews"

Caiaphas and the others obviously objected, but it was too late. Clearly, Pilate would not change the inscription and, besides, he says Jesus told him that he was King of the Jews.

Pilate would teach them a lesson, which they should have learned before committing this act of injustice, that by crucifying Jesus they would establish his kingship throughout the world for generations to come.

The garments are gambled for and this represents the wrestling for power among the factions. They choose by lots as the disciples would at Pentecost when they would choose Matthias to replace Judas in Acts after the Crucifixion.

The four parts mean the four positions of the compass. This was the metaphor the wheel of Ezekiel that would be used in Revelation to describe the sending out of the horsemen priests to the four corners of the earth with the four Gospels. As the Gospels had not been written yet it referred to dividing the territories of the Diaspora with the apostles as soldiers.

Apparently the leadership of these apostles would remain unified under one king, therefore a 'seamless kingly robe' akin to Joseph's coat of many colors. Such a person would be James, the crown prince, moving up to kingship at Jesus' death. James had always been manipulated by the followers of John the Baptist and others who did not accept Jesus as king because of his 'illegitimate' birth and his policy of peaceful coexistence with Rome.

Casting of lots (continued)

(Gospel of Luke: Luke 23:34b) And they parted his raiment, and cast lots.

(Gospel of Peter: Gospel of Peter 12) And having set his garments before him, they parted them among them, and cast lots for them.

Two thieves on both sides.

(Gospel of John: John 19:18b) (Where they crucified him,) and two other with him, on either side one, and Jesus in the middle.

(Gospel of Peter: Gospel of Peter 10a) And they brought two malefactors, and they crucified the Lord between them.

(Gospel of Matthew: Matthew 27:38) Then were there two thieves crucified with him, one on the right hand, and another on the left.

(Gospel of Mark: Mark 15:27,28) And with him they crucify two thieves; the one on his right hand, and the other on his left. And the scripture was fulfilled, which saith. And he was numbered with the transgressors.

(Gospel of Luke: Luke 23:32,33c) And there were also two other, malefactors, led with him to be put to death. There they crucified him and the malefactors, one on the right hand, and the other on the left.

Father forgive them

(Gospel of Peter: Gospel of Peter 10b) But he held his peace, as though having no pain.

(Gospel of Luke: Luke 23:34a) Then said Jesus, 'Father, forgive them; for they know not what they do.'

People revile Jesus

(Gospel of Matthew: Matthew 27:39,40) And they that passed by reviled him, wagging their heads, And saying, Thou that destroyest the temple, and buildest it in three days, save thyself. If thou be the Son of God, come down from the cross.

(Gospel of Mark: Mark 15:29,30) And they that passed by railed on him, wagging their heads, and saying. Ah, thou that destroyest the temple, and buildest it in three days, Save thyself, and come down from the cross.

(Gospel of Luke: Luke 23:35,37) The people stood watching. The rulers with them also scoffed at him, saying, 'He saved others. Let him save himself, if this is the Christ of God, his chosen one!' And saying, If thou be the King of the Jews, save thyself.

Since Pilate had put the words 'King of the Jews' on the cross of Jesus, it was clear that his intent was to have Jesus in the center cross. This also is confirmed by the order in which they were sent out to be crucified, with Jesus being first.

With the right being mentioned first before the left, Simon Magus must have been on Jesus' right hand and Judas Iscariot on his left.

The Gospel of Peter at this point says "But he himself remained silent, as if in no pain". It is this statement that has been used to dismiss the Gospel of Peter to be a Docetic statement similar to that of 'The Second Treatise of the Great Seth' where all is illusion. This is, in fact, a fallacy because according to the prophecy of Isaiah, 'the suffering servant' in Isaiah 53:7 is expected to passively accept God's will. Luke is similar, expressed as 'forgiving the ones responsible'.

Next the ones reviling Jesus are "passers-by" which were shown to be apostles. This indicates that they are closely related to Jesus' group, but on the other side of the split, probably the followers of James, his brother, who would later become Jewish-Christians.

Although Peter is suspiciously absent, having 'denied Jesus thrice', he would assuredly be in the background thinking that there is quite a bit of truth in what these taunting brothers are saying. For what is the sense of believing in a Messiah, if that Messiah cannot ask God to rescue him.

148

**********Reference Column**********
Priests revile Jesus

(Gospel of Matthew: Matthew 27:41-43) Likewise also the chief priests mocking him, with the scribes and elders, said, He saved others; himself he cannot save. If he be the King of Israel, let him now come down from the cross, and we will believe him. He trusted in God; let him deliver him now, if he will have him: for he said, I am the Son of God.

(Gospel of Mark: Mark 15:31,32a) Likewise also the chief priests mocking said among themselves with the scribes, He saved others; himself he cannot save. Let Christ the King of Israel descend now from the cross, that we may see and believe.

**********Reference Column**********
Thieves reproach Jesus

(Gospel of Matthew: Matthew 27:44) The thieves also who were crucified with him cast on him the same reproach.

(Gospel of Mark: Mark 15:32b) And they that were crucified with him reviled him.

(Gospel of Luke: Luke 23:39-43) And one of the malefactors who had been crucified railed on him, saying, If thou be Christ, save thyself and us.
But the other answering rebuked him, saying, Dost not thou fear God, seeing thou art in the same condemnation? And we indeed justly; for we receive the due reward of our deeds: but this man hath done nothing wrong.
And he said unto Jesus, Lord, remember me when thou comest into thy kingdom.
And Jesus said unto him. Verily I say unto thee, 'Today shalt thou be with me in paradise.'

(Gospel of Peter: Gospel of Peter 13,14) And one of those malefactors reproached them, saying, 'We for the evils that we have done have suffered thus, but this man, who hath become the Saviour of men, what wrong hath he done to you?'
And they, being angered at him, commanded that his legs should not be broken, that he might die in torment.

**********Reference Column**********
The Marys at the cross

(Gospel of John: John 19:25-27) Now there stood by the cross of Jesus his mother,and his mother's sister, Mary the wife of Cleopas, and Mary Magdalene. Jesus, then perceiving the mother and the disciple standing by, whom Jesus loved, is saying to the mother of him, Behold the son of you! From that hour, the disciple took her to his own home.

Next the Chief Priest Caiaphas, smugly thinking that Jesus will not bother him anymore, also taunts him.

As shown earlier, the two thieves crucified with Jesus were Simon Magus and Judas Iscariot. It is easy to see what a rotten mood Judas would be in. The Gospel of Peter says, "And they, being angered at him, commanded that his legs should not be broken, to die in torment." (Actually, a crucifixion lasts longer with legs unbroken because the legs keep the lungs from collapsing.) The Gospel of John indicates that the two thieves had their legs broken later on.

The thief who stood up for Jesus would be Simon Magus and he confirms that Jesus did not deserve to be up there. The Sadducees did not believe in the after-life, but Simon Magus did. Actually, Paradise has a deeper meaning that alludes to a possible escape plan.

In their plan, Antipas Herod has promised to see if he could convince Pilate of the need to observe the Jewish law of not leaving bodies on the cross during the Sabbath to shorten the time on the cross.

Hell in Jesus' parable of the Rich Man and Lazarus was the chasm below the tombs, thus Paradise was the caves above. One of these caves would be the place where they could be suggested to be taken to die as it had no air once the stone was put in place, being designed as tomb.

To take this metaphor further, Judas would be dumped out of the cave to the chasm below for his treachery, thus to Hell. (Acts 1:16-20).

The next event has been already covered. It shows that Jesus is taking solace in the knowledge that Mary Magdalene is carrying his child and heir.

12 NOON Jewish Time (clock forward 3 hours).

Three hours of darkness

(Gospel of Matthew: Matthew 27:45) Now from the sixth hour there was darkness over all the land unto the ninth hour.

Three hours of darkness (continued)

(Gospel of Mark: Mark 15:33) And when the sixth hour was come, there was darkness over the whole land until the ninth hour.

(Gospel of Luke: Luke 23:44,45) And it was about the sixth hour, and there was a darkness over all the earth until the ninth hour. And the sun was darkened, and the veil of the temple was rent in the midst.

(Gospel of Peter: Gospel of Peter 15a,18,22) And it was noon, and darkness came over all Judaea: And many went about with lamps, supposing that it was night, and fell down. Then the sun shone, and it was found the ninth hour:

At noon real time, the Gospel of Mark catches up to the Gospel of John and the Four Gospels and the Gospel of Peter now agree that it is noon, having all completed their three hour time adjustment.

The explanation given is that there was 'darkness from the six to the ninth hour'. Time is always confusing. When the clocks were synchronized at noon, the Jews lost three hours which they referred to as darkness. For theatrical effect this darkness would now run from noon to 3PM.

The 'stumbling' is the confusion that happens in ones own head when thinking about how it is possible to lose three hours. The lamps were clocks with gradated candles that show the time of day.

At noon real time Jesus had only been on the cross for less than a minute because the candle-lamp clock moved forward from 9AM to noon at that moment. Keep that wine flowing to Pilate! Before he knows it, it will be 3PM.

But wait prior to the time that the clock had been changed, the people were used to sundown occurring at 3PM on their clock. Thus when Jesus faints shortly at 3PM as if dead, the people begin thinking that the evening of Passover is almost upon them and panic that they must remove the corpses from the cross by Jewish law before sundown.

3 PM Jewish Time: 3 PM Roman Time (Jesus asks for the poison).

Jesus asks for the poison

(Gospel of Matthew: Matthew 27:46) And about the ninth hour Jesus cried with a loud voice, saying, Eli, Eli, lama sabachthani? that is to say, 'My God, my God, why hast thou forsaken'

(Gospel of Mark: Mark 15:34) And at the ninth hour Jesus cried with a loud voice, saying, 'Eloi, Eloi, lama sabachthani' which is, being interpreted, 'My God, my God, why hast thou forsaken me?'

(Gospel of John: John 19:28) After this, Jesus knowing that all things were now accomplished, that the scripture might be fulfilled, saith, I thirst.

(Gospel of Peter: Gospel of Peter 19a) And the Lord cried out, saying. 'My power, my power, thou hast forsaken me.'

₽ Jesus has now been on the cross for three hours and in Matthew he quotes Psalm 22:1 in Aramaic, "Eloi Eloi lama sabachthani?" meaning "My God, my God, why hast thou forsaken me?" Matthew parallels this with a slight variation. Jesus is speaking in Aramaic because he would not want to let the Romans think that he was forsaking Yahweh. He also did not want Caiaphas and his cronies to know that this was a code for the beginning of the escape plan and thus he appeared to be just quoting from Psalms.

The God he was referring to was his Abba Father, Jonathan Annas. The Aramaic verb 'to forsake' also means 'to allow' so Jonathan's followers knew immediately that this was a request for the poison. The Gospel of John has the same intent in the expression: 'I Thirst' (give me the poison).

The Gospel of Peter confirms that 'God' is Jonathan Annas because it uses the word 'Power' for 'God'. 'Power' is part of the finale of the Lord's Prayer: 'For thine is the kingdom, the power, and the glory', which shows the three positions of the hierarchy in order of importance: the second being the 'power' or 'Son of God' and the third is 'glory' or 'Son of Man'. Jesus is the 'Son of Man' thus the 'Glory' to the 'Power'.

(Gospel of Matthew: Matthew 27:50) Jesus, when he had cried previously with a loud voice, yielded up the Spirit.

(Gospel of Luke: Luke 23:46a) And when Jesus had cried with a loud voice, he said. Father, into thy hands I commend my spirit: ...

(Gospel of John: John 19:29) Now there was set a vessel full of vinegar: and they filled a sponge with vinegar, and put it upon hyssop, and put it to his mouth.

(Gospel of Peter: Gospel of Peter 16,17) And one of them said, Give him to drink gall with vinegar. And they mixed and gave him to drink, and fulfilled all things, and accomplished their sins against their own head.

(Gospel of Matthew: Matthew 27:47-49) Some of them that stood there, when they heard that, said, This man calleth for Elijah And immediately one of them ran, and took a sponge, and filled it with vinegar, and put it on a reed, and gave him to drink. The rest said. Let be, let us see whether Elias will come to save him.

(Gospel of Mark: Mark 15:35,36) And some of them that stood by, when they heard it, said. Behold, he calleth Elijah. And one ran and filled a sponge full of vinegar, and put it on a reed, and gave him to drink, saying. Let alone; let us see whether Elias will come to take him down.

(Gospel of Mark: Mark 15:37) After crying in a loud voice, he expired.

(Gospel of Luke: Luke 23:46b) and having said thus, he gave up his spirit.

(Gospel of John: John 19:30) When Jesus therefore had received the vinegar, he said. It is finished: and he bowed his head, and gave up his spirit.

(Gospel of Peter: Gospel of Peter 19b) And when he had said it he was taken up.

(Gospel of Mark: Mark 15:38) And the veil of the temple was rent in twain from the top to the bottom.

(Gospel of Peter: Gospel of Peter 20) And in that hour the veil of the temple of Jerusalem was rent in twain.

The Gospel of Mark does not say 'gives up the ghost' or even the 'spirit, 'pneuma'. It merely says, 'expires'. Nor does it mean 'gives up the ghost' in the Gospel of Matthew when it says Jesus 'yields the spirit' ('pneuma') or in Luke 'he commends his spirit' ('pneuma'). The word spirit, 'pneuma' is the third position as in Father, Son, and Holy Spirit with Jesus being the 'Holy Spirit'. Jonathan is 'Son' as in 'Son of God' and thus Jesus' request is "As the 'Holy Spirit, the Son of Man', I accept that you are the 'Son of God'. I will take the poison". The 'loud voice' is merely a voice of authority.

In Matthew, Mark, and Luke, a mixture containing vinegar is offered to Jesus before the Crucifixion. (John and the Gospel of Peter are silent on this.) Just before Jesus faints on the cross, Matthew mentions he is given only vinegar, but earlier it had included gall (poison). Mark also only mentions vinegar when before it was wine mixed with myrrh, the standard analgesic administered under humane Jewish provisions. Luke is silent again. John and the Gospel of Peter now show the mixtures for the first time: John has vinegar and hyssop and the Gospel of Peter has vinegar and gall (poison). It was clearly not simply poison like Jonathan's.

The Gospel of John makes a point of 'the vessel sitting there' and that it was a mixture but "vinegar and hyssop" is not satisfactory. It has been sitting there for three hours since the start of the Crucifixion waiting for Jesus to ask for it. Now that the signal is given they act and give it to Jesus on a reed with a sponge attached to the top. It clearly was a lethal brew to act so quickly from a few drops.

The 'some people' who thought he said 'Elijah' would have been Thomas and the women at the cross. My grandmother Mary Magdalene said she had been informed of the rescue plan by John Mark-Bartholomew. She did not suspect the earlier deception of Jonathan Annas and thought he was assisting in the plan of Simon Magus and Herod Antipas to rescue the three from the cross. It is not surprising that they would think that Jesus was calling Elijah because this was also the name that Jonathan Annas called himself as the replacement for John the Baptist.

Jesus had fainted according to plan from the carefully mixed poison that would create a coma-like state and now the pressure was on to make Pilate believe that he was dead and get Jesus removed from the cross to a cave where he could be revived.

The splitting of the veil of the temple is, of course, symbolic of the split between the Jews of Caiaphas and the Jewish-Essenes of Peter and James and John.

(Gospel of Matthew: Matthew 27:51-53) Behold, the veil of the temple was torn in two from the top to the bottom. The earth quaked and the rocks were split. And the tombs were opened; and many bodies of the saints which slept arose, And came out of the graves after his resurrection, and went into the holy city, and appeared unto many.

(Gospel of Matthew: Matthew 27:54) Now when the centurion, and they that were with him, watching Jesus, perceived the earthquake, and those things that were done, they feared greatly, saying, Truly this was the Son of God.

(Gospel of Mark: Mark 15:39) And when the centurion, which stood over against him, saw that he so cried out, and yielded the spirit, he said. Truly this man was the Son of God.

(Gospel of Luke: Luke 23:47,48) Now when the centurion saw what was done, he glorified God, saying, Certainly this was a righteous man. And all the people that came together to that sight, beholding the things which were done, smote their breasts, and returned.

(Gospel of Matthew: Matthew 27:55,56) And many women were there beholding afar off, which followed Jesus from Galilee, ministering unto him: among whom was Mary Magdalene, Mary the mother of James and Joses, and the mother of the sons of Zebedee.

(Gospel of Mark: Mark 15:40,41) There were also women looking on afar off: among whom was Mary Magdalene, and Mary the mother of James the less and of Joses, and Salome; Who also, when he was in Galilee, followed him, and ministered unto him; and many other women which came up with him unto Jerusalem.

(Gospel of Luke: Luke 23:49) And all his acquaintance, and the women that followed him from Galilee, stood afar off, beholding these things.

The Gospel of Matthew has something of a prophecy that 'the saints' (the Jewish-Essenes) would arise from their sleep and come out of their graves after Jesus' resurrection, go to Jerusalem and be seen by many. These 'saints', of course, would be Jesus and Simon Magus, assisted by Peter and John-Bartholomew and Theudas.

There obviously was a centurion overseeing the Crucifixion, but here it is clearly referring to John Mark-Barthomew, the beloved disciple and physician of Jesus, declaring that Jesus is dead so that he can be taken down. He also says that Jesus deserves to be the 'Son of God', therefore moving from third to second position to take Judas Iscariot's position under Simon Magus.

He looks over to Theudas, who would gain the nickname 'Earthquake' shortly and signals for him to gather the medicines to revive Jesus according to plan.

The women at the cross are now shown in Matthew and Mark. They were shown earlier in John 19:25 and will appear at the Resurrection in Mark 16:1 and Luke 24:10. They are Mary Magdalene, Helena-Salome-Joanna, and Mother Mary, grandmother and two great-grandmothers. They will be important in helping to disguise the fact that Jesus is still alive by dressing him in a hooded gown.

Joseph asks for Jesus' body.

(James, the brother of Jesus: Josephus Antiquities XX. 9,1) ... the brother of Jesus who was called Christ - James was his name; Ananus delivered to be stoned.

One of the means by which Jesus' presence after the Crucifixion would be hidden was to use his brother James' as a substitute thus he is called the Christ. Sometimes he helped, but often times, James acted as his arch rival, compelling Ananus to have him killed.

Certainly, James was already feeling remorse for betraying his brother by the time he was marched off to be crucified. The Gospel of Peter has James' request for the body before the Crucifixion, so it was likely that Theudas had persuaded James to request Pilate's permission for Jesus' body even before the Crucifixion. Once Jesus was supposedly dead, James would have the best chance of persuading Pilate for his body as he would move up to be the David King and he was also Jesus' brother.

The disguising of James' name, whose real name was Joseph, as being Joseph of Arimathaea is because he had officially sided with Caiaphas, who had promised to recognize him as the David King. This is why he is called 'a member of the council' and why he had 'secretly' asked. The expression that he was a 'good and just man' is the proof that it is James as he would be called James the Just as crown prince.

It is unlikely that James knew of the secret plan or that Jesus was still alive because later after the Resurrection he did not recognize Jesus on the road to Emmaus. It would have been too dangerous to tell him the truth as he was ostensively on Caiaphas' side.

Although he had done this service, even then the eleven disciples did not trust him enough to vote him as the twelfth in place of Judas, but chose his younger brother Joses-Matthias. He would later be in charge of the Jewish-Christians in Jerusalem carrying on a quasi-relationship with the Christian Church. He met his death by stoning in 62 AD by Ananus the Younger, an associate of Paul in the Christian Church.

Surprised that Jesus should be dead already, Pilate asked the centurion to check. He passes this task to a soldier, but John Mark-Bartholomew intervenes as a physician to Jesus. It is clearly John Mark testifying as he changes the narrative to 'he' as the speaker in the Gospel assigned to him as scribe.

Pricking Jesus with a lancet, not a spear, John Mark carefully inserts it into the lung where fluid has gathered, hoping to help Jesus to breathe, but also as a pretence to check for life. Since apparently there is no flow of blood, but fluid, he claims that Jesus' heart has stopped pumping and that he is dead.

When James requests Jesus' body, Pilate confers with Herod Antipas. This gives Herod a chance to tell Pilate another Jewish rule, which actually is real: "it is written in the law, that the sun set not upon one that hath been put to death." With Pilate wanting to be done with the situation and with his 'King of the Jews' prodigy dead, Herod Antipas finds it easy to convince him to merely break the legs of the other two, so that they can also be taken off under Jewish law.

153

**********Reference Column**********
Jewish rules to the rescue (continued)

(Gospel of Peter: Gospel of Peter 4,5a,15b) And Pilate sent to Herod and asked his body. And Herod said. Brother Pilate, even if no one had asked for him, we purposed to bury him, especially as the Sabbath draweth on: for it is written in the law, that the sun set not upon one that hath been put to death. and they were troubled and distressed, lest the sun had set, whilst he was yet alive: [for] it is written for them, that the sun set not on him that hath been put to death.

**********Reference Column**********
Legs of the other two are broken

(Gospel of John: John 19:32,33) Then came the soldiers, and brake the legs of the first, and of the other which was crucified with him. But when they came to Jesus, and saw that he was dead already, they brake not his leg

The breaking of the legs was a common method used to speed up death. Chains are normally wrapped around the legs and the pole to allow the crucified person to push upward with the legs to prevent the body from being pulled at the wrists too long, which puts all the weight of the body on the chest and lungs resulting in quick suffocation.

Pilate announces that Jesus is to be taken down and for the legs of the other two to be broken. With a wave of his arm, he walks away to prepare to leave, wanting to be done of this tiresome process.

This verse in John confirms that Jesus' legs were not broken. The other two, with their legs broken, would linger on, but needed to be removed quickly.

Jesus is taken down.

**********Reference Column**********
Pilate has released the body

(Gospel of Matthew: Matthew 27:58b) Then Pilate commanded the body to be delivered.

(Gospel of Mark: Mark 15:45) And when he learned it of the centurion (John19:34), he gave the body to Joseph.

(Gospel of John: John 19:38b) and Pilate gave him leave. (To take the body)

(Gospel of Peter: Gospel of Peter 23) and the Jews rejoiced, and gave his body to Joseph that he might bury it, since he had seen what good things he had done.

**********Reference Column**********
Nails are removed

(Gospel of Peter: Gospel of Peter 21) And then they drew out the nails from the hands of the Lord, and laid him upon the earth, and the whole earth quaked, and great fear arose.

**********Reference Column**********
Jesus wrapped in a shroud

(Gospel of Matthew: Matthew 27:59) And when Joseph had taken the body, he wrapped it in a clean linen cloth,

(Gospel of Mark: Mark 15:46a) And he bought fine linen, and took him down, and wrapped him in the linen,

(Gospel of Luke: Luke 23:53a) And he took it down, and wrapped it in linen,

(Gospel of Peter: Gospel of Peter 24a) And he took the Lord, and washed him, and wrapped him in a linen cloth,

Instructions having been given by Pilate to take Jesus down, the soldiers begin their task under the supervision of Theudas and John Mark-Barthomew. They ask the soldiers to be careful as they lift the cross from its hole and place it on the ground.

The Gospel of Peter shows the nails being removed. Then Theudas (Earthquake) and John Mark lift him up onto the palanquin like the one that Jonathan uses when he is among the unclean Gentiles.

The four Marys (Mary Magdalene, Mother Mary, Mary Salome, and Mary the betrothed of James) push James out of the way and stand around Jesus to prevent the others from seeing that Jesus is still breathing. They wrap Jesus in a linen shroud. As he was still alive, his wounds began to show through, so they also drape his cloak over him with its hood over his face.

Jesus wrapped in a shroud (continued)

(*Gospel of John: John 19:38c,40*) He (Joseph) came therefore, and took the body of Jesus. Then took they the body of Jesus, and wound it in linen clothes with the spices, as the manner of the Jews is to bury.

***********Reference Column***********

Nicodemus brings the hospital

(*Gospel of John: John 19:39*) And there came also Nicodemus, which at the first came to Jesus by night, and brought a mixture of myrrh and aloes, about an hundred pound weight.

Nicodemus, who is Theudas-Barabbas, gathers up the medicines, pretending that they are for burial rites. He has an antidote for poison and bandages and salves. Clearly the huge amounts of aloe and myrrh are also for the other two still on the crosses. He places the medicines on the palanquin. Now the palanquin is weighing over a hundred pounds! They carry Jesus down to the end of the esplanade.

Jesus is put in the cave (7Q). The other two will be in the adjacent cave (8Q) with guards placed.

***********Reference Column***********

Laid in the tomb

(*Gospel of Matthew: Matthew 27:60,61*) And laid it in his own new tomb, which he had hewn out in the rock: and he rolled a great stone to the door of the sepulchre, and departed. And there was Mary Magdalene, and the other Mary, sitting over against the sepulchre.

(*Gospel of Mark: Mark 15:46b,47*) and laid him in a sepulchre which was hewn out of a rock, and rolled a stone unto the door of the sepulchre. And Mary Magdalene and Mary the mother of Joses beheld where he was laid.

(*Gospel of Luke: Luke 23:53b,54,55*) and laid it in a sepulchre that was hewn in stone, wherein never man before was laid. And that day was the Preparation, and the Sabbath drew on. And the women also, which came with him from Galilee, followed after, and beheld the sepulchre, and how his body was laid.

(*Gospel of John: John 19:41,42*) Now in the place where he was crucified there was a garden; and in the garden a new sepulchre, wherein was never man yet laid. There laid they Jesus therefore because of the Jews' Preparation day; for the sepulchre was nearby.

(*Gospel of Peter: Gospel of Peter 24b*) and brought him into his own tomb. which was called the Garden of Joseph.

Although not explicitly stated, Simon Magus and Judas pretend to faint and, since Pilate has left the scene, the disciples convince the soldiers to take them down, assuring them that they will quickly die when they are sealed in the tomb as it has no window.

The cave in which Jesus will be placed is the cave that James (Joseph) hides the Church money. The Gospel of Peter shows that the tomb is called the "Garden of Joseph", being the latrine for the monastery members, carrying with it the euphemism of 'going to the garden'. It was an appropriate place for the money that Joseph kept there because it was considered unclean also. This explains how Mary Magdalene would later think that Jesus was the gardener James and also why she did not go into the cave.

The Gospel of John clarifies that this cave has never been used as a tomb and, considering that it is almost 6 PM, it is implied to be the latrine, which is soon to be closed for the Passover Sabbath.

Mary Magdalene and Mother Mary stand outside the cave as Theudas and John Mark place Jesus inside. Their presence would also force any Church member to go on further down the hill to relieve themselves.

There was actually one entrance way with a common floor and two separate trap doors to each cave. The blocking stone would be rolled in front of this common entrance because rolling was exempt from the no lifting rule of the Sabbath. Jesus was in Cave 7Q and Simon Magus and Judas would be placed in Cave 8Q.

The cave of Jesus had a window, but the other cave had no window so those inside would suffocate once the smaller stone was over its entrance.

Once Jesus had been brought into the cave, John Mark and Theudas worked to revive Jesus. After Jesus expelled the poison, they bandaged his hands. They needed to hurry before anyone would see that Jesus was still alive in his cave.

***********Reference Column***********

Simon Magus is cared for

(Gospel of Luke: Luke 23:56) And they (the women) returned, and prepared spices and ointments; and rested the Sabbath day according to the commandment.

(Gospel of Peter: Gospel of Peter 26,27) And I with my companions was grieved; and being wounded in mind we hid ourselves: for we were being sought for by them as malefactors, and as wishing to set fire to the temple. And upon all these things we fasted and sat mourning and weeping night and day until the Sabbath.

***********Reference Column***********

Caiaphas asks Pilate for guards

(Gospel of Matthew: Matthew 27:62-66) Now the next day, that followed the day of the Preparation, the chief priests and Pharisees came together unto Pilate, Saying, Sir, we remember what that deceiver said, while he was yet alive, After three days I will rise again. command, then, the sepulchre to be made secure till the third day, lest his disciples, having come by night, may steal him away, and may say to the people, He rose from the dead, and the last deceit shall be worse than the first.'
You can have a guard,' said Pilate: 'go and make all safe, as best you can.'So they went and made the sepulchre secure, sealing the stone besides setting the guard.

(Gospel of Peter: Gospel of Peter 25,28-33) Then the Jews and the elders and the priests, perceiving what evil they had done to themselves, began to lament and to say. 'Woe for our sins: the judgement hath drawn nigh, and the end of Jerusalem.' But the scribes and Pharisees and elders being gathered together one with another, when they heard that all the people murmured and beat their breasts, saying. 'If by his death these most mighty signs have come to pass, see how just he is', — the elders were afraid and came to Pilate, beseeching him and saying,
Give us soldiers, that we may guard his sepulchre for three days, lest his disciples come and steal him away, and the people suppose that he is risen from the dead and do us evil.
And Pilate gave them Petronius the centurion with soldiers to guard the tomb. And with them came the elders and scribes to the sepulchre, and having rolled a great stone together with the centurion and the soldiers, they all together who were there set it at the door of the sepulchre; And they affixed seven seals, and they pitched a tent there and guarded it.

As the time moved closer to sunset at 6 PM, the other disciples had brought Simon Magus and Judas to their tomb. With Jesus resting, but alive, Theudas and John Mark rolled the stone over Jesus' trapdoor so that no one could look down and discover that he was alive. Theudas, and John Mark would now help to revive Simon Magus and to splint his legs and bandage his hands. Judas was given a sedative.

Caiaphas, seeing Simon Magus removed and fearing that he might escape and also that Jesus' disciples might violate Jewish law and steal away Jesus's body to pretend that he has risen from the dead, asks Pilate for guards at the tombs. Since sundown was upon them with the Sabbath Passover, he could not send guards of his own to the tombs.

When the soldiers arrive Theudas stays in the lower cave with Jesus while John Mark quickly slides the stone over the trapdoor. The soldiers check to see that Simon Magus and Judas are in the other cave and place the stone on top. They roll the blocking stone in front of the two caves. At this point Theudas slides the stones on both trap doors to allow air to circulate. Then the soldiers pitch their tents and stand on guard.

The Gospel of Peter names the centurion guard as Petronius, but this is spurious and is probably an allusion the Petronius, who had avoided violence in AD 40 by ignoring Caligula's command to have his effigy placed inside the Temple, but fortunately Caligula had died before the execution for his insubordination could be carried out.

Midnight, Saturday begins.
Mary Magdalene comes to the tomb.

***********Reference Column***********
Mary Magdalene visits the tomb

(Gospel of John: John 20:1,2) To the yet one day of the Sabbaths cometh Mary Magdalene early, when it was yet dark, unto the sepulchre, and seeth the stone taken away from the sepulchre. She ran therefore, and came to Simon Peter, and to the other disciple whom Jesus loved, and said to them, 'They have taken away the Lord out of the tomb, and we don't know where they have laid him!'

(Gospel of Peter: Gospel of Peter 50) And at dawn upon the Lord's day, Mary Magdalen, a disciple of the Lord, fearing because of the Jews, since they were burning with wrath, had not done at the Lord's sepulchre the things which the women are wont to do for those that die and for those that are beloved by them -

***********Reference Column***********
Peter and John Mark race to the tomb

(Gospel of Luke: Luke 24:12) And Peter having risen, did run to the tomb, and having stooped down he seeth the linen clothes lying alone, and he went away to his own home, wondering at that which was come to pass.

(Gospel of John: John 20:3-8) Peter and the other disciple started at once to go to the tomb, both of them running. And the two ran together, and the other disciple ran forward faster than Peter, and came first to the tomb. And stooping down he sees the linen cloths lying; he did not however go in. Simon Peter, therefore, cometh, following him, and he entered into the tomb, and seeth the linen cloths lying; and the cloth that was on his head, not lying with the linen cloths, but rolled up in a place by itself. Then the other disciple also entered in therefore, who came first to the tomb, and he saw, and believed.

(Gospel of Peter: Gospel of Peter 35-38) And in the night in which the Lord's day was drawing on, as the soldiers kept guard two by two in a watch, there was a great voice in the heaven; And they saw the heavens opened, and two men descend from thence with great light and approach the tomb. And that stone which was put at the door rolled of itself and made way in part; and the tomb was opened, and both the young men entered in. When therefore those soldiers saw it, they awakened the centurion and the elders, - for they too were hard by keeping guard;

Though not shown, Theudas, at midnight, pushed the large blocking stone from the inside as it could not be rolled except from the outside. It had crashed to the ground and broke. From this he was given the nickname 'Earthquake'. The frightened guards thought that the dead were rising! Using the money from James' tomb, Theudas would bribe the soldiers, telling them to say that an earthquake had moved the stone. They had gone back to their tents.

In the middle of the night, Mary Magdalene came up the hill to the cave from the Queen's House. Being pregnant, with my mother Phoebe, she was not under Sabbath restrictions. When Mary passed by on her way up the hill, the soldiers repeated to her the cover story of an earthquake. Seeing the stone rolled away from Jesus' tomb as the guards had told her, she immediately thinks that Jesus' body had been stolen. Theudas was sleeping inside the upper level to assist if necessary and did not hear her. She runs back down to hill to the Queen's house to tell John Mark, the beloved disciple.

Mary Magdalene was so agitated that she could hardly get the words out as she told the story to John Mark. Peter, who had stayed in the sidelines until now, having denied Jesus three times at the cock crowing and thinking that Jesus was dead, had walked up from Ein Feshkha to go up to the caves and see what was going on. He happened to be approaching the Queen's House as he saw John Mark speaking with Mary Magdalene in the light of the full moon and then start running off. When Magdalene repeated the story to him, he ran after John Mark.

The beloved disciple immediately went into the upper chamber and woke Theudas to find out what had transpired since he had left early in the night. Peter came in after him. As the Gospel of Peter confirms, the soldiers saw two young men enter into the tomb. Peter went down the trapdoor to the Jesus' cave below. He was amazed to see Jesus standing there.

₽ Jesus spoke to him, "Has Jonah come to see me inside the whale? Were you foolishly waiting three days?"

Peter replied, "I am so sorry for my unbelief. This is truly a joyous day! I will never doubt you again."

Mary weeps

(Gospel of John: John 20:11-13) But Mary was standing outside at the tomb weeping. So, as she wept, she stooped and looked into the tomb, And she saw two angels in white sitting, one at the head, and one at the feet, where the body of Jesus had lain. And they say to her, 'Woman, why dost thou weep?' she saith to them, 'Because they took away my Lord, and I have not known where they laid him;'

(Gospel of Mark: Mark 16:9) Now when Jesus was risen early, the first day of the week, he appeared first to Mary Magdalene, out of whom he had cast seven demons. (not in Vaticanus)

Mistakes Jesus for the gardener

(Gospel of John: John 20:14-17) And these things having said, she turned backward, and seeth Jesus standing, and she had not known that it is Jesus. Jesus saith to her, 'Woman, why dost thou weep? whom dost thou seek? She, supposing that he is the gardener, saith to him, 'Sir, if thou didst carry him away, tell me where thou didst lay him, and I will take him away;' Jesus saith to her, 'Mary!' having turned, she saith to him, 'Rabbuni;' that is to say, 'Teacher.' Jesus saith to her, 'Be not touching me, for I have not yet ascended unto my Father; and be going on to my brethren, and say to them, I ascend unto my Father, and your Father, and to my God, and to your God.'

Mary Magdalene, being pregnant, was not able to run as fast as the two disciples and arrived after they had gone inside to prepare Jesus for exiting the cave. She ventured further in this time and looked into the trapdoor to Cave 8Q thinking it was the cave that Peter and the beloved disciple had entered. Being confused at which cave was which, she was actually seeing Simon Magus and Judas. Since both Simon Magus and Judas were officials of the Jewish-Essene order, they could be referred to as 'angels' and having a lantern were illuminated brightly in the dark. Having initially gone to the caves with the body of Jesus, she had no idea that the Simon Magus and Judas had been rescued.

Since she thought it was Peter and John Mark and then not seeing Jesus with them, she began sobbing. Simon Magus, one of the 'angels' in her vision, asked her why she was crying. She explains that Jesus' body has been stolen.

She recognizes Simon Magus' voice and realizes that she has been looking into the wrong trapdoor. Peter and John Mark and Theudas had just helped Jesus up from the tomb to the floor above while Mary is talking. As Mary Magdalene turns around she sees a person standing on her level just outside the trapdoor. Since she is still thinking that Jesus' body was stolen, she immediately thinks it is James, the keeper of the tomb in the Garden of Joseph.

Jesus says to her, "Mary" and she suddenly realizes that it is Jesus. She says "Rabbuni" which is Aramaic for "Teacher", in other words "excuse me for being so stupid".

Being filled with joy she immediately starts to hug her beloved and give him a kiss, but Jesus stops her saying "Do not touch me". This strange statement that seems to make Jesus a hard-hearted person instead of the loving Jesus that everyone wants to emulate is actually proof that Mary Magdalene was three months pregnant with Jesus' child. Even if Jesus was not dirty and bloody from the cross, the Essene rule said that they could not touch each other once she was pregnant three months. Thus it had been for Joseph and Mary, when she was found with child.

Peter and the Beloved Disciple help Jesus out from the Tomb

Jesus is helped out of the tomb

(Gospel of Peter: Gospel of Peter 39-42) And, as they (the soldiers) declared what things they had seen, again they see three men coming forth from the tomb, and two of them supporting one, and a cross following them. And of the two the head reached unto the heaven, but the head of him that was led by them overpassed the heavens. And they heard a voice from the heavens, saying. 'Hast thou preached to them that sleep?' And a response was heard from the cross, 'Yea.'

After all these preceding proofs, there is no greater proof that Jesus survived the Crucifixion than in the Gospel of Peter: "two men descend" and now "three men coming forth from the tomb, and two of them supporting one, and a cross following them."

The two men are Peter and the beloved disciple John Mark, who had gone down into the cave, helping Jesus out. Jesus, still weak and needing support, is between them with his arms around their shoulders as they come down the cliff to the Queen's House, his place of birth. Although Peter had slept when Jesus was troubled about the cup the night before. All was forgotten. It was a new day. He had his disciples with him. And like my grandfather I say, "Yeah".

**********Reference Column**********
Jesus is helped out of the tomb (continued)

(Gospel of Mark: Mark 16:12,13 - not in Vaticanus) And after these things, to two of them, as they are going into a field, walking, he was manifested in another form, They (the two of them) went away and told it to the rest. They didn't believe them, either.

**********Reference Column**********
Simon Magus is brought out

(Gospel of Peter: Gospel of Peter 43,44) They therefore considered one with another whether to go away and shew these things to Pilate. And while they yet thought thereon, the heavens again are seen to open, and a certain man to descend and enter into the sepulchre.

**********Reference Column**********
Soldiers afraid

(Gospel of Matthew: Matthew 28:4) And for fear of him the keepers did shake, and became as dead men.

(Gospel of Peter: Gospel of Peter 45) When the centurion and they that were with him saw these things, they hastened in the night to Pilate, leaving the tomb which they were watching, and declared all things which they had seen, being greatly distressed and saying, Truly he was the Son of God.

**********Reference Column**********
Dogma of Resurrection not created yet

(Gospel of John: John 20:9) For not yet did they know the scripture, that it behoveth him out of the dead to rise again.

**********Reference Column**********
Mary tells the disciples

(Gospel of Mark: Mark 16:10,11) She having gone, told those who had been with him, mourning and weeping; And they, having heard that he is alive, and was seen by her, did not believe her.

(Gospel of John: John 20:18) Mary Magdalene came and told the disciples that she had seen the Lord, and that he had said these things to her.

Once this verse is known it is easy to spot two verses out of place in the Gospel of Mark that describe the same occurrence: "And after these things, to two of them, as they are going into a field, walking, he was manifested in another form". See how 'he is manifested in another form' compares well with the line in Gospel of Peter: "And of the two the head reached unto the heaven, but the head of him that was led by them overpassed the heavens." This a strong proof that the Gospel of Peter is the original and the Gospel of Mark is the edited version.

These verses were left in the Gospel of Mark, but moved forward as the editors needed more material for Jesus' appearances as a Spirit after the Resurrection. They also fit quite well after the true ending of the Gospel of Mark: Peter always a pragmatist): "And they (the women) went out quickly, and fled from the sepulchre; for they trembled and were amazed: neither said they any thing to any man; for they were afraid." To add the visit of the Spirit of Jesus being seen was much more uplifting.

As this point the Gospel of Peter shows only one man going into the cave. Since Jesus has already been removed from the cave 7Q, it must assuredly be cave 8Q and, since Peter and the John Mark-Bartholomew are gone with Jesus, it must be Theudas who enters the trapdoor to help Simon Magus. He dresses his hands again and helps put on his white priestly raiment, that he had gone back for, so that Simon can present himself again as the Pope. Theudas, having replaced Judas as is shown in the Last Supper as 'Judas not Iscariot' was now officially Simon's levite, second in the hierarchy.

Next it is the development of the cover-up story on the soldiers' part. By pretending that it is all a supernatural occurrence, they will be excused.

The verse in John "For not yet did they know the scripture, that it behoveth him out of the dead to rise again" is an amazing statement as it refers to scripture in the New Testament that has yet been written. Thus Jesus' death and resurrection would be added later, but John Mark and Peter knew the truth. So did Mary Magdalene.

Mary Magdalene rushes back to tell the disciples and the women the good news.

159

The women visit the tomb.
Simon Magus says "he is risen!"

***********Reference Column***********
The women visit the tomb

(Gospel of Matthew: Matthew 28:1) Evening yet of the Sabbaths lighting into one Sabbath, came Mary Magdalene and the other Mary to see the sepulchre.

(Gospel of Mark: Mark 16:1,2) Very early in the morning of one of the Sabbaths, Mary Magdalene, and Mary the mother of James, and Salome, had bought sweet spices, that they might come and anoint him. And very early in the morning the first day of the week, they came unto the sepulchre when the sun had risen.

(Gospel of Luke: Luke 24:1) To the yet one day of the Sabbaths of early of deep, they came unto the sepulchre, bringing the spices which they had prepared, and certain others with them.

(Gospel of Peter: Gospel of Peter 34,51,52) And early in the morning as the Sabbath was drawing on, there came a multitude from Jerusalem and the region round about, that they might see the sepulchre that was sealed. She (Mary Magdalene) took her friends with her and came to the sepulchre where he was laid. And they feared lest the Jews should see them, and they said, Although on the day on which he was crucified we could not weep and lament, yet now let us do these things at his sepulchre.

***********Reference Column***********
The stone is heavy

(Gospel of Mark: Mark 16:3) And they said among themselves. Who shall roll us away the stone from the door of the sepulchre?

(Gospel of Peter: Gospel of Peter 53,54) But who shall roll away for us the stone that was laid at the door of the sepulchre, that we may enter in and sit by him and do the things that are due? For the stone was great, and we fear lest some one see us. And if we cannot, yet if we but set at the door the things which we bring for a memorial of him, we will weep and lament, until we come unto our home.

***********Reference Column***********
Earthquake rolls the stone

(Gospel of Matthew: Matthew 28:2a) And, behold, there was a great earthquake:

(Gospel of Mark: Mark 16:4) And when they looked, they saw that the stone was rolled away: for it was very great.

With the Sabbath over at end of the day, the three women who were at the cross: Mary Magdalene, Mother Mary, Helena-Salome-Joanna and Mary of James go to the cave of Simon Magus.

As they walk up they are concerned that the stone may have been rolled back onto the tomb of Simon Magus and that they would not be able to move it.

The women, having heard about the earthquake from the soldiers, are amazed to see that the front entrance of the tomb is open.

Earthquake rolls the stone (continued)

(*Gospel of Luke: Luke 24:2*) And they found the stone rolled away from the sepulchre.

(*Gospel of Peter: Gospel of Peter 55a*) And they went away and found the tomb opened,

Women enter the sepulchre

(*Gospel of Mark: Mark 16:5a*) And entering into the sepulchre,

(*Gospel of Luke: Luke 24:3*) And they entered in, and found not the body of the Lord Jesus.

(*Gospel of Peter: Gospel of Peter 55b*) and coming near they looked in there;

Simon as angel

(*Gospel of Matthew: Matthew 28:2b,3*) for the angel of the Lord descended from heaven, and came and rolled back the stone from the door, and sat upon it. His countenance was like lightning, and his raiment white as snow:

(*Gospel of Mark: Mark 16:5b*) they saw a young man sitting on the right side, clothed in a long white garment; and they were affrighted.

(*Gospel of Luke: Luke 24:4,5a*) And it came to pass, as they were much perplexed thereabout, behold, two men stood by them in shining garments: And as they were afraid, and bowed down their faces to the earth,

(*Gospel of Peter: Gospel of Peter 55c*) and they see there a certain young man sitting in the midst of the tomb, beautiful and clothed in a robe exceeding bright;

The Lie of the Resurrection

(*Gospel of Matthew: Matthew 28:5-7*) And the angel answered and said unto the women, Fear not ye: for I know that ye seek Jesus, which was crucified. He is not here: for he is risen, as he said. Come, see the place where the Lord lay. And go quickly, and tell his disciples that he is risen from the dead; and, behold, he goeth before you into Galilee; there shall ye see him: lo, I have told you.

(*Gospel of Luke: Luke 24:5b,6-8*) they said unto them, 'Why seek ye the living among the dead? He is not here, but is risen: remember how he spake unto you when he was yet in Galilee, Saying, The Son of Man must be delivered into the hands of sinful men, and be crucified, and the third day rise again.' And they remembered his words,

They peer into the upper level and, looking in, they do not see Jesus, who, of course, is no longer there.

Then they look over and see the shattered round blocking stone lying flat and with Simon Magus sitting on it like a throne. His "white shining garments" having been scrubbed with frankincense make him look like a true angel even though Simon and Theudas were already Essene 'angels'. Simon is shown as a young man because, having been Lazarus, he is still at the level of initiate and must work his way back to officially be the Pope.

Helena says to Simon, "Now I see, Great Seth, you did not die in reality, but in appearance; for you were altering your shapes, changing from form to form. You were laughing at their ignorance and empty glory. And now you have joined with Sophia once again." (Quoted from 'The Second Treatise of the Great Seth, Nag Hammadi Library)

Mother Mary says, 'What is to happen now? Once my son was the Savior of the World, now he is merely rescued and dishonored. The mission is empty as his tomb.'

Simon replies, "Why seek ye the living among the dead? He is not here, but is risen! Remember how he spoke to you when he was yet in Galilee, saying, 'The Son of Man must be delivered into the hands of sinful men, and be crucified, and the third day rise again.' He goeth before you into Galilee; there you shall see him."

"He is risen!" This was the myth that had trapped Jesus in a lie. He was not a resurrected body; he had merely escaped death.

In the real story, Jesus, being free from his marriage commitments because Mary Magdalene was three months pregnant, could now return to the monastery. In that he would "Ascend" in his clergical status. He would not return until the next child in either three or six years depending on whether it was a girl or a boy. I guess you know it was three years, thanks to the birth of my mother Phoebe.

***********Reference Column**********

The Lie of the Resurrection (continued)

(Gospel of Mark: Mark 16:6,7) And he saith unto them, Be not affrighted: ye seek Jesus of Nazareth, which was crucified: he is risen; he is not here: behold the place where they laid him. But go your way, tell his disciples and Peter that he goeth before you into Galilee: there shall ye see him, as he said unto you.

(Gospel of Peter: Gospel of Peter 55d,56) who said to them, 'Wherefore are ye come? Whom seek ye? Him that was crucified? He is risen and gone. But if ye believe not, look in and see the place where he lay, that he is not here; for he is risen and gone away thither, whence he was sent.'

***********Reference Column**********

Women return from the sepulchre

(Gospel of Mark: Mark 16:8) And they went out quickly, and fled from the sepulchre; for they trembled and were amazed: neither said they any thing to any man; for they were afraid.

(Gospel of Luke: Luke 24:9-11) And returned from the sepulchre, and told all these things unto the eleven, and to all the rest. And it was the Magdalene Mary, and Joanna, and Mary of James, and the other women with them, who told unto the apostles these things, and their sayings appeared before them as idle talk, and they were not believing them.

(Gospel of John: John 20:10) The disciples therefore went away again unto their own homes.

(Gospel of Peter: Gospel of Peter 57-59) Then the women feared and fled. Now it was the last day of the unleavened bread, and many were going forth, returning to their homes, as the feast was ended. But we, the twelve disciples of the Lord, mourned and were grieved: and each one, being grieved for that which was come to pass, departed to his home.

(Gospel of Matthew: Matthew 28:8-10) And they departed quickly from the sepulchre with fear and great joy; and did run to bring his disciples word. and as they were going to tell to his disciples, then lo, Jesus met them, saying, 'Hail!' and they having come near, laid hold of his feet, and did bow to him Then Jesus said to them, 'Don't be afraid. Go tell my brothers that they may go into Galilee, and there they will see me.'

***********Reference Column**********

Judas is punished with death

(Judas Iscariot is hurled out of the cave (Acts 1:18) Now having bought a piece of ground with the money paid for his wickedness he fell there with his face downwards, and, his body bursting open, he became disemboweled.

When it says that the women feared it means that they were amazed at the reality of this great event. Now they would repeat to everyone the story that Jesus had risen from the dead.

As they came from the caves to Ain Feshkha, they met Jesus walking toward them.

Although Judas is also rescued from the cross, he will not survive the wrath of Simon Magus. The next night Theudas returned and pulled the body of the traitor Judas out of the dungeon and threw him over the cliff. He had already suffocated to death. His body "fell headlong" and "all his bowels gushed out". He had earned himself a plot of land in Hell, the Qumran version of Jerusalem's Gehenna.

162

Soldiers are bribed

(Gospel of Matthew: Matthew 28:11-15) Now while they were going, behold, some of the guards came into the city, and told the chief priests all the things that had happened. When they were assembled with the elders, and had taken counsel, they gave a large amount of silver to the soldiers, telling them to say, 'His disciples came during the night and stole his body while we were asleep.' And if this,' they added, 'is reported to the Governor, we will satisfy him and screen you from punishment.' So they took the money and did as they were told. This saying was spread abroad among the Jews, and continues until this day.

(Gospel of Peter: Gospel of Peter 46-49) Pilate answered and said, I am pure from the blood of the Son of God: but ye determined this. (Matt 27:24) Then they all drew near and besought him and entreated him to command the centurion and the soldiers to say nothing of the things which they had seen: For it is better, say they, for us to incur the greatest sin before God, and not to fall into the hands of the people of the Jews and to be stoned. Pilate therefore commanded the centurion and the soldiers to say nothing.

Now Caiaphas had to cover this up, being afraid of word getting back to Pilate Thus the soldiers would receive more bribes to keep quiet. Pilate had already washed his hands of the whole event.

Fabled Appearances of Jesus' Spirit

Peace be unto you

(Gospel of John: John 20:19-25) When therefore it was evening, on that day, the first day of the week, and when the doors were locked where the disciples were assembled, for fear of the Jews, Jesus came and stood in the midst, and said to them, 'Peace be to you.' When he had said this, he showed to them his hands and his side. The disciples therefore were glad when they saw the Lord. A second time, therefore, He said to them, 'Peace be to you! As the Father sent me, I also now send you.' When he had said this, he breathed on them, and said to them, 'Receive the Holy Spirit! Whoever's sins you forgive, they are forgiven to them. Whoever's sins you retain, they are retained.' But Thomas, one of the twelve, called Didymus, was not with them when Jesus came. So the rest of the disciples told him, 'We have seen the Master!' His reply was, 'Unless I see in his hands the wound made by the nails and put my finger into the wound, and put my hand into his side, I will never believe it.'

Next Jesus is just attending a Church service after the Resurrection and the doors, by custom, were locked when the service started. A little belief in ghosts and you imagine he passed through the door, but he was already inside.

That he had the marks on his hand and side certainly makes it appear as if he is alive. If it is possible to triumph over death, why not heal the scars? Clearly, the congregation would know what he looked like and many reliable witnesses had seen him crucified and appear to die.

Doubting Thomas

(Gospel of John: John 20:26-31) And after eight days again his disciples were within, and Thomas with them: then came Jesus, the doors being shut, and stood in the midst, and said, Peace be to you. Then he saith to Thomas: Put in thy finger hither, and see my hands; and bring hither thy hand, and put it into my side; and be not faithless, but believing. 'My Lord and my God!' replied Thomas. Jesus said to him, 'Because you have seen me, you have believed. Blessed are those who have not seen, and have believed.' Therefore Jesus did many other signs in the presence of his disciples, which are not written in this book; but these are written, that you may believe that Jesus is the Christ, the Son of God, and that believing you may have life in his name.

The Emmaus meeting

(Location of Emmaus: Josephus War 7:6.6) Emmaus, is distant from Jerusalem threescore furlongs (60 stadia). **(Gospel of Luke: Luke 24:13-49)** Behold, two of them were going that very day to a village named Emmaus, which was sixty stadia from Jerusalem. They talked with each other about all of these things which had happened. And it came to pass, that, while they communed together, and reasoned, Jesus himself drew near, and went with them. But their eyes were kept from recognizing him. 'What is the subject,' He asked them, 'on which you are talking so earnestly, as you walk?' And they stood still, looking full of sorrow. And one of them, whose name was Cleopas, answering, said to him, Art thou only a stranger in Jerusalem, and hast not known the things which have come to pass there in these days? And he said unto them, What things? ...

Still there was a need to have Thomas put his hands on the scars to verify that they were real to prove that Jesus was on the cross.

This story had to be an addition to combat the Gnostics who were saying that Jesus' crucifixion was an illusion. It was very shrewd to use the disciple Thomas upon whom was built a whole cult of gnosticism!

Thomas would prove that Jesus had either resurrected with his physical body or was just his physical body. Jesus was the Holy Spirit before he died and now he was the same. But does the Spirit World exist? It does not tell us that.

The road to Emmaus is a cute story of two disciples: James (Cleopas) and another, both were not part of Jesus' Church. Meeting Jesus' Resurrected Spirit on the road near Emmaus, a place equidistant between Jerusalem and Qumran.

The significance being that Jesus is centered at Qumran and James is centered at Jerusalem. It was an opportunity to give a synopsis of the invented story. Amazingly there are eleven disciples that they tell the story to and the only one who has seen Jesus and that is Peter! John Mark-Bartholomew and Theudas "Earthquake" are two of the eleven, but apparently count for nothing.

Ascension: returning to monastery.

Meeting at the mountain

(Gospel of Matthew: Matthew 28:16-20) But the eleven disciples went into Galilee, to the mountain where Jesus had sent them. When they saw him, they bowed down to him, but some doubted. Jesus came to them and spoke to them, saying, 'All authority has been given to me in heaven and on earth. Go, and make disciples of all nations, baptizing them in the name of the Father and of the Son and of the Holy Spirit, and teach them to obey every command which I have given you. Remember, I am with you always, until the Close of the Age.

At last we have reached the Ascension. It appears to be an accepted fact that resurrected spirit-bodies have a time limit to be on earth with their physical bodies. This time limit might have been made up in the interest of convenience because the visitations of Jesus' resurrected Spirit were so hard to invent without being discovered. Perhaps, it was supposed to be a necessary proof that heaven exists. Even so, Jesus clearly keeps returning in visions.

The easiest explanation is, of course, that Jesus went back to the monastery, needing time for his hands to heal, and to contemplate the future of his Church. He also would have time to compose the Gospel of John with the help of Simon Magus.

(Gospel of Mark: Mark 16:14-20) Afterward he was revealed to the eleven themselves as they sat at the table, and he rebuked them for their unbelief and hardness of heart, because they didn't believe those who had seen him after he had risen. And he said to them, Go into all the world, and give the good news to all mankind. He who believes and is baptized shall be saved, but he who disbelieves will be condemned. These signs will accompany those who believe: in my name they will cast out demons; they will speak with new languages; They shall take up serpents; and if they drink any deadly thing, it shall not hurt them; they shall lay hands on the sick, and they shall recover. So then the Lord Jesus, after he had spoken to them, was received up into heaven, and sat down at the right hand of God ...

(Gospel of Luke: Luke 24:50-53) He led them out as far as to Bethany, and he lifted up his hands, and blessed them. It happened, while he blessed them, that he withdrew from them, and was carried up into heaven. They worshipped him, and returned to Jerusalem with great joy, ...

Feed my sheep

(Gospel of John: John 21:1-3) After these things Jesus showed himself again to the disciples at the sea of Tiberias: and in this manner did he show himself. There were together Simon Peter, and Thomas who is called Didymus, and Nathanael from Cana of Galilee, and the sons of Zebedee, and two others of his disciples. Simon Peter said to them, 'I'm going fishing.' They told him, 'We are also coming with you.' They immediately went forth, and entered into the boat. That night, they caught nothing.

(Gospel of Peter: Gospel of Peter 60) But I, Simon Peter and Andrew my brother, took our nets and went to the sea; and there was with us Levi the son of Alphaeus, whom the Lord . .
.

In Mark are predictions of future events, obviously added later: "casting out devils" (the split of the Church of Peter and Paul with Simon Magus in AD 44); "speaking in new tongues": Acts 2:1-11; "taking up serpents":Paul with the viper in the fire Acts 28:2-5, "drink any deadly thing it shall not hurt them": alluding to Jesus' poisoning on the cross; "laying hands on the sick": Peter' miracles beginning in Acts 3. The 'viper' was clearly placed this addition after Paul's Journey to Rome in AD 60-61.

Then the disciples returned to Jerusalem with Mary Magdalene ('great joy': pregnant with Jesus' child).

This last event has to do with the restructure of the Church now that Jesus was entering back into a monastic existence. It concerned Peter, Thomas, Jonathan Annas (Nathanael), James and John, Andrew and John Mark-Bartholomew. During the lesson that Jesus taught to Peter about agape-love using the image of 'feeding of his sheep', he made Peter the Pope and John Mark-Barthomew the head of the monasteries. (The lesson was shown earlier.)

This final chapter 21 of the Gospel of John was the result of the huge edit of this gospel in order to remove Simon Magus and John Mark. The purpose of adding this chapter to the Gospel of John was to temper the predominance of Mary Magdalene and Thomas in the previous chapter and to raise the importance of Peter. It was assembled using material that had been deleted from the Gospel of Peter (traces remain at verse 60) in the editing of the Gospel of Mark. This is why some believe that this final chapter of John was added much later.

dear Grandfather Jesus, "May you be free from all regret that ties the Spirit to this mortal realm. May you truly ascend to the Kingdom of heaven where we all will meet one day. Know that your struggle has not been in vain for your truths have been revealed again in my book.

Once people are freed from the chains of dogma, they will find themselves again in that place, which was once your Church, where the pureness of agape-love transcends all time and space. Amen"

Postscript

I do not know if this book will find its way to you, dear reader, but I pray that it will. The greatest danger would be for it to be found by the Church, as they will certainly want to burn it for fear that it will uncover the myths which they have spun to fulfill their own propaganda. Yet, I am hoping that, even then, there will be some members of the Church, who will hide it in some secret archive to protect it and maintain its integrity; and, when the time is right, let it be discovered.

The intent of my writings is to reveal the truth as told by my grandfather Jesus. Yet, I know that there exists a collective force, which is underlying and often even unconscious. This force, like the book of 'Revelation', sets its own time to be discovered and to awaken the consciousness of humankind.

There exists a sacred trust between the leaders and the congregation of all religions and it is important that it be based on purity and truth. When religion abuses this trust and speaks lies, it must be cast aside like 'salt that has lost its flavor' and be replaced by a new paradigm.

Inevitably, there will be the non-believers who will cry out that all religion should be replaced by civil law while the blind followers of the empty shells of religious dogma will try to use force to preserve it.

As for Christianity, its truth can be revealed by applying the principles of the 'Pesher of Christ' as laid out in this book. Using its principles, there is revealed a new New Testament, yet this is really the old New Testament, as my grandfather Jesus, my father Paul, my mother Phoebe, and Peter meant it to be. These same principles can also be applied to every other religion, to uncover its own true roots. Within these roots, we will find that we are all part of the same genesis, which is the 'Tree of Life'.

Many will vehemently dispute this book, for change is difficult for some; but the 'collective unconsciousness' will be made more manifest to our waking consciousness from this process. As my grandfather Jesus said, "If you have faith as a grain of mustard seed, you will tell this mountain, 'Move from here to there,' and it will move; and nothing will be impossible to you."